Dear Eric,

You are one of the dearest,
most generous, most talented
students I've taught (and we
know how long I've been teaching!).
I hope you enjoy reading this
teacher's rendition of some of
the tricks of the trade.

With fond regard and
affection,

Judith Summerfield

April 1991

# Texts
# and
# Contexts

## A Contribution to the Theory and Practice of Teaching Composition

## Judith Summerfield
## Geoffrey Summerfield

*Queens College, The City University of New York*

RANDOM HOUSE  NEW YORK

**For**
**Jimmy Britton**

*"Where,—O for pity,—we shall much disgrace,*
*With four or five most vile and ragged foils,*
*Right ill dispos'd in brawl ridiculous,*
*The name of Agincourt."*

First Edition
987654321
Copyright © 1986 by Random House, Inc.

Library of Congress Cataloging in Publication Data

Summerfield, Judith, 1941–
  Texts and contexts.

  Bibliography: p.
  1. English language—Rhetoric—Study and teaching.
I. Summerfield, Geoffrey.    II. Title.
PE1404.S86    1986    808.042'071173    85–28203
ISBN 0-394-35159-2

Manufactured in the United States of America

Designer: Glen M. Edelstein

Cover Design: Marsha Cohen

# Permissions and Acknowledgments

# Foreword

## The Theory of Composition
## and the Composition of Theory

What do our students really know when they walk into their first writing class in college? Too often we tend to think they know nothing at all—that their implicit scholarship in pop music, sports, fashion, even the semiotics of motorcycle repair, is altogether beside the point when they arrive in our midst. *Texts and Contexts* makes no such assumptions, and tells us why by appealing to the developments in the theories of human discourse that have contributed so much to the history of contemporary thought in the last two decades and more. Thanks to such developments—and, of course, to their own imagination and good sense—the Summerfields have generated a text and a practice very likely singular among efforts of its kind.

Crucial is the book's delicate but decisive adjustment in our pedagogy by moving it away from the usual "process" approach to composition and onto the student's—and the teacher's—growing recognition of what the Summerfields shrewdly call our "enabling constraints." These enabling constraints are the sediments of convention in everything we do, even in what we are, and in forcing them out into the open, the Summerfields show how useful a theoretical background can be in clearing up the muddle that has confronted us for years over the problem of teaching composition. Reading and writing, maintain the authors, are both products of concrete social exchange. Text production and text reception are a common process that makes the theory of reading—criticism—and the theory of writing—composition—virtually one and the same.

The implications of such a pedagogy are almost innumerable, but we can isolate at least two chief effects among them. The first is the degree to which the Summerfields tactfully but efficiently integrate the lessons to be had from structural linguistics, narratology, psychoanalysis, and philosophy; the second is the degree to which they can thereby go on to alter our frequent reflex manner of sustaining models of composition based on outmoded notions about hitherto uninterrogated categories such as essential selfhood, autonomous being, spontaneous expressiveness, and the supposed transparency of language itself.

First, then, the assumption throughout—as the title tells us—that any text always already has its context; nothing, in short, makes sense except in relation to something else. By virtue of subscribing so diligently to this axiom of structural linguistics in the tradition of Saussure and Jakobson, the Summerfields presume in all their suggestions for teaching the existence of a larger—and largely unconscious—cultural context looming up to determine what we do in even the most apparently marginal of writing exercises. This context the

Summerfields call "funding," a term borrowed from the American philosopher John Dewey; other familiar terms for it include ideology, Chomsky's "competence," Foucault's "episteme," Lacan's "Symbolic," or, most recently, what Stanley Fish calls the presuppositions shared by "interpretative communities." To recognize this determining context startles us into realizing how entirely implicated we are in the social languages we normally oppose to our privacy. It is quite clearly the authors' intent, then, to make us hesitate about continuing to insist upon the notion of the "solitary" life of the author as it is usually mystified by our culture; instead, the Summerfields describe the real nature of the scene of reading and writing as a function of the "social production of discourse."

Thus, central to the theoretical recapitulations contained in the Summerfields' pedagogy is their reassessment of the status of the self, that fragile vessel to whom all of our teaching is addressed. Following one of the chief philosophical implications of structural linguistics (those made especially evident by the linguist Emile Benveniste and the philosopher Jacques Derrida), the Summerfields conclude that the self comes into being as a belated function of the various discursive situations in which it gets positioned—whether as father or mother, daughter or son, lawyer or doctor, student or teacher. The self is not—as the psychoanalysis of Jacques Lacan is most exact in articulating—what we usually think it is, an essence independent of time and history, "beyond culture," to use Lionel Trilling's phrase. The self is instead a bundle of conventions from the start, and its location in language is fundamental to its very coherence. The implications for teaching make the philosophical ones even more readily apparent.

Second, then, the results at the practical level of pedagogy proper: the "inner process" for the Summerfields is not what we customarily think it is in our usual attempts to theorize the self in the theory of composition. The authors are in fact exact and explicit about their lack of belief in a Rousseauesque kind of freedom in which an essential self may be said to exist independent of the community that otherwise sustains it—another way of saying that even the most private of personal experiences is at the same time also necessarily social, since it takes place as the result of discursive conventions that don't just express but actually shape what feelings we have. Thus, the otherwise familiar usefulness of notebooks and journals in composition class is, for the Summerfields, less the function of the students' discovery of an "authentic" self than it is of their discovery "that as their jottings accumulate, they come to constitute a representation of the self." This is not normative "process" pedagogy, then, but one designed instead to produce a more contemporary—and, for our students, a more faithful—view of the nature of experience than the liberationist ethic of spontaneity can provide. It is, as the Summerfields say, an "effective alternative to the current orthodoxies offered by the term *process.*"

Indeed, the book has a luminous figuration for why "internal process" is not really monological or self-sufficient, a figuration theoretically precise as well as reminiscent of the psychological companions that haunt our Romantic literary heroes from Keats to Pater to T. S. Eliot—that of our "ghostly interlocutor," as the Summerfields call it, even in the solitude of idleness or despair. The "inner process," conclude the authors, is itself always already dialogical or polylogical, since "any 'personal' experience is," as they say, "inescapably saturated, informed, packed by public meanings."

The production of a systematic pedagogy in accord with the contemporary climate in criticism was, of course, bound to happen anyway—the demands of the real are too acute to have prevented it. If there is a reason why our renewed attempts to teach writing in the last decade have frequently failed, it is that we have relied too largely on outworn models of reading, writing, and selfhood that force us into appealing to categories that our students are predisposed to reject on the basis of what their lives are like in an overtly systematic and media-oriented world. While neo-conservatives imply that any devolution in reading and writing skills is a function of open admissions policies and affirmative action, the real truth is that such devolution is actually a function of our clinging to precisely the kinds of essentialist notions that the Summerfields put so plainly into question. The point, therefore, is not to lead students of composition—or of literature—into a realm of absolutes, but into an awareness of historicity and cultural particularities instead. Our students' various knowledges or "fundings" are not only systematic, but, given today's communications society, knowingly so. What may well separate us from our students is our lingering humanist belief in a realm beyond systems to which our students no longer assent. Thus a pedagogy of "enabling constraints" is one that is sufficiently paradoxical to correspond to the world as it presents itself in the present. "We bring them," say the Summerfields of their own students, "to a certain place in their heads wherein certain structures become," not restraints or ornamental annoyances, but, rather, "appropriate," and, indeed, "necessary." The text of the self and those of the world are in ever-shifting relation, and pedagogy consists in bringing students to an awareness of the manifold structures those relations can and may take.

It is not, however, only a practical absorption of theory or even a winning pedagogy that distinguishes *Texts and Contexts*. Its plasticity as a text in its own right also requires recognition as a reflexive instance of what it has to say. After all, any ordering of its series of recommended writing exercises, each of them ingenious in itself, is provisional and experimental. Like Hugh Kenner's description of any given reading of Joyce's *Ulysses*, any given use or reading of *Texts and Contexts* is only one of so many "trial alignments," none absolute, none nugatory. In its refusal to construct itself upon any fixity, the book does what it says: the "various interacting dialectics" that may, as the authors put it, give shape to the book are always a function of how the teacher reads and uses it. The text, in other words, can, like any text, address itself only to particular, never universal, contexts; to put it another way, every text is a function of its reading, of its place in a signifying chain determined by a specific reader or audience. To discover, moreover, that the plastic structure of *Texts and Contexts* resembles the structure of a postmodern novel such as Cortazar's *Hopscotch* is hardly surprising given the commonalty of their projects. Like modernism and postmodernism themselves, the best pedagogy is clear about the socially necessary, if metaphysically random, orderings that language and society require of us no matter what our particular or momentary beliefs.

The range of the book's implications, then, are as striking for the criticism of literature as they are for the teaching of composition. Chief among them is the plain inevitability of our having to recognize that texts are different by virtue of degree rather than of kind, that a student essay and a poem by Ted Hughes — the kind of juxtapositions the Summerfields are fond of supplying us — in fact occupy or overlap equivalent discursive spaces despite what differences may otherwise separate them. But, of course, one can't measure that distance — one can't evaluate either Hughes's poem or one's own composition — without the presumption that both texts belong to similar fields of signification. Such a presumption is no less than the very precondition of measuring one's ability to perform in any discursive field at all, and the precise educational yield of the Summerfields' approach. In the process, it forces us to rethink, too, not just the relation of the literary to the paraliterary text, but also the reason we privilege literature as an object or study in the first place. We do so because literature is the locus par excellence for the production of persuasive rhetorical effects upon others, a microscope of the field of power in all its realms of play in life and letters alike, even in the semiotics of motorcycle repair. This position is perhaps difficult to accept wholeheartedly because of its raw truth; its inevitabilities are, however, inescapable. As a teacher, one cannot hesitate to explore every possibility.

Perry Meisel
New York University

# Preface

*Primitive sources of satisfaction must be steadily converted into more complex and humanly significant joys.*
*Anton Semyonovich Makarenko*\*

There are at least two ways to read this book. If you can tolerate, or even enjoy, delayed disclosure, we suggest that you simply read it from beginning to end; if, however, you are the kind of reader who prefers to have a solution before a mystery, a sense of the whole before exploring the parts, we suggest that you read Chapter 12 *first*.

We have ventilated the guiding ideas of this text both by discussing them with colleagues and friends at all levels of teaching, and also by applying them in composition courses with students from a great variety of backgrounds. In doing so, it was gratifying to be met with many recognitions, positive inclinations, and a sense of practical usefulness. But we hasten to add that we claim neither a sense of fixity nor a sense of completion. What we offer is a *contribution* to a continuing discussion, not a total theory of composition. We are sure of only one fact: we offer no one the last word.

Since the basic frame or template for our thinking and doing is dialectical, we would be inconsistent if we failed to acknowledge our expectation that this, our thesis, will generate, in others' minds, various antitheses, and that, when one fine day we all appear to have reached the ultimate synthesis, that synthesis will in the event promote the emergence of some necessary antithesis. Meanwhile, our belief in the necessity of the dialectic of practice and theory, of participation and spectatorship, is supported by nothing less than the example of Henry James—far enough removed from pedagogical concerns, indeed, yet continuously a source of illumination. Not least is his celebration of the gifts afforded by life to "the participant at once so interested and so detached as to be moved to a report of the matter," and his commitment to walking with one's eyes "greatly open."

Four (or five) propositions seem to us to be immediately and continuously useful (that is, usable) in thinking about the meanings and purposes of composition:

1. It seems likely that our best hope for a productive and coherent model of composition is to be derived from the nature and variety of human discourse as a primarily social fact; we produce discourse in context.

---

\*Preface to *The Road to Life, an Epic of Education* (Moscow: Foreign Languages Publishing House, 1955).

2.  Much of our discourse is *reactive*. It comprises a more or less appropriate reaction to some precedent action, invitation, arousal, or provocation.

3.  It seems equally likely that one of the primary features of social interactions—those interactions wherein we use language to construct and share a sense of what is commonly termed "reality"—is that we perform them, engage in them, in a variety of roles.

4.  Again, it seems that of all the various roles we occupy or inhabit, whether they be social, familial, intimate, or professional/institutional, the most radical distinction we experience is that which separates the role of participant from the role of spectator, and that these two superordinate or fundamental roles shape or determine the crucial features of our discourse.

We propose here to explore the implications and consequences, both theoretically and practically, of these four propositions. We shall attempt a little fine-tuning and elaboration, to try to show how they contribute to a basic rationale for work in composition and to exemplify them as working for students of composition at a daily level.

As for the relationships between theory and practice for student writers, our position is quite simple: as participants, they produce texts; as spectators, they reflect on those texts, and on others' texts, which may be seen to exemplify, to substantiate, certain key features of text *as* text, signifying meaning. We work to promote not self-consciousness but rather a more active, more subtle awareness of the constituent features of texts—their textuality—as a way of organizing discourse in order to take effect.

Composition courses, for us, are not occasions for confession, self-revelation, narcissism, or therapy of any kind, though we do believe that an effective course can generate a remarkable sense of community and even cheerfulness. Rather, they are occasions for the production of texts and for the promoting, in the writers, of an awareness not only of some of the crucial *features* of textuality but also of both the numerous options that at any moment the writer can see as available, as occasions for choice, and of the constraints that inhere in any social act.

As for "process," we agree that "One law for the ox and the lion is oppression," and that most discussions of process—even allowing for the inherent limitations of the word's connotations—are vitiated by two weaknesses: one, an apparently irresistible inclination to talk about "the writer" (as if we were all identical and as if all writing contexts were the same); the other, a promotion of inappropriate and counterproductive forms of self-consciousness.

What follows, then, is (a) an attempt to spell out realistically some of the possibilities that await us whenever we teach a composition course; and (b) an attempt to ventilate some new theoretical possibilities in the rationale of composition teaching. If you will read what we offer as representing a small step in what may be a useful direction, you will be accepting our words in the spirit in which they are offered.

We would like you to read all the pages of this text simultaneously, but like us, you are trapped in the necessity of linearity.

What kind of line, then, can we offer you? As in fishing, a line has two ends and a lot of stuff in between, with some knots. In the line of a text, the ends are "to begin" and "to end." Where to begin? Since we would like you first to enjoy some particularities, rather than the abstractions of generalizations, we begin *in medias res*, in the classroom, with an attempt to evoke the ethos of a composing class. The words on the page, however we manage them, fail inevitably to register all the nuances of response, of energy, of commitment that are actually present.

## A Note on Student Texts

The student texts in *Texts and Contexts* fall mostly into two categories:

(1) Texts written by students in Freshman Composition at Queens College are marked *Q*. Most of the students in these courses are "college age," 18–25. A few texts are by students at New York University and are marked *NYU*.

(2) Texts written by students at Utah State University are marked *U*. In the courses and workshops we have given at Utah, many of our students were "mature" individuals, some of them teachers themselves. They did not, however, consider themselves "writers"; yet many of them discovered (perhaps rediscovered) the joys, frustrations, and challenges of writing texts—particularly in the context of the classroom. "A leveling experience," many of the teachers said, as they felt the terror and exhilaration of "doing assignments." No better way, they agreed, of being reminded what it feels like to be "on the other side of the desk." And as they themselves experienced the interactions of a composing class, they agreed, as well, that texts produced in the context of a congenial classroom were spirited, fired, and inspired by the energy and the attentiveness of the group.

We would like to point out that the majority of student texts quoted are unrevised first drafts.

## Acknowledgments

Our first debt is to our students in New York, Utah, Oxford, York, and other places where we have either taught or offered workshops for teachers; to friends and colleagues who responded in various useful ways as we were shaping our ideas: Lil Brannon, Edmund Epstein, Joyce Kinkead, John Mayher, George McCulley, Donald McQuade, Donald Murray, Joyce Nelson, Thomas Newkirk, Richard Perry, and Gordon Pradl; and to those who read an early draft and offered generous criticism: Perry Meisel of New York University, David Bartholomae of the University of Pittsburgh, and Patricia Bizzell of Holy Cross. We are grateful to Perry Meisel also for writing the Foreword.

One of our basic dialectics is that of participant/spectator, and here a word of explanation is called for. We owe these terms to the pioneering work of Denys Harding and James Britton, but we have extended and modified their uses, their meanings, in accordance with our own purposes.

The practical aspects of our text draw primarily on our work in Freshman Composition at Queens College, New York; but we also draw on work we did in a very different place—Utah. In both places, our students, in effect, translated Marianne Moore's famous lines so that they read: "Writing? We too dislike it: there are things that are important beyond all this fiddle. Doing it, however, with a perfect distaste for it, we have discovered in it, after all, a place for the genuine." We are grateful for their generous collaboration, and for their permission to quote their texts.

Finally, we want to thank Steve Pensinger and Cynthia Ward at Random House, who helped our text develop; and Tina Barland and Evelyn Katrak for a scrupulous and clear-headed editing of our copy.

Our primary intellectual debt is acknowledged in our dedication.

J. S.
G. S.

# Contents

# CHAPTER ONE

# CONTEXT
## A Composing Class

*According to the current way of thinking (or non-thinking), it seems that if we are to enjoy anything then we must not have to think about it, and, conversely, if we are to think about anything, then we mustn't enjoy it. This is a calamitous and idiotic division of functions.*

*Barbara Wright*

# ETHOS

The kind of composition classroom we endorse is less like a lecture room and more like a workshop or studio. It's a place where texts get made: the air is experimental, tonic, collaborative, athletic, genial, sometimes urgent, always productive. It's not without tension, but if things go well, the tension is not destructive but generative. Utterance is dialogical rather than monological.

It's a place where students find meanings in differences and recognize something *as* something: as representative, as typical (or atypical); where reflection starts, and goes home to roost with them, and comes back to deliver an egg.

It's a place where competition does not rear its ugly head, where students can cut a dash without feeling foolish and take risks without feeling mortally vulnerable.

It's . . . well, it's not like the place represented in the following student text:

### ECONOMICS 1

It is time now. The clock clicks to the noon hour and it is time. The noon hour, how odd it is. All of the working people rejoice in this hour. It is a time to get rid of inefficient parts. It is a time to watch the show.

A show with a new star each day. How interesting it was. I used to get to the show early every day to get a good view. Today, I am in the furthest seat. The show has just started.

My friend Jake has the worst seat. He is the star. There he sits naked. His body completely shaven. Two men come out and make him lie down on the table. His name and history are read aloud to the audience. He has just finished his last day of his tenth working year. He is marked inefficient. The crowd starts a slow chant of "Inefficient! Inefficient!" I sit silent.

The two men slowly start to dismember his body as if he were an old machine. They start with his feet and then his legs. Each part is separately auctioned off to a buyer who will use it for its chemical properties. As they work upwards on the body, the crowd's chant grows louder and louder. Finally, they reach the skull, and it is auctioned off at a high price. The show is over.

The people rejoice in the effectiveness of the show in

another chant, screaming EFFICIENCY! EFFICIENCY! All of the people, all but me. For tomorrow, tomorrow, I am the star.

Steve Micozzi (Q)

## *Reflections*

"Economics 1" is the story of my economics class, believe it or not. The whole story came about by my thinking of the distaste I have for that class. . . . The class is, of course, at noon, and just as the story goes, it's a time to watch the show. The show in real life is this: the teacher picks each student apart and humiliates him in front of the whole class. He picks on a different person each day. I always used to get to class early until he started getting closer to my name. The day I wrote this, I was the next person in line, after my friend got it. The terms "efficiency" and "inefficiency" were the trademark of the teacher's lectures.

Steve Micozzi (Q)

This is not to say that blood does not flow in our classrooms. Here is how one student perceived her participation in our class:

## *TO MY CLASSMATES*

I am a carnivore. I feed off the entrails of my new friends' ideas. These last two days have been a magnificent carnage. Your creations, your possessions, I selfishly devour—a foot, three toes, a chunk of hair. Your soul children, precious offspring, I swallow greedily. Never satisfied, I hungrily reach for more.

Each new limb is offered eagerly, graciously. This puzzles me, but I grab it, dissect it, roll it about in my mouth— intestinal ambrosia. I eagerly reach for more. I am a monster. I am insatiable. You willingly offer me more, and more.

How brave you are, how bold, to allow your vitals to be strewn here and there for me to lay my eyes upon, and desire. Do you feel a sadness as I snatch your dear cherubs away? Do you sense a longing as I split them open and feast on those richest organs? Doesn't it tear at your heart to see me consume your darlings?

And you offer me more? How *can* you offer me more?

3

Don't you know they can't be replaced. THEY CAN'T BE REPLACED. I can't give them back. I am sorry. They are mine now. They have become a part of me. I turn away from you, ashamed to see the anguish, the yearning in your eyes. But again and again, you offer me more. Again I take, but am not filled.

I am a carnivore. Day after day, I feed on the sweet meat of your innermost parts. I am enriched, but never satisfied. I demand more. Please, forgive me. I cannot control this huge appetite of mine. I am a monster. I am an endless chasm where your precious thoughts are deposited. And now they are mine. All mine . . . forever, and ever, and ever . . .

Katherine Green (U)

## *What Happens in Our Classroom*

What is it that *could not* happen if the class did not meet? By asking this question, we can pinpoint some of the jobs we have to do:

1. Students write texts within constraints of time and place. We need to exploit these constraints positively. (See page 7.)

2. Students read each others' texts and discuss them, nonjudgmentally.

3. Students make conversation—a collaborative act. As the philosopher Michael Oakeshott says:

> As civilized human beings, we are the inheritors, neither of an enquiry about ourselves and the world, nor of an accumulating body of information, but of a conversation, begun in the primeval forests and made more articulate in the course of centuries. It is a conversation that goes on both in public and within each of ourselves. . . . It is the ability to participate in this conversation, and not the ability to reason cogently, to make discoveries about the world, or to contrive a better world which distinguishes the human being from the animal and the civilized man from the barbarian. . . . Education, properly speaking, is an initiation into the skill and partnership of this conversation in which we learn to recognize the voices, to distinguish the proper occasions of utterance, and in which we acquire the intellectual and moral habits appropriate to conversation.[1]

4. Texts are read *aloud*. Many of the distinctive features of a text can often best be apprehended through / by the *ear*. We encourage students both to write and read with the ear. We believe that the use of the ear is profoundly, consistently beneficial, and that silent reading misses a great deal, especially if it shifts into speedy reading.

   The expressive features of *any* text—its rhythms, its textures, its tones, its pace, its modulations, its structures, its effects on the reader—all these are more vividly apprehended through getting the words off the page. Many features, then, by being uttered and heard, present themselves, come to the surface, are made manifest. To neglect such possibilities is to try to wrestle with one hand tied behind the back.

   Every text generates expectations and proceeds to satisfy (or disappoint) them. Many texts "play with" the reader, by using such devices as suspense, an unexpected turn, "effective surprise." Again, these can be *heard*, and when one hears them, one discovers that, after all, there is some useful truth in the notion that text is displaced speech.

5. Students assume or enter many actual roles, as tellers and listeners, as readers and writers. They read, both silently and aloud; alone and in groups. They write, both rough drafts and texts that will not be revised: they make notes, keep journals, jot down reactions, prepare questions. They write and become the first readers of their own texts. They invite or allow others to become readers of their texts. They compare notes on their experiences of writing and hearing / reading other texts, both primary texts and reactive. They read their texts to the whole class or hear them read by someone else.

   They feel the effects of their own texts and of others'. They are moved in various ways. They have moments of insight, recognition, illumination.

   They enter vicarious / virtual roles; they even become "possessed" by them. And they write texts that they could not have written *in propria persona*. (See Chapters 9 and 10 for more on role work.)

6. When things go well, the students become part of a dynamic community—not cloned into homogeneity, but stimulated by the lively interactions that occur when minds are aroused, alert, on the qui vive, provoked, responsive, light-footed.

   Whenever students look back at the end of a semester in which things have gone well—positively, productively, faring

forward—it is to this experience of good-humored lively interaction that they direct our attention. One of our students,
John Roundy, remembers a writing workshop in Utah:

> The rapport of the participants became closer than any
> group I have ever seen. From two "exercises" we did, many
> of the participants know Ron Fowler, Roger Haderlie, Vickie
> Edgar and Ijeoma Ahanonu, all John Does of the literary
> world, better than they will ever know Ernest Hemingway.
> We remember each other's stories; we listen and we laugh
> and are moved. I don't remember hearing such laughter in
> a classroom.

7. The class develops an identity and acquires a history. The
   context is not simply the group here and now; it is also temporal and developmental—a sense of where they were and
   how far they've come, a sense of some kind of change for the
   better. Their texts acquire extravagant ambitions.

    And always there is a counterpoint of action and reaction:
   the student who reads aloud sees the listening, responsive
   faces of his or her peers.

8. Nor, as teachers, do we try for homogeneity. There are two
   distinctive voices in this text, and we, the two of us, are two
   distinctive personalities in the classroom: male, female; soft,
   loud; patient, impatient, etc. One of us may suddenly jump
   onto a chair to make a point, the other would never dream of
   it. One of us may read work in progress to the class; the other
   says, "No way!" We take and give and learn from each other
   but do not try to become the other; that is why we cannot,
   dare not, offer recipes. We offer ingredients and principles;
   and you, our colleagues, stew in your own juices, your own
   ovens, your own translations, your own classrooms.

We end where we began. ("In our end is our beginning.") A composing classroom is not a lecture room. So the first thing we do is put the
chairs in a circle.

# ENABLING CONSTRAINTS

*In our society . . . it is felt that, with the possible exception of pure fan-
tasy or thought, whatever an agent seeks to do will be continuously con-
ditioned by natural constraints, and that effective doing will require the
exploitation, not the neglect, of this condition.*
*Erving Goffman*

"**A** rtificial limits create a crisis, which rouses the brain's resources: the compulsion towards haste overthrows the ordinary precautions, flings everything into top gear, and many things that are usually hidden find themselves rushed into the open. Barriers break down, prisoners come out of their cells." Thus writes Ted Hughes, on how we can help students get words onto the page.[2] He goes on to suggest that all else (e.g., concern for grammar and syntax) should be sacrificed in "an attempt to break fresh and accurate perceptions and words out of the reality of the subject chosen." And that is remarkably close to William Carlos Williams's advice: "Write carelessly so that nothing that is not green will survive."

Our students *are*, willy-nilly, constrained. Universities depend for their survival on constraints; otherwise buildings would go up in flames and some of us would be hanged, drawn, and quartered. What interests us is the distinction to be made between constraints that disable and constraints that enable. Young tomato plants are firmly tied to wooden stakes—constraints that serve to support the plant when the fruits ripen.

We have no objection to arbitrary constraints ("Do this because I say so") as long as the doing is seen to bear fruit *that the students themselves can value*. The important thing is to reap a quick modest harvest so that the students can come sooner rather than later to believe in the efficacy of the procedure. "Trust me," we can say, once or twice. But unless the giving of trust pays off soon, is justified by its product, we shall end up talking to the walls. Pragmatically, through texts getting made and being valued, we work to build belief, and through belief, students discover commitment to this strange act of urgent, silent scribbling. Blessedly, they have no time for self-consciousness.

The constraints that we don't believe in, that we think are fraudulent, misleading, or counterproductive, have been keenly anatomized by John Warnock and Tilly Eggers in their exhilarating account of freshman writing at the University of Wyoming,[3] and we are content to let their words speak for us, too.

## Constraints That Enable

To involve one's students in a short bout of unhappiness, frustration, and tension is an effective way of bringing them to appreciate some of the crucial differences between constraints that they feel to be legitimate and those that they feel to be illegitimate. They come to recognize legitimate constraints as fruitful, as yielding good results (like playing tennis with a net). They come to recognize illegitimate constraints as *merely* arbitrary, as inexplicable impositions, rules that are not susceptible of rationalizations that they can endorse.

Here now are some examples of short-term, modest exercises of the kind that we use to nudge, provoke, impel students into writing in the early stages of the semester.

## Eight Words and No More

Occasionally, we start our work with a new class by asking students to write a short text whereby they "introduce" themselves: the arbitrary proviso is that no sentence (or T. unit) in the text shall exceed eight words. The results are always fascinating. Here are some comments by the students (U) themselves:

> I sit thinking of the text I produced. There were frustrations involved with the eight-word limit. I struggled with the limit imposed on my writing. I am usually not as conscious of constraints. I sensed a little better how students can feel with assignments. What seems natural to me may seem totally unnatural to students. Back to the text. I begin a sentence. Then stop. One word; two, three, four, stop. Reread, five. Pause, count words. How can I finish in eight words or less? Name that word! Cross out a word; Cut the thought off. The sentence stops in midthought—the eight-word limit. The limit is unreasonable. I run out of things to say. Cover the bases with short sentences. I try to elaborate, but the limit. I start a new sentence and a new idea. See Dick run! I'm regressing. After ten sentences, what more do I have to say? Change directions. What's the purpose of the assignment? Too heavy use of "I." I, I, I, I, me, me, me. Egocentric. Get rid of I. I do it and it goes passive. I have just been working with style. Eliminate the passive. Avoid is, are, was, were, etc., etc. I find myself editing the text as I go. I want to get it out and then go back. But there's a time constraint. I want the assignment to be what's wanted. I want to make a good impression. I want to give an accurate picture of myself, my goals, my plans, my uniqueness. The constraints seem to limit; or is it inhibit? I feel demoted ten grades as I reread the text. I want to put a big "THE END" at the

bottom. I have finished. Closure! I want to announce the fact. Now you are subject to reading my ramblings.
THE END

*I am beginning*—good, only three words so far—why is he doing this, anyway? I suppose he wants our writing to be simple—brief—to the point—let's see—*I am beginning my twelfth year of teaching.* There—perfect—eight words—but teaching what? Can't I say English? Wait a minute, I'm not conserving words—I'm expanding. *My current assignment is ninth and tenth grade English.* Dammit—nine words—had to tag that word English on the end of a sentence after all—or should I go back and try it again? How about—*I currently teach ninth and tenth grade English?* There—did it. Was it worth it? Not so sure. *Also I have recently been appointed English Department Chairman*—Egad, can't I even tell where without starting again—and what? Nine words again. Go back? Take out the *also?* Nah—surely he'll count the label *English Department Chairman* as one word. Geez—sounds like I'm bragging myself up—titles and all. Can't I say it but soften it a little? Not in eight words I can't. Oh well—*For the past eight years I have coached swimming*—nine words again. Well, at least I've struck a pattern—nine words is pretty good—heck of a lot more economical than I've been with words for some time—good enough—keep going—*This spring I resigned as swimming coach.* This is horrible——Heavens, I at least want to sound like Hemingway—not a third grader. It's driving me crazy—I quit.

Eight words. He's got to be kidding. What does he think this workshop is? A remedial workshop? Let's see, who am I? *Anna Barbieri.* Well, I did that in four words. I feel like an idiot. I can't think of anything to say—let alone in eight-word sentences. I hope no one is going to read this. It makes me sound like a babbling idiot. Let me think . . . *I've enjoyed my education.* . . . Oh, good, Anna, we're getting deep now. I wonder if the writing time is up? Better yet, I wonder if I'm in the wrong workshop? *Adolescents are a species of their own.* How profound, Anna. You're right about their being their own species. It's what kind of species they are that worries me. I did that sentence in eight words or less, though. Boy, how exciting it is to digress in time and ability. Did I hear him say "time"? Thank God!

## Three-Word Riddles

*Scene:*   The students sit in the classroom.

*Action:*   "Choose any object in this room and write a three-word riddle for it." The constraint here is one of *extreme* economy.

*Time:*   Three minutes.

*Reaction:*

1. Riddles are composed, on scraps of paper.
2. These are thrown into a hat.
3. Each student takes one piece of paper randomly from the hat.
4. Reads it aloud.
5. Tries to solve it.
6. Solves or fails to solve it.
7. Discussion follows: was the riddle too easy or too difficult? How so? How do our minds have to work when we decipher the "code" of a riddle?

*Examples:**

1. slap slap slap
2. Hickory Dickory Disney
3. fill empty full
4. little bo peep
5. black coarse smelly

After attempting to guess the objects referred to by the riddle—with the writer assisting if necessary—we discovered that:

1. *slap slap slap* referred to Marge's navy blue mules. The writer tried to present the sound the mules made as Marge walked.

2. *Hickory Dickory Disney* referred to Donna's Mickey Mouse watch. The three-word riddle called up the world of nursery rhymes, playing on the notion of clocks. "Hickory, Dickory, Dock, the mouse ran up the clock." Donna had a mouse on her clock. The writer here called upon allusions and metaphoric leaps.

3. *Fill empty full:* The basic states of a cup: fill (verb), empty (verb and adjective), full (adjective); an echo of the optimist and pessimist: half-empty, half-full.

---

*The whole of *Examples* is derived from a student's record of the class.

4. *Little bo peep:* A reference to toes peeping out of a sandal. When retracted, they were lost; when exposed, they lay like a flock of sheep, peeping out.

5. *black coarse smelly:* An evaluative account of someone's pipe.

## The Tension Between Inner Feelings and Social Conventions

What we want to say and what we feel we *can* say, given social constraints (politeness, sobriety, appropriateness, tact) demand a balancing act. We might want to blow our top, but we don't; instead we choose language to clothe our feelings in socially acceptable conventions. Here, we offer a situation where students are given an opportunity to explore those tensions between the needs of the inner world and the constraints of the social world.

A typical assignment in this category would be:

1. Read the account of Melvin's baptism (see p. 35).

2. Go into role as Melvin's mother.

3. Write a letter to Virginia's mother, letting off the steam of indignation, rage, or whatever.

4. Write your letter *in accordance with the social rules of a polite society.*

It is in the tension between 3 and 4 that the students find the focus of constraint.[4]

Here are extracts from two such letters:

> Furthermore, aside from the sacrilege involved in permitting your daughter to profane our sacred religion by mocking the holiest of holy ceremonies dear to our faith, whereupon a newborn child receives God's grace, I find it to be totally reproachable and reprehensible that you should have allowed your daughter, who was at that time in charge of my Melvin, to have jeopardized my child's life by having put him into a dangerous situation through negligent, foolhardy, and unpardonably careless actions that could have been avoided, if only self-restraint and proper control had

been exercised in the very first place both on the part of your daughter as well as yourself.

Ira Kleinman (Q)

Have you not taught your child the sanctity of life? That life is precious? That it should be cherished? Particularly, the life of an innocent, defenseless child? Your daughter practically murdered my son! He might have drowned in that rain barrel. All for a childhood prank. And in the name of God! You may say Virginia is only a child: she didn't know any better. It is about time that she finds out; her actions were wrong, wrong, wrong, and she must know. Let her know that she defiled life and made a mockery of the church. Let her know before it is too late, before she is too old to know, and let her know in such a way that she will remember.

George (Q)

## Commentary

We enjoyed both of those texts—both Ira's extravagant hypotaxis, and George's staccato parataxis. Ira doesn't let Mrs. Hudson off the hook. He goes on and on, until Mrs. Hudson must have begun to wonder how much more she could take before she would get a chance to catch her breath—at the end of the sentence. George's is a series of quick, sharp jabs or hooks—left, right, left, right—staccato, unrelenting, which leave the reader *impressed!*

Both seem to us to work, partly because both exploit rhythm to carry part of the meaning—not the meaning of individual words but the meaning of the whole, the tone, mood, or feeling that is the essential energy of the utterance. As Michael Halliday has observed, sentences do not compose a text, they *realize* it.[5]

## Constructing the Middle

We give students two sentences, either composed for the occasion or borrowed from an already existing text. They must start with the first of the two sentences and end with the second. In between, they are on their own, but they must move their text irresistibly to the terminus of the given line.

For example, we offer the opening and closing lines of a remarkable paratactic poem by Dave Etter: "The house smells like we had smelly socks for dinner" and "Monday night and I feel already I've worked a week."

Here is one student's reaction:

> The house smells like we had smelly socks for dinner. Sweat beads on the ceiling and grandfather absentmindedly peels the soft painted skin from the walls. A wet forearm glides across a sopping brow, as I look at the black shade, which the sun has turned to scalding platinum. Everywhere I turn, I see the sun, or an equally potent likeness blazing from a window across the way, or from the fender of a car feeling its way through the bloated air. When I was younger, I fried an ant or two under a magnifying glass; everyone did, I suppose. So you could say we all deserve this, but I had no idea that God had the sick sense of humor of the average eleven-year-old. Grandfather chimes in, uninvited, "Haven't seen a stretch like this since '37." "Enough," I shout, "when it's cold, it hasn't been this cold since '37, when there's a drought, it hasn't been this dry since '37; that must have been some year. I know, you lived in Iceland, worked in a car wash, and went to the sauna to unwind." Was I too harsh? Grandpa rocks back and forth in silence; perhaps I've hurt him. "Nope, hasn't been this hot since '37." I walk to the window, see the sun is finally losing its grip on the sky. Monday night and I feel already I've worked a week.
>
> Marc Kieselstein (Q)

## A Tight Repetitive Structure

Consider the following poem by Edwin Morgan:

### SPACEPOEM 3: OFF COURSE

> *the golden flood    the weightless seat*
> *the cabin song    the pitch black*
> *the growing beard    the floating crumb*
> *the shining rendezvous    the orbit wisecrack*
> *the hot spacesuit    the smuggled mouth-organ*
> *the imaginary somersault    the visionary sunrise*
> *the turning continents    the space debris*
> *the golden lifeline    the space walk*
> *the crawling deltas    the camera moon*

*the pitch velvet    the rough sleep*
*the crackling headphone    the space silence*
*the turning earth    the lifeline continents*
*the cabin sunrise    the hot flood*
*the shining spacesuit    the growing moon*
    *the crackling somersault    the smuggled orbit*
    *the rough moon    the visionary rendezvous*
    *the weightless headphone    the cabin debris*
    *the floating lifeline    the pitch sleep*
    *the crawling camera    the turning silence*
    *the space crumb    the crackling beard*
    *the orbit mouth-organ    the floating song*[6]

The structure of this poem is fairly obvious: two blocks or stanzas of 14 and 7 lines, the stanza shift marked by a literal shift, a typographical move from left to right—a kind of indentation. Each line consists of two equal parts, and each part consists of determiner (definite article), adjective, and noun. Semantically, the topic or subject remains consistent throughout. Relationship between noun and adjective in the first block produces an effect of harmony, efficiency, normality. The same relationship in the second part creates an effect of tension, unease, calamity, distress. Some of the nouns in part 2 are the same as in part 1, but in part 2 they have "dissonant" adjectives modify them.

As a piece of lexicogrammatical description, that all sounds pretty abstract. But as soon as you choose a topic and proceed to represent it in accordance with that given structure so as to replicate the *form* of Morgan's poem, something very interesting begins to happen. Your choices are entirely and exclusively *semantic*; you have absolutely no structural choices to make. The pattern exists a priori. What is left for the writer to present is entirely a matter of meaning.

As the bit of the world and its meaning begins to find its way onto the paper, the writer finds himself or herself, willy-nilly, increasingly interested in the act—especially in terms of the crucial shift from positive-normal to negative-abnormal.

Here now are some student texts written after only the structural instructions had been offered—that is, the students had not yet met Morgan's poem:

The woman's smile.        The steaming pot.
The vapored smells.      The heated coils.
The tasting spoon.        The added salt.
The dinner call.           The wooden chairs.

The Delft china.
The fresh bouquet.
The dinner call.
The cooling food.
The untied apron.
The rumpled bed.
The man's snoring.
The folded arms.

The shining silverware.
The wrapped present.
The quiet room.
The wiped hands.
The creaking stairs.
The wrinkled suit.
The sturdy door frame.
The sobbing sigh.

Craig Shertloff (U)

## Reflections

This assignment was fascinating. The constraints seemed to force a focus upon one situation. I chose an anniversary. A woman cooking a special meal (the Delft china), some detail about the careful cooking of the dinner. My moment of discord is the repetition of the dinner call. She has called her husband to the special dinner; he does not answer. I pictured her concerned look as she wipes her hands and unties the apron to investigate his whereabouts. "The cooling food" is probably the "thesis" statement of this piece. Their relationship is cooling; he has forgotten, or is just unconcerned about, the special occasion and preparations going on downstairs. I pictured the couple as well-to-do; stairs in the house, to me, always connote success. He has simply fallen asleep. It's not that she can't wake him, not that the dinner can't be salvaged, it's just that he makes no contribution of his own will. I see her leaning against the door frame (sturdy, which she is not). The folded arms are some kind of resentment statement, and the sobbing sigh sums up her options and possibilities.

Craig Shertloff (U)

## RECITAL

The ebony keys, the accurate fingers
The envisioned pages, the hollow room
The distant breathing, the harmonious rhythm
          The unsuppressed giggle, the broken spell
          The forgotten passage, the hollow rhythm
          The mounting terror, the fearful shame.

Katherine Green (U)

The silky fabric.　　The earthy colors.
The loved colors.　　The unusual design.
The daring pattern.　　The backless back.
The large buttons.　　The elegant sleeves.

The damned sleeve.　　The left sleeve.
The three attempts.　　The damned sleeve.
The laughing friend.　　The damned friend.
The torn fabric.　　The abandoned fabric.

Anna Barbieri (U)

A palpable tension arose as the students came near to concluding and closing their texts. For the required structure is consistently (i.e., exclusively) paratactic; but many students felt the need to *modify the structure* so as to signal some kind of closure, to represent a conclusion—to represent closure not only semantically but also structurally: either with cadence ("and they all lived happily ever after") or in one of the various ways that Barbara Herrnstein Smith has so fully explored in *Poetic Closure*. The consensus was that at the shift from part 1 (positive) to part 2 (negative), there was no felt need to *change the structure*, because part 2 was a negative "mirror-image" of the positive part 1. It was only on approaching and effecting closure that the need for a marked change of structure was felt.

Similarly, when students write *reactive* texts, either after reading a passage from Beckett's *Watt* (see p. 148) or after being given structural instructions (the "program" for a pattern of syntax), they generally drift toward one or the other tendency: they either have little or no difficulty in replicating Beckett's patterns, both at a macro- and at a microlevel; or they feel impelled to modify it in certain ways, of which they themselves gradually become aware *as they are writing* (see p. 192).

## Words from the Dictionary, Randomly Lifted

We take about ten words, more or less at random, from any one page of a good dictionary, give them to the class, and discuss their meanings.

The students' task is then to produce a text that incorporates each of the given words and *as few others as possible*. Here is an example:

Flow fearless and free
Forget me not, oh fluid flamingo!
I in my firkin, thou in thy fire
Fester in my flanks.

*16*

Flagrant, oh faithless one!
My friend, my foe.
Flaccidly, I lie fallow
Waiting to be filled.
Flamboyantly flabbergasted,
I fish for fulfillment
And fork feathers.

April Ivy Krassner (NYU)

## Responses to an Image

We distribute reproductions of paintings that seem to us rich in human meanings. Then we simply ask students to give their picture as full and close an attention as possible and to "let something happen." Here are two reactions to the same picture:

### THE LADY WITH THE PRIMROSES

Oh god, she was beautiful!
I wanted to rush and close her in my arms.
I wanted the curve of her cheek
In the curve of the curve of my palm
And to feel the warmth, the flush.
But no, that wouldn't have worked.
Rushing was sound and she would have turned;
The movement would have dissolved it.

I saw the flared nostrils,
The cord of nerve running through her forehead
Tight and smooth,
Not tension but intensity.
She just kept looking and looking
Clutching the primroses to her chest.

April Ivy Krassner (NYU)

### LADY WITH PRIMROSES:
### INTERROGATION AND MEMORIES

Upon turning it over, I was disappointed. Surely a gracious lady with primroses should be permitted a few vivid spots of color.

With senses gasping and suffocating, I gaze at the neuter gray museum card. And where is the ambience of the garden, the bushes and trees hanging with ripe fruit, wet moss, and fragrant blossoms? (Her skirt swished down the garden path amidst the scattering of soft petals on either side.)

Would she so purposefully clasp the primroses and thereby ruin their dimensionality? Doesn't the marble allow for parted petals to *fall* in disarray from the subject?

The unitary figure clasps the primrose treasures lovingly, yet they are crushed. So what is the "raison d'être" of this primrose lady, trapped paradoxically in the marble form?

If I consider the action itself, I find some meaning. Her quiet, sensitive face and her preserving gesture—Did she pluck them herself, or are they perhaps the gift of a child?

. . . I remember the wild flowers presented to me each day by my four-year-old son, Jake. It was during the one summer that I spent at the "fisa" site. Sweaty hands squeezed the wilting stems. They sustained themselves only temporarily, even when placed in the icy spring water. The gritty hands, the tan streaked face and the eager voice piping, "I picked some pretty flowers for you, mum."

Dreary days with leaking rain followed by sunny days when the sand blasted its way through the cracks of the cabin. The liquor ridden, blue and white Delft vase stands constant—filled with blue starflowers, wild clover and fuchsia fireweed. The narrow neck has been subservient to the tightly grasping fingers.

But when presented, I don't clasp them to my bosom as the lady with primroses does—What difference between fifteenth- and twentieth-century flower-holding poses? Is it an affected pose, a mere prop to the sculptor's design, or does it have a real function?

Really, it is the action of giving and receiving the primroses which has meaning. This action precedes the pose and emits emotion, just as my memory does for me.

Mary Anne Kendall (NYU)

## Writing in the Dark

This is an extreme situational constraint, an experience of sheer eventfulness. We literally plunge the room into darkness and tell students to write. Darkness, like nighttime, has powerful effects on us all. Some students find themselves lapsing into erotic fantasy, some are discomfited, others feel very comfortable. Again, as in the eight-word sentence assignment, students discover a great deal about their own habitual, daylight, unexamined procedures as writers. In the eight-word case, they discover above all their habitual dependency on, their *intuitive* commitment to, sentence variety. In the dark, they discover that invariably when they write, whatever they write, they read recursively even as they write. The onward flow of their text, moving forward into empty space, moment by moment, depends on a rapid review of what is already, most freshly, a text on the page.

Consider Denise Levertov's poem:

## WRITING IN THE DARK

*It's not difficult.*
*Anyway, it's necessary.*

*Wait till morning, and you'll forget.*
*And who knows if morning will come.*

*Fumble for the light, and you'll be*
*stark awake, but the vision*
*will be fading, slipping*
*out of reach.*

*You must have paper at hand,*
*a felt-tip pen—ballpoints don't always flow,*
*pencil points tend to break. There's nothing*
*shameful in that much prudence: those are your tools.*

*Never mind about crossing your t's, dotting your i's—*
*but take care not to cover*
*one word with the next. Practice will reveal*
*how one hand instinctively comes to the aid of the other*
*to keep each line*
*clear of the next.*

*Keep writing in the dark:*
*a record of the night, or*
*words that pulled you from depths of unknowing,*
*words that flew through your mind, strange birds*
*crying their urgency with human voices,*

*or opened*
*as flowers of a tree that blooms*
*only once in a lifetime:*

*words that may have the power*
*to make the sun rise again.*[7]

Here are a few reactions to darkness at noon:

### *WRITING IN THE DARK*

Abyss down —
        a hole without name
No one's been back to tell us more than the surface.

If they're lost below that, they're gone,
Never to return to the world of light.

The abyss rims and then darkness eternally down.

We pushed Wodwo in during the Renaissance.

But sometimes when the sun goes down, and
the lights go out . . . darkness crawls out of the hole.
It throws down a chain and hand over hand Wodwo returns
and lurks just beyond our window pane for us to come out
into the woods, where darkness is his domain until light.

Charlotte Miller (U)

### *Reflections*

I still love a good horror story, I guess. Actually when the lights went out I thought of the middle ages, lost in the dark. Wodwo came to my mind and I wondered if we are really all that much more civilized today than then. After all, Wodwo has just changed shapes and names. We call him "Sasquatch," "Yeti," "Abominable Snowman," or "Bigfoot." Wodwo is still being sought for by teams of scientists. Who knows, maybe he isn't just a bogeyman. This needs Vincent Price to read it.

Charlotte Miller (U)

I'm not sure I like this. I'm in a section of the room that is totally dark. Wow, so much blackness. I kind of like the dark sometimes. It's so . . . thick, and velvety. It's hard to really explain the feeling. Sometimes when I'm sitting alone in the darkness, and I'm *sure* that I'm alone, I can relax in a way that daylight would never allow. I can really participate in a special kind of communion with the quiet and the solitude.

I'm getting a little flaky. Must be all of this darkness with the little scratching noises from the pens floating out of it. Pretty weird . . .

Ho hum, I wonder when he's going to turn the lights on again. It's funny, watching the small glow from his pipe float around the room. It reminds me of "Tinkerbell" from the production of Peter Pan dad took me to see when I was a kid. Just a little light floating around in the dark. Nice thought to end on.

Ah, here are the lights.

Jennifer Kirk (U)

I love the dark. I wish we could play out this last hour in the dark. Everyone seems uninhibited and I bet we'd share our best thoughts with each other.

Darkness is a funny thing. I remember fearing the dark at a time when I believed a green slimy monster would attack me. Now . . . now, darkness is my escape from a brutal world where I'm always on display. No one can see me in the dark. It's like a shroud of security. Security that can't be taken away and is only a light switch away.

Sometimes in the dark I can see things more clearly. I guess by shutting out all the world, it's just me. Me and all my thoughts. I'm quite entertaining, you know. No one makes me happier than me. I remember the first time I was introduced to myself. It was in the dark. I was quite pleased. I knew I'd hit it off right away.

Anna Barbieri (U)

Who knows what evil lurks in the hearts of men? The Shadow knows. Cackle, cackle!

And here we all sit, writing in the Shadows of Merlin. How does Merlin feel about the Connecticut Yankee—now? Is he still threatened sometimes? Some here think so. I hope not. Even Merlin can grow. Even Merlin writes in the dark.

Up theme music. And we are in the Inner Sanctum. Cre e e e ch! Welcome.

Red glow. Sunset. Hot Coals. Burned feet. Fakir. Nirvana. Kosmos.

Judy Lord (U)

### WRITING IN THE DARK

I am a creature of the light.
I have absolutely no interest in writing
in the dark.
Wait!

I have made an interesting discovery.
I am such a recursive reader I sometimes
can't even remember what letters I have already
put on the page. . . .
This is not as silly an exercise as I
had originally thought—
I don't like it but
I want to know why.
Is it that I trust the page
more than the memory?

Lind Williams (U)

It is through inviting our students to compose with such constraints that we educe a repertoire of relatively modest texts of a desired variety. Should you wish to see how such work may fit into a semester's schedule, you may wish to do a quick reading of Chapter 12, but, meanwhile, what of the absence of constraints?

# LOOK! NO CONSTRAINTS! WRITING FOR ONESELF
## Writing Whatever You Want, Need, or Feel the Impulse to Write

Sentimentalists—teachers of a Rousseauesque persuasion—espouse a dubious absolute: freedom. We believe freedom in such terms to be an illusion. But it's not our present purpose to knock straw men down. Rather, we simply wish to offer here a few reflections on the more spacious elbowroom that comes with relatively random, serendipitous, unsupervised writing.

Writing within minimal constraints, and doing it regularly, is clearly one of the high roads to the unburdened confidence that comes with familiarization and can conduce to certain kinds of fluency. We think of Trollope, in successful middle age, opening a chest and looking over the thousands of pages of text he had written during his early years. He had preserved them, and now, as he read them again, he quickly decided to destroy them. They were, he said, rubbish; but he acknowledged that in producing them, he had acquired a fluency, a certain comfort and ease: writing had become second nature—an old-fashioned way of saying he had become acculturated.

The "free" text will, by definition, absolve itself of many of the constraints appropriate to social writing. At its most extreme, it will be solipsistic, rambling, incomprehensible to anyone other than the writer, uncontextualized, unbuttoned, unself-consciously unguarded, self-consciously reflexive, yet almost irresistibly providing a location for experiments in addressing others, so deeply social is the impulse of all discourse.

There is clearly a place for such discourse in our lives—indeed, we produce it as the more private form of inner speech. But how does such discourse emerge as text? Our guess is that it usually occurs in the form of the journal. At its best, it can be enjoyed as literature—as in the journals of Virginia Woolf, Arnold Bennett, Henry David Thoreau, F. Scott Fitzgerald. What place, then, is there for the journal in a composition course? How can it become useful? Useful to the student? Useful to the instructor?

We prefer to call it a notebook rather than a journal. We encourage students to see it as more than a bed-to-bed accounting of their lives; we encourage them to get out of their own dailiness and look around, take note, reflect upon, debate, *react to,* ask questions about, their own worlds and the worlds they encounter in texts. And we suggest that the journal not tyrannize, that they need not write daily. We ask for a total number of pages by the end of the semester: 50, 75, 100. We note that students often balk at the number, and we remember many open-admissions students in the early 1970s insisting that they could not/ would not be *able:* the feat was impossible. By the end of the semester, many had written well over 100 pages. And they took with them their *books*—their writings, their texts—to keep writing in. Numbers of students, in fact, return to us, after our semester with them has ended, to share their new notebooks. (We, as instructors, can choose to read, if we wish, and usually, we wish, out of sheer interest and curiosity; if not, we can simply tally the number of pages, as one of the required texts for the course.)

So the notebook, for many, becomes a sacred object, a text to keep and reread, a way of keeping track, of holding on to the "data" of their minds, a way of experimenting, daring, allowing out private thoughts that are rarely made public. Here, for example, is Meg lashing out at M—, a student in one of her classes. She lets him have it, and feels better for having done so. Her "voice" is unstoppable, dynamic, lambasting—a rush of unbridled energy:

> If M— was not such an ass, I could handle his comments
> with more patience. He is a cheesey Argentine who still
> wears his hair like the 1978 John Travolta. His shirts are

always made of rayon with a sleeveless tee-shirt underneath. Jesus Christo hangs around his neck on a gold chain that is not very different from my own St. Barbara. I suppose all Latin Americans bring with them a common mark of their culture. But on his neck, the religious tradition—that Ave-Maria-between-every-word tradition—is cheesey as well. He rapes his heritage with his stupid grin, his disrespect for promptness, and above all, with his worthless arrogance.

So he didn't like my story? Well, that is anyone's right. But if anyone is going to criticize my work, it should be someone who is bright—someone who can write himself. Criticism from an ass is asinine. He has proved this: the remarks were empty. No ending!?! There is always a positive way of delivering criticism. If Pat had offered negative criticism, I could have handled it. And certainly I would have reviewed my work.

He is startlingly unable to understand things that are not S P E L L E D OUT. He is such a *shithead*.

Well, I feel much better.

Margaret Medina (Q)

And there are bits and pieces of overheard conversations. We invite students to record *utterances* in their notebooks, to pay attention to language all around them—to hear the rhythms, the intonations, the patterns, the repetitions; to observe the social interactions, the meanings beneath the surface. Here is Elaine's eavesdropping on a bus from the Bronx to Manhattan:

*Woman:* Look at your shirt. How can you go out in the street like that?

*Girl:* Like what?

*Woman:* It's so wrinkled. You don't iron your shirts?

*Girl:* Ma, will you leave me alone. You're embarrassing me. Uch, just leave me alone.

*Woman:* That's it, you just never want to talk to me.

*Girl:* What are you talking about?

*Woman:* Never mind. Listen, did you tell Eddie about the car?

*Girl:* What about it?

*Woman:* About tomorrow.

*Girl:* Yeah, he said he'd let me have it.

*Woman:* Good. It's a shame he doesn't know how to keep it. He's so filthy, the car needs a good long wash and I keep telling him to go to a car wash at least. At least to wash the windows. I'm afraid to sit in that car.

*Girl:* You're impossible.

*Woman:* I'm impossible. I'm impossible, she says. I'M impossible.

*Girl:* Why don't you speak a little louder? That man over there in the front didn't hear you.

*Woman:* Now, listen . . .

*Girl:* Ma, I'm getting off at the next stop if you don't quit. You're making me crazy.

*Woman:* Okay, be that way. It's wonderful to speak, to talk that way to me.

*Girl:* Okay, listen. . . .

Elaine Marton Diller (Q)

And here is Roger's eavesdropping on a conversation overheard during lunch:

What'd he say?
Nevermind.
Now c'mon tell me.
Can't say.
Was it about you and me?
No.
At least lie.
O.K., he said you were fantastic.

Roger Gonzalez (Q)

Meg, in her notebook, reflected on her "skull's voice," which keeps on going and going and going:

Sometimes I can't shut my skull's voice. It keeps whispering quickly, or changing subjects too rapidly, or overlapping so that I can't understand, forget or remember. I close my eyes and it yells to "WAKE UP." Once up, it asks "AREN'T YOU TIRED?" He is handsome, she is ugly, such is life,

Ralph's moustache is crooked, I don't like Hinda, Javier doesn't write: all this at once. On and on and on and on and *then* it suddenly dies.

Margaret Medina (Q)

One of the chief virtues of the notebook is the capturing of that "skull's voice," the insistent pressures inside our head, the nonstop jabbering that comprises most of the life of the mind. When it is turned into text, in the unbridled realm of the notebook, students have, for themselves, at the end of the semester, a text of their own to read and reread.

David Bartholomae has highlighted this use of the journal:

> *A teacher at a school I recently visited gave what I thought was a wonderful assignment—and she gave it knowing that her students, at least most of them, would have to write their papers over again, perhaps several times, since in many ways it was an impossible assignment. She asked students to read through the journals they had been keeping over the semester and to write about what they had learned about themselves from reading the journal. What I admired in this assignment, and what makes it such a difficult assignment, is that students were asked to write about what they had learned by reading the journal and not what they learned by writing in the journal. This is a nice stroke, since it defines the journal as a text and not an experience, and it defines the person writing as a composite of several people and not as a moment of feeling or thought. The assignment defines the student as, simultaneously, a textual presence—the "I" in a passage dated September 3rd and the "I" in a passage dated October 5th—and as an interpreter of texts, someone who defines patterns and imposes order, form, on previous acts of ordering. Who is to say quickly what that person might learn.*[8]

The notebook, seen this way, *is* text, offering its pages for immediacy and reflection, for participation and spectatorship, for acting and reacting, for reading and rereading, for the writer *now* to reflect upon the writer *then*. At its best, sustained unhurriedly over a generous period of time, it allows the student writer to recognize the sheer benefits of the report, the record, the commonplace, the cameo, the sketch—fragments of life, of actuality, rendered quickly as experience, as text snatched from the jaws of evanescence. Above all, it can come to constitute an informal but revealing representation of the evolution of the writer's mind and character.

# A
# CONCEPTUAL FRAMEWORK

W e propose now to offer a brief outline of the conceptual framework, on which our teaching and the rest of this book depend.
We have suggested in our Preface that human discourse is primarily
social. This needs to be stressed because, ever since the days of the
Romantic movement in Western literature, art, music, and thought, we
have inherited a preconscious inclination to think of one who produces
words (i.e., literature) as inherently and emphatically solitary.

The social production of discourse involves various patterns of interaction. Most of our lives involves us in reactions rather than actions. In
its segments—episodes, scenes, meetings—we react far more than we
initiate action from scratch. In teaching composition, our inclination,
therefore, is to offer an "action" (especially a verbal representation) to
which our students may react in a variety of ways. They don't have to
*start* anything: the propulsion is in the action that we offer them. But
the students are never merely passive recipients or mere commentators.
Their reactions (i.e., texts) enjoy the same status as the initial actions
(the primary texts).

All our actions are always performed *in role*. We are, none of us, never
nobody, always somebody; and that somebody involves role, whatever
it may be. In our daily lives we move easily from one role to another,
without even having to think about the shift. Our moves from one role
to another are so deeply habituated that some innocent individuals
have serious difficulty in even accepting the notion of role when it is
pointed out to them. Any role, and the context that requires or provokes it, takes effect not only in actions but in language, or speech acts.
We notice the fact of congruence between role, context, and discourse
only when that congruence breaks down. Someone produces inappropriate language—too colloquial, too intimate, too pretentious, or whatever—and we flinch with embarrassment or entertain a sense of their
ridiculousness. Presidents, for example, sometimes get this wrong.

Our case is that when we effectively occupy or live in a role, it is as
a result of our well-tuned responsiveness to the particular constraints
and demands of that role that we produce appropriate discourse.

The two radical or overarching categories of the role—the definitive
existential roles—are those of participant—someone involved in the
enactment of a segment of life—and spectator—someone "off to the
side," not directly involved in the action. For every second since birth,
we have been participants in our own lives. When, however, we stop
to reconstruct a segment or strip of our past lives, an episode, a

happening—we become spectators of our representation of our own past lives. It is as spectators that we reconstruct our past and rehearse our future.

The participant produces a particular kind of discourse; the spectator produces a quite different kind of discourse. Participant texts are long on particularity, sensation, impression, and vivid "realization"; spectator texts are long on reflection, generalization, and above all, evaluation. The burden or delight of the participant is to be in it; the privilege of the spectator is to stand back and to evaluate.

The linguist Michael Halliday offers some startling observations on the early emergence of the participant/spectator distinction. His category "interpersonal/intrusive" corresponds to our "participant," while his "ideational/observer" corresponds to our "spectator."

The child that Halliday observed first created his own protolanguage, in which Halliday observed six functions—instrumental, regulatory, interactional, personal, heuristic, and imaginative. At about 18 months, the child switched from his own protolanguage—"his own special system"—to English:

> *Simultaneously with this switch, he generalized out of his original range of functions this very general functional opposition between . . . the pragmatic and the mathetic. With this child the distinction was very clear . . . he used a rising intonation for all pragmatic utterances, and a falling one for all mathetic ones. So he knew exactly what he was doing: either he was using language as an intruder, requiring a response . . . which he did on a rising tone; or he was using language as an observer, requiring no response . . . and with these there was a falling tone.*[9]

The beauty of the "adult language," as Halliday explains, is that it is "polyphonic," and allows one to be a participant-observer, producing discourse that is simultaneously pragmatic and mathetic.

It is our case that if we wish to involve students in the production of a greater variety of texts, to nudge them toward *repertoire expansion,* the best way to do it is to involve them in a variety of roles that will themselves, inescapably, generate a variety of modes of discourse. In other words, we need to start *not* with the text but with that which in itself gives rise to the text. When students produce participant texts, they write more vividly, with a keener sense of sharp, concrete immediacy: texts that lack context, that sometimes baffle, but that are often very dramatic. Their structures are generally paratactic—that is, a series of coordinate parts without any inherent syntactic hierarchies.

When they produce spectator texts, they contextualize, see the whole picture, are explicit. They move from the concrete toward the abstract, make a variety of connections between the parts, present some features as more significant than others, and so generate various subordinating and superordinating structures—hypotaxis. Thus they exercise the conventions of "academic" prose.

Their texts have audiences: actual audiences—ourselves and other students—and vicarious audiences, which correspond to the vicarious roles that, in writing, they will have assumed.

Figure 1 (see p. 30) shows the diagram we offer to our students as a way of alerting them to some of the constructive interactions that can take place in a composition course. At level A, we recognize that the activity of the mind is fairly promiscuous, so that daydreaming, for example, can be expected to occur alongside, say, surmising and speculating. Level B alerts students to some of the uses of a notebook and to the possibility of useful feedback from classmates. At level C, we encourage students to consider their text as provisional, still open to revision.

When we generalize with them about such matters, we prefer to use the term "act" (or "action"), rather than "process." The advantage of "act" is that it affirms the student as agent; the disadvantage of "process"—for the currency of which we confess to feeling a not inconsiderable distaste—is that (a) it can too easily suggest passivity ("being processed") as opposed to activity; and (b) its current use (misuse?) can too easily give rise to the dangerous fallacy that there is a homogenized entity: "*the* writing process"—just as that there is but one straw for the drowning person to clutch at.

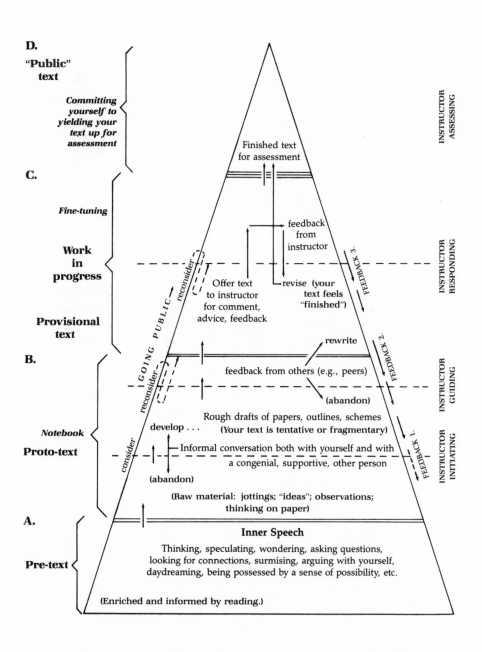

**Figure 1:** The three "levels" of text that prove useful in a composition course. Level A (inner speech) is active even when you don't have a pen in your hand.

# NOTES

1. Michael Oakeshott, *The Voice of Poetry in the Conversation of Mankind* (London: Bowes and Bowes, 1959), p. 11.
2. Ted Hughes, *Poetry in the Making* (London: Faber and Faber, 1967), p. 23.
3. John Warnock and Tilly Eggers, "The Freshman Writing Program at the University of Wyoming," in *Options for the Teaching of English*, ed. Jasper P. Neel (Urbana, Ill.: NCTE, 1978).
4. For the interactions of 3 and 4, cf. Michael Halliday, *Language as Social Semiotic* (London: Arnold, 1979), pp. 187–88.
5. "Sentences are, in fact, the *realization* of text rather than constituting the text itself. Text is a semantic concept." Ibid., p. 135.
6. Edwin Morgan, *Poems of Thirty Years* (Manchester: Carcanet New Press, 1982), p. 260.
7. Denise Levertov, *Candles in Babylon* (New York: New Directions, 1982), p. 101.
8. David Bartholomae, "Writing Assignments: Where Writing Begins," in *Fforum*, ed. Marc Pachter (Upper Montclair, N.J.: Boynton/Cook, 1983), p. 302.
9. Halliday, *Language as Social Semiotic*, p. 55. For a full account of Halliday's observations, see his *Learning How to Mean — Explorations in the Development of Language* (London: Arnold, 1975), where he observes that the "distinction between two broad generalized types of language use, the mathetic and the pragmatic, that Nigel [the child he observed] expresses by means of the contrast between falling and rising tone, turns out to be the one that leads directly in to the abstract functional distinction of ideational and interpersonal *that lies at the heart of the adult linguistic system. . . .* It seems likely that the ideational component of meaning arises, in general, from the use of language to learn, while the interpersonal arises from the use of language to act" (p. 53; italics added).

# CHAPTER TWO

# GENERATIVE FRAME
## Actions and Reactions

*. . . contemplated till, by a species of reaction, the tranquillity gradually disappears, and an emotion . . . is gradually produced, and does itself actually exist in the mind. In this mood successful composition generally begins, and in a mood similar to this it is carried on.*

*Wordsworth*

The whole world waits to be "read" and to be reacted to—as we see, for example, in Roland Barthes's *Mythologies*. But as teachers, we must accept and choose limits or constraints. We therefore select those "actions" to which we wish our students to react; and since we are paid to help them produce *texts*, we choose to offer them actions as embodied in, represented by, texts. Furthermore, since we wish to promote the production of a variety of texts—a variety of types, functions, and forms—we offer them a corresponding variety to react to. We do not aim to promote slavish imitations; but this is not to deny that a certain amount of unconscious modeling will take place.

Our "primary" texts certainly include some of the dominant literary forms. But, as exemplified in the case of the L'Anselme and Hudson texts that follow, one of our criteria of choice involves the use of texts that are obviously provocative, dramatic, disconcerting, and open-ended. By "open-ended" we mean unresolved; the reactions of the students will include an attempt at resolution, at "finishing the business." L'Anselme and Hudson also exemplify another of our cardinal principles—they are comedic. We believe that a composition course that is not ventilated by sporadic bouts of comedy is thereby diminished. A sense of community can be promoted when we laugh together.

# PRIMARY TEXTS
## (Short-Term Funding)

When we offer students others' texts—we call these *primary texts*—through, by, and in these, they have access to virtual experiences. If we choose the texts well, the students are moved—to laughter, astonishment, wonder, horror, puzzlement, and so on.

The arousal or provocation that such reactions constitute—this energy finds expression in their writing of *reactive texts*. The dialectic in their psyches seems to be something like this:

Arousal → Energy or Tension → Resolution or Appeasement

(We're grateful to Seamus Heaney for that last word.) In other words, we start by following the advice of William James: "No reception without reaction, no impression without correlative expression—this is the great maxim which the teacher ought never to forget."

Here now are two of our favorite primary texts. The first is by Jean L'Anselme, the second by Virginia Cary Hudson.

## FALLING BRICKS

*Dear Sir,*

*By the time I arrived at the house where you sent me to make repairs, the storm had torn a good fifty bricks from the roof. So I set up on the roof of the building a beam and a pulley and I hoisted up a couple of baskets of bricks. When I had finished repairing the building there were a lot of bricks left over since I had brought up more than I needed and also because there were some bad, reject bricks that I still had left to bring down. I hoisted the basket back up again and hitched up the line at the bottom. Then I climbed back up again and filled up the basket with the extra bricks. Then I went down to the bottom and untied the line. Unfortunately, the basket of bricks was much heavier than I was and before I knew what was happening, the basket started to plunge down, lifting me suddenly off the ground. I decided to keep my grip and hang on, realizing that to let go would end in disaster—but halfway up I ran into the basket coming down and received a severe blow on the shoulder. I then continued to the top, banging my head against the beam and getting my fingers jammed in the pulley. When the basket hit the ground it burst its bottom, allowing all the bricks to spill out. Since I was now heavier than the basket I started back down again at high speed. Halfway down, I met the basket coming up, and received several severe injuries on my shins. When I hit the ground, I landed on the bricks, getting several more painful cuts and bruises from the sharp edges.*

*At this moment I must have lost my presence of mind, because I let go of the line. The basket came down again, giving me another heavy blow on the head, and putting me in the hospital. I respectfully request sick leave.*[1]

## MELVIN'S BAPTISM

*One day we got tired of playing hop-scotch and skin the cat, so Edna Briggs said, "Let's play Baptizing." I said to Mrs. Williams, "Can we, I mean may we play Baptizing in your rain barrel?" And she said to me, she said, "Yes, indeed," and she just went on tatting. So I put on my father's hunting breeches and got Judge Williams' hat off the moose horn rack, and I dressed up like the Baptist preacher. That was when Edna ran to get all the kids. And I said to them I said, "The Lord is in his Holy Temple, keep silent and shut up." And then I said, "All you sinners come forward and hence." And nobody came but Melvin Dawson. He is just two years old. Poor little Melvin. He is so unlucky. I got him by the back of*

35

*his diaper and dipped him in the rain barrel once for the Father,
and once for the Son, and when it came time for the Holy Ghost,
poor little Melvin's safety pin broke and he dropped in the bottom
of the rain barrel, and everybody ran, and nobody would help me,
and I had to turn the rain barrel over to get him out, and then I
galloped him on his stomach on my pony to get the water out of
him, and then I sat him inside his house, and then I went out to
Mrs. Harris' house and got under her bed, and when she looked
under there and saw me, all soaking wet, Mrs. Harris said, she said,
"Rain and hail in Beulah land, what has happened now?" And when
I told her what had happened she just patted her foot and sat, and
sat, and then she said, "You know what?" and I said, "What" and
Mrs. Harris said, "The Bishop sure needs just such a barrel in the
church yard to give some members I know just what little Melvin
got." And then Mrs. Harris said, "Let's talk about fishing." And
we did.*

    *Thank God for fishing. Thank God for Mrs. Harris and God bless
poor little Melvin. Amen.*[2]

We would like to consider, briefly, two questions: what happens to
us when we read those texts? And what happens that invites, allows,
or impels us to turn toward writing?

## Reading "Falling Bricks"

    Gradually, irresistibly, we move toward laughter. What kind of laughter is it? Even if the text were not a fiction, we, as readers, are as *free* as if it were. Free from pain, from calamity, from the shamefacedness of incompetence. We have, however, known pain, suffered calamity, and felt ashamed of our incompetence. Our laughter comes in part from our noninvolvement, from the fact that we are privileged observers. It also comes from the interplay of our expectations or anticipations, and their fulfillment. Indeed, as we move through the text, we generate such expectations (What *will* he do next? Surely, it will get worse?), and the text more than fulfills those expectations: it is hyperbolic.

    But what do we respond to in the "facts" of the event—the chaos, the mess, the destruction, the breakages? Our case is that our response depends for its richness on our prior *fundings*—a term we borrow from John Dewey. Our reading is an inseparable melding of memory and desire, past experience and unfolding text. We are already funded with memories of little domestic mishaps, both directly in our own lives and vicariously through the stories we have heard and read. The text invites us to be spectators (we are not the bricklayer, nor are we "Sir"); and as it proceeds, it seems to tell us, "Read this as a joke, as farce." Our pleasure is re-cognition—an act of knowing again, and of knowing *this* event as one of a type (cf. Chaplin, Tati, Keystone Cops, Feydeau, etc.). Our atavistic desire for chaos—our pyromanic fantasies, our wild dreams of demolition—this desire, since we are civilized, is rarely satisfied. Here, it is. And so is our desire for peace and quiet, for survival, for appeasement. We don't wish to fall off a roof and break a leg; but the unfortunate writer will do it for us. It is a licentious experience for us, no less vivid and compelling because it is "merely" vicarious or virtual.

Such is the mediating power of words that, like the fluttering images of the cinema, they can create vivid illusions of actuality—realization; it is *as if* we can see it, hear it, feel it. We are spectators, outside the text or image, and yet can feel a powerful, even disconcerting, sense of involvement, of participation. Marks on paper can make us laugh and cry, temporarily blind and deaf to the demands of the world. When we offer texts to our students, we are offering them *short-term funding*, to add to (and call up) their various *long-term fundings*, both in life and in texts.

And when they laugh with us, something important happens. As Stanley Cavell puts it:

> *We learn and teach words in certain contexts, and then we are expected, and expect others, to be able to project them into further contexts. Nothing insures that this projection will take place (in particular, not the grasping of universals nor the grasping of books of rules), just as nothing insures that we will make and understand the same projections. That on the whole we do so is a matter of our sharing routes of interest and feeling, modes of response, senses of humor and of significance and of fulfillment, of what is outrageous, of what is similar to what else, of what is rebuke and what is forgiveness, of when an utterance is an assertion, an appeal, or an explanation—all the whirl of organism that Wittgenstein calls "forms of life."*[3]

When we share texts, then, we share what they signify, namely, "forms of life." And when students create texts, they share "forms of life"—what they and we understand to be indignation, disgust, awe, optimism, and so on. And such forms of life—mediated and provoked, intensified and sharpened, even midwifed, by the virtual experiences afforded by primary texts—these themselves constitute the raw material of the students' reactive texts.

# REACTIVE TEXTS

Hudson's story also is a calamitous one and also is comical. Notice how many characters are involved in some degree in Melvin's misfortune: Melvin, Virginia, Edna, Mrs. Harris, Mrs. Williams, Virginia's mother and father, Judge Williams—not to mention Melvin's parents. Depending on how we react to Virginia's pranks, we unconsciously role-play, siding more with those who condone or with those who condemn, with those who merely shrug or with those who punish. What would Melvin's mother want to say to Virginia's mother? Does Judge Williams set great store by his hat? When we read Virginia's text, such little (or large) questions—implicit in the narrative—nudge us, enliveningly. It is from that sense of arousal and enlivenment that we ask our students to produce their reactive texts.

Such texts will *not* be subordinate to, or imitative of, Hudson's text, as would a parody or a critical commentary, but will take on lives of their own. Hudson's text and all that happens inside us as we read and react—these launch us into our own possibilities.

How, then, when students take up the story, do they choose who they will "become"? How do they choose their vicarious role? In general, we prefer to treat this matter as a preconscious enigma; but it is nevertheless clear that women students tend to take on a female role, and men a male role. Occasionally, we deliberately prevent this and specifically ask them to reverse or invert their roles.

The role seems to be entered/assumed/realized initially and primarily as a "voice": the role is *heard* rather than seen or otherwise realized. And in such a matter, women know as well as men do what men tend to sound like, how grandfathers talk, or the jargon of male enclaves; and vice versa: 18+ years of funding (see end-of-chapter appendix).

A voice, then, is "heard" and becomes the first draft of a text. Since the attention is focused on something other than the voice, there is rarely any significant degree of self-consciousness about the voice as such: it comes "naturally." We are all funded with hundreds of voices—both those we hear and those we use—and to get a range of them onto paper, authentic simulations, is, we have found, inherently satisfying.

## *Reacting to "Falling Bricks"*

Here now are some reactions to "Falling Bricks":

Inspector #G6287
Report #29
March 3, 1983

The recent epidemic of poorly trained bricklayers has not found its end in District 23. The following report of incompetence in this district may seem like fantasy, but I assure you it is not. Out of the 34 bricklayers whom I inspected this week, only 7 met the Department's standard qualifications check. It would be understandable for you to assume my judgment harsh based on the ratio of those failed to those passed. I insist that this is not the case. As you surely know from my long career in the Department, I always test by the book.

Where these inept bricklayers are receiving their training I do not know. In one case the problem was so severe that I checked with personnel to make sure the bricklayer's license was not a forgery. Without going into too elaborate an account of the incident: the workman had either not received or had completely forgotten the most elementary brick hoisting techniques. This ignorance almost cost the man his own life in the course of lowering bricks from the roof of a two story unit he had been repairing. An accident resulting from a simple hoisting operation can only represent total incompetence in more complicated procedures. Surely you must agree that my credentials check was not overzealous.

I feel, out of a sense of fraternity, that I must leave names out; however, on checking this man I found he was indeed licensed. The only possible way he could have procured one is through bribery. I'm sure you are aware of the seriousness of this inference. However, my duty as a professional leaves me no choice but to insist that you pursue this matter with the licensing department.

John Lynch (Q)

"Do you remember back in 1959? We were working on a brownstone on Frederick Street."

"We were younger then."

"A storm had taken eighty bricks from the roof. We were sent to repair it."

"I could repair all kinds of things in those days. Kept my old place runnin', AND the neighbors'."

"You got concussion; do you remember that?"

"I helped old Jonas stop his outdoor tap. It was spraying like a good geyser. I built Fluffy a two-story dog house out of left-over shingles and two by fours."

"After we had finished, and you lowered the basket of unused bricks, the rope caught and you were propelled into the air, hanging madly to the rope. The basket of bricks hit you on its way down and then again on its way back up again."

"That was some winter in '59."

"Ha. You really banged your head and got your fingers jammed in the pulley."

"We still had four inches of snow on April 21st."

"It was comical to see you bobbing away up there."

"It took till July for the garden to dry out for planting."

"I nearly carried you all the way to the hospital. You DO remember me carrying you? You were bleeding and bellering."

"Had a great crop of early Betsy peas that year."

"You kept saying that your head ached. Boy! You sure complained. And laid up for two weeks! Complained, and how!"

"Lost the corn to summer drought . . . what? Complained about what?"

"The accident. You know, that time with the basket of bricks."

"Hmmm. I don't recollect. . . . You must be thinking of someone else."

Katherine Green (U)

Dear Sir:

A fortnight ago we contacted your business about repairing the damage done to our roof during a storm. You sent 'round a young man to make these repairs, and we must admit they were done properly. However, we have just received your bill and we object most strongly to the labour charge. The chap in question spent as much time playing Tarzan with his equipment as he did in actual repair. Should we be expected to pay £10 an hour while someone swings about on a rope attached to a basket of bricks? We shall not.

By our records, your man spent one hour on the roof, a half-hour setting up his play toys and a good twenty minutes swinging about—up and down, up and down. Another thing, we shall not pay for the basket. Take it out of his pay, we say. We shall not pay for the bricks young Tarzan broke with his nonsense either. Is it our fault you hire children to do men's work? Because of his foolishness, we must now arrange to have the eaves repainted and windowpanes replaced in the second floor bedroom. Did he tell you he put his foot through two perfectly good panes of glass while trying to emulate Johnny Weismuller?

We are enclosing a cheque to cover the cost of the bricks used—only the bricks used, mind you—and for one hour of labour. We strongly suggest that in the future you hire grown men with their feet planted firmly on the ground.

Sincerely,
Lady Jane
Pat Campbell (U)

As a commentary on how she had written her "Lady Jane" letter, Pat wrote the following memo to the class:

Writing this was an unusual experience. I did not know where to begin on the Bricklayer. So, as all letters start, I started: "Dear Sir:". The first line and a half were lifted from the main text, but before I finished writing them, I was possessed. (Go ahead and laugh.) I was myself, but not myself. The letter flowed as "she" wrote. I was more absorbed by the character writing the letter, more "her" than I have been able to achieve in any acting role. With "Sincerely," she left. The letter was completely serious. She—I?—did not write it to be funny. I made a concession to irony with her name—a play on the Tarzan theme of the letter.

Your reactions took me by surprise. I have never been successful with humor. You gave me a great gift—your laughter. Thank you.

During the evening after the class in which she had composed her text, Pat elaborated on her memo:

## *Reflections*

At last! I was beginning to worry. It was as if the pool of creativity with intelligence and sensitivity had dried up. But today, I found it again. Or perhaps it found me. I have struggled with the assignments, never quite getting them right, always just a bit off the mark. Today I found it again. We discussed reactive texts and I began to feel at home. Here was meat I could get my teeth into. Here was a medium I could relate to on paper. Discussion of "Melvin's Baptism" primed the pump. Geoffrey gave us the text that has been running through my head for a year. Not on the surface, but always there under the tests, papers to be written for profs., books to be read. The idea first presented itself when Geoffrey read "Falling Bricks" and discussed reactive texts last year. At the time the word was alien, but I saw such rich possibilities for the owner of the house. She has grown through the year via letters from our former caretaker's wife in England and my part in a Neil Simon play *(The Good Doctor).* Today she was born on paper in all her pompous glory. I could almost feel "the other" taking control, melding my mind with its power, getting me ready to transcribe its dictation. I did not think of her as funny. Just very proper, very aristocratic, very upper-class British. It is my first successful (can I call it successful?) humor, and it was an accident. The letter seemed to flow on the page by itself. There was a sense of being "possessed"–of Lady Jane writing it through me. Revisions were from "I" to the royal "we," and there were only four small areas scrapped and rewritten. And they happened during, not after, the original writing. Where did it come from? The year of subconscious work? How could it flow so freely when most of the time my writing takes multiple revisions? Was it the voice that allowed it to come uninhibited? Was it the limitations set by the original text, the language necessary to mark the voice? Why? (Side note: In looking at the text, I find I have, without conscious knowledge, spelled *check* c-h-e-q-u-e, and *labor* l-a-b-o-u-r, English spellings I have not used since I was thirteen.) If I can find the answers to these questions, perhaps I can open the door to writing. Perhaps then I can get on paper the hundreds of stories racing about in my head.

There is a sense of power in lifting the words off a page and creating a living, breathing being. As an actor, I revel in my power to give birth to new life, life alien to my everyday existence, to convert words into being. Today I had a double dose of power. I was the actor playing a role, giving life to the character who had penned the letter, making Lady Jane a flesh and blood human. The words took on life and Lady Jane lived and breathed. But a new power, a very heady POWER pumped adrenalin through me as I realized *I* had written the words. *I* wrote the words which *I* then used to create a being. God, what a feeling!

# PRODUCING A REACTIVE TEXT: WHAT SEEMS TO HAPPEN

*Active/reactive*

*In what he writes, there are two texts. Text I is reactive, moved by indignations, fears, unspoken rejoinders, minor paranoias, defenses, scenes. Text II is active, moved by pleasure. But as it is written, corrected, accommodated to the fiction of Style, Text I becomes active too, whereupon it loses its reactive skin, which subsists only in patches (mere parentheses).*

                              *Roland Barthes*

When we ask students to write reactive texts, after their experience of a primary text, they are not being subjected to a disabling constraint: their reactions to the primary text are as various in point of view, degree of intensity, tone, and so on, as they are themselves. Even as they hear or read the primary text and allow it to work in their minds, in a kind of rapid fermentation, they are in a useful sense already "writing," even though they hold no pen. In the ebb and flow of their sympathies, they are already constructing an alternative reactive text. To put it simply, they don't have to "make anything up." Their theme or subject is already opening its wings. None of them has ever said, "I couldn't think of anything." When they move to write, it is because they have indeed thought of it—their subject, their theme. It has come to them, possessed them. They don't have to make choices.

Helen Vendler, the poetry critic, has written illuminatingly on the nature of the writer's choices. What she offers is by way of a commentary, specifically, on Keats, but it is entirely appropriate, and convincing, as a general account:

> *The poet's first choice is the choice of theme: "I sought a theme and sought for it in vain; / I sought it daily for six weeks or so," says Yeats, allowing us a glimpse of the long searching for the first, and crucial, choice—the choice of subject (which may, of course, and often does, follow on the inchoate choice of rhythm, about which both Hopkins and Valéry have given testimony). . . .*
>
> *The subsequent compositional choices (the angle of vision, the method of self-representation, the proportions of the treatment, the length and structural shape of the work, the level of diction, the registers of discourse, the manner of initiating, delaying, and resolving the work, and so on) all have metaphysical and ethical meaning for the artist, and therefore for us as well.*[4]

In a totally different context, Henry Glassie in his classic account of the storytellers of Northern Ireland, *Passing the Time in Ballymenone*, observes that effective storytellers "begin the creative process by selecting a group of words."[5] Selection is often a matter of the words selecting and offering themselves—a voice is "heard." The *immediate* context, for a student's reactive text, is provided by the primary text in all its suggestive richness, its sense of more and other possibilities. The larger context is the long-term funding that each student brings to the moment. As for the "selecting [of] a group of words"—it seems that students "hear" them, in the form of a tone of voice, an exchange, a rhythm, etc.

Let us risk an oversystematic schema for a moment and offer an approximate sequence of how a reactive text gets written:

1. A primary text and/or scenario provides short-term funding.

2. Students experience 1 as a vicarious/virtual experience of "forms of life" and as an act of re-cognition. At a preconscious level, the primary text interacts productively with elements of their long-term funding.

3. Students observe or infer "states of mind" present in 2.

4. Students react to 2 and 3. "Forms of life" and "states of mind" are provoked/aroused by 2 and 3. The reaction is generally experienced either as (a) one inescapable reaction, nothing else being appropriate or possible, or as (b) a repertoire of choices, a variety of possible responses, from which the student chooses one or more (see the Bogarde example, below).

5. "States of mind" (4) take form as frames of mind.

6. Frames of mind provide the organizing context or focus for acts of mind.

7. Acts of mind shape a reactive text: primarily a sequel to 1 or an alternative to 1.

Let us illustrate this sequence with a simple example: In Dirk Bogarde's memoirs, *A Postillion Struck by Lightning,* he tells of his unhappy early years. His father had insisted on his staying with an unsympathetic aunt and uncle so that he could attend a convenient technical high school and acquire a useful skill. He is chronically unhappy and homesick. One day at the end of a semester, his uncle tells him that his school report is unsatisfactory:

> *In short, I was wasting everyone's time, money and patience.*
> *The fact that I never, at any time ever, saw my school reports—they were always addressed to him, correctly, as my Guardian and he sent them on to my parents—nor ever had any discussions with anyone about them didn't seem to occur to either of us at the time. I was simply struck dumb with shock. As far as I was aware, I had worked as hard as possible and had tried my best.*
> *The next morning, after an anguished night watching the patterns flicker on the ceiling from the Valor Perfection Stove, my uncle and I parted company as usual at Queen Street Station. At the bookstall I bought a stamp and a picture postcard on which, leaning against a pile of magazines, I wrote in pencil, "I am very unhappy here. Please, please let me come home." A swift Burberry'd arm shot over my shoulder and lifted it up.*
> *My uncle's face was expressionless, a nicotined finger brushed his little moustache.*
> *"Well now, Sonny," he said kindly, "why not post it?" He flipped it on to the magazines and walked away.*
> *Dismay and guilt gave way to rising desperation. I did exactly as he said and went on to school.*[6]

So the postcard is mailed and duly arrives at his parents' home. For our purposes, the postcard is the primary text, and the context of situation is the contingent scenario, the determining environment. Early in the semester students were asked to respond to Dirk's postcard in role as mother or father, and *dash off* a reply: the situation is urgent.

The results are very interesting. In general, at stage 4, in the above sequence, students in role as father have no doubt at all about what to write. The "mothers," conversely, are torn by conflicting needs: most of their replies attempt to resolve those conflicts.

When we look at the reactive texts, we find a confirmation of the view that the meanings are often to be found in the differences: given two types of text—affectively different, purposively different—the characteristics of each type are highlighted by the characteristics of the other. In isolation, such features would be less conspicuous; it is in the collocation that they are most emphatically obvious.

For example, we first offer you some severely edited texts from which we have removed all salient clues as to the role of the writer. Given these depredations, see if you can identify them:

> My dear son,
> The mailman delivered your letter today. I could tell its contents simply from the quivering handwriting. . . . I knew then what I know now; you should never have left home.
> You must realize that I think of you each evening. . . . Such thoughts a . . . never forgets. . . .
> I want you to come home. . . . Come home, Dirk. I miss you.
>
> Lovingly yours,

> Dirk:
> Got your letter. I do not understand. Unhappy? When I have sent you to get an education in a job which most certainly is the best for you? . . . How dare you?
> Certainly you may come home. I am your . . . , and this is your home. . . .
> Yesterday, I mailed your food and lodging money to your uncle. Get the return fare from him, if you are so foolish as to wish to return.

Did you have much difficulty in allocating each of those texts appropriately, plausibly, to a "mother" or a "father"? What kinds of clues did you depend on? Were they in what was being written—semantic? Or were they in how it was written—syntactic? What, then, is the relationship between syntax and tone? What is it in the shaping of discourse that effectively represents an impulse, a sense of distance, an unkindness, a warmth? To what extent did you recognize stereotypes?

Let us now come clean and offer you the complete texts. First, Nick (Q) as the "mother":

My dear son,

The postman delivered your letter today. I could tell its contents simply from the quivering handwriting on the envelope. I knew then what I know now; you should never have left home.

You must realize that I think of you each evening. I still remember cradling you in my arms, all wrapped up in a small, woolen blanket, resting your weary head on my bosom. Such thoughts a mother never forgets. A son will never be forgotten by a mother.

I want you to come home. I will aid you in every conceivable way. You have no life there, at least a chance here. Your father will give in, I know. He will allow you to become an actor. Dirk, you belong here with me. I am as discontented as you, and my greatest joy will be when I receive you at my front door. Come home, Dirk. I miss you.

Lovingly yours,
Mother

Now, Michael (Q) as the father:

Dirk:

Got your letter. I do not understand. Unhappy? When I have sent you to get an education in a job which most certainly is the best for you? When I have taken care of you, seen to your lodging with your mother's sister? I am appalled at your rebelliousness and stupidity, you ungrateful wretch! *How dare you!*

Certainly, you may come home. I am your father, and this is your home. But I will not try to help you anymore, as you refuse my assistance. You'll have to learn your own trade. And *mark my words:* When you reach the age of a printer's apprentice, I will support you no longer. Out you shall go.

Yesterday, I mailed your food and lodging money to your uncle. Get the return fare from him, if you are so foolish as to wish to return.

Father

Finally, for extra measure, here is John (Q) as the mother:

47

My dearest Dirk,

I can only hope you receive my letter first, because I'm sure the one your father is writing will make you feel worse. I'm so sorry, Dirk. I've pleaded with your father to let you come home, but there is nothing I can do.

When I read your post card, I was in tears. Your father looked at it, tossed it aside, and asked me when dinner would be ready. When I asked him about you, he asked if I was joking. Under no circumstances are you to return, he said, until you've set your life in order.

An orderly life, to him, would be one which follows his orders. He still wants you to take up an "honorable profession." I still haven't told him of your hope to become an actor; I probably never will. He won't find out until you become a successful matinee idol. I know you can do it, son, even without his support.

I wish there was something I could do, but there is nothing. When you are a bit older, he will no longer be able to keep you at your uncle's house. Then I'll take you around to the studios, and who knows?

I have faith in you, son. I know you'll get through this and make me proud of you. I can't wait to see you again. I wish it could be sooner.

Love,
Mom

# WHAT TO "DO" WITH REACTIVE TEXTS

When such texts as those above have been written, what can we do with them? What is it useful to do with them?

We have three elements: the new texts, their writers, and their readers. The readers know "effects"—the ways in which those texts have affected them, how they have struck them; the writers know intentions and purposes—to produce an "authentic forgery" of this or that person's expression of his or her forms of life, states of mind.

In such a triangular context, there is enough to keep us busy for a semester. But we have to choose, because we don't want to kill the matter with an excess of analysis. One of our choices is to ask questions of the readers—for example:

When Nick as mother writes "The postman delivered your letter today," is he doing more than stating the obvious?

What is the tone of Nick's letter—"strong" or "weak"?

Where do you find the expressive evidence for your finding?

In face-to-face situations, we touch people and meet their eyes: these are ways of maintaining or intensifying the contact between us and them. Does Nick use any written equivalents of such contact-maintenance signals?

Turning to Michael, what features of his text are stereotypically masculine?

If you read Michael's letter aloud in a tender loving voice, what is the effect? If you read John's letter aloud in a harsh or unsympathetic voice, does that change the effect?

Of the two "mothers," Nick's and John's, which do you find more sensible? helpful to Dirk? reckless? conspiratorial?

If you didn't know, could you *confidently* infer that the letters of Nick and John had been written by men? Or do you find their impersonations plausible? Do they appear to be prey to stereotypes?

The enabling constraint that we imposed on the students was simply this: that their reaction *must* be expressed as a letter from either father or mother; it was not to be expressed in any other way. *Within* that constraint, they had an important option—to "become" either father or mother. What they wrote, in role, was not a "response" to a "stimulus"; it was the expression of a state of mind, partly inescapable and partly chosen.

Our case is that whenever students effectively enter, take on, or are possessed by a form of life and a state of mind, the features of the text they produce can be shown to be effectively expressive of the initiating state of mind. The text exemplifies the more or less obvious, more or less subtle conventions of language that comprise "our way of talking." The text achieves the status of authentic forgery even when it is stereotypical. The appeal is, inescapably, to recognition—to the students' familiarity with cultural conventions as they control or determine language and take effect in language. Those who recognize what we appeal to—who already "know"—enjoy the confirmation of their knowing; those who don't know, who cannot yet recognize such things—some foreign students, for example—learn or are alerted to the possibility of learning.

Given a sufficient range and variety of primary texts/scenarios, a corresponding range of reactions is called up, resulting in a range of various texts, characterized by various forms/degrees/kinds of roles, voices, and textuality. The "voice" is an expression, a realization of the role—its tone, its purpose, its mood, its status—and the text is a representation of the "voice." Whatever we say or write is said or written in role, either actual or vicarious.

# REPERTOIRE EXPANSION

In a justly famous essay, "Teaching a Native Language," Jerome Bruner makes a compelling case for the recognition of repertoire expansion as one of the first priorities of English teaching:

> *The point is, simply, that language serves many functions, pursues many aims, employs many voices. What is most extraordinary of all is that it commands as it refers, describes as it makes poetry, adjudicates as it expresses, creates beauty as it gets things clear, serves all other needs as it maintains contact. It does all these things at once, and does them with a due regard to rules and canons such that a native speaker very early in life is usually able to tell whether they are well done or botched. I would like to suggest that a man of intellectual discipline is one who is master of the various functions of speech, one who has a sense of how to vary them, how to say what he wishes to say—to himself and to others.[7]*

And again:

> *The way of language in knowing is the most powerful means we have for performing transformations on the world, for transmuting its shape by recombination in the interest of possibility. I commented earlier that there should be a special birthday to celebrate the entrance of the child into the human race, dated from the moment when he first uses combinatorial grammar. Each of the functions of language has its combinatorial necromancy, its enormous productiveness. It is with the cultivation of these combinatorial powers that I am concerned.[8]*

How, asks Bruner, "does one achieve awareness, mastery, and finesse in the various functions to which language is devoted? How indeed does one become masterfully adept at the rules for forming functionally appropriate utterances for the consumption of others or for one's own consumption, save by exercise?" It is a splendid, central question; and here is what Bruner proposes:

*Many of us have delighted over the years in the weekend competitions of the* New Statesman. *"Write the Declaration of Independence in the style of the Old Testament." Or, "Do a prose rendering of the 'Charge of the Light Brigade' in the style of Henry James." There is a comparable delight in Max Beerbohm's* Christmas Garland *or Raymond Queneau's* Exercises in Style. *To write in different styles and in different voices—a beseeching account of evolution, an expressive account of Newton's Law of Moments, whatever—surely this is one right path.*[9]

Beerbohm's *Christmas Garland* is a fine collection of wicked parodies, exemplifying a very high level of textual sophistication. It is not, however, a text that we would feel comfortable with in our freshman composition classes, since its point, to be taken, depends on an intimate knowledge of the writers being parodied. What, then, of Raymond Queneau? His *Exercices de Style* (1947) has been brilliantly translated by Barbara Wright, and it is a delightful bundle of verbal fireworks, owing something to the ingenious coruscations of Bach's *Art of Fugue.* Briefly, Queneau offers ninety-nine variations or versions of an event: The narrator sees a man on a bus. He is having a mild argument with another man, whom he accuses of jostling him. When a passenger gets off, he takes the empty seat. Two hours later, in another part of the city, the narrator sees the same man with a friend; the friend is telling him to sew another button on his overcoat.

Queneau's texts start with "Notation," a kind of notebook prose:

> *In the S bus, in the rush hour. A chap of about 26, felt hat with a cord instead of a ribbon, neck too long, as if someone's been having a tug-of-war with it. People getting off. The chap in question gets annoyed with one of the men standing next to him. He accuses him of jostling him every time anyone goes past. A snivelling tone which is meant to be aggressive. When he sees a vacant seat he throws himself on it.*[10]

The "Metaphorical" variation reads:

> *In the centre of the day, tossed among the shoal of travelling sardines in a coleopter with a big white carapace, a chicken with a long, featherless neck suddenly harangued one, a peace-abiding one, of their number, and its parlance, moist with protest, was unfolded upon the airs. Then, attracted by a void, the fledgling precipitated itself thereunto.*
>
> *In a bleak urban desert, I saw it again that self-same day, drinking the cup of humiliation offered by a lowly button.*[11]

51

Queneau's "Awkward" text (effectively a meta-text) begins:

> *I'm not used to writing. I dunno. I'd quite like to write a tragedy*
> *or a sonnet or an ode, but there's the rules. They put me off. They*
> *weren't made for amateurs. All this is already pretty badly written.*
> *Oh well. At any rate, I saw something today which I'd like to set*
> *down in writing. Set down in writing doesn't seem all that mar-*
> *velous to me. It's probably one of those ready-made expressions*
> *which are objected to by the readers who read for the publishers*
> *who are looking for the originality which they seem to think is*
> *necessary in the manuscripts which the publishers publish when*
> *they've been read by the readers who object to ready-made expres-*
> *sions like 'to set down in writing' which all the same is what I*
> *should like to do about something I saw today even though I'm only*
> *an amateur who is put off by the rules of the tragedy the sonnet or*
> *the ode because I'm not used to writing. . . .*[12]

His "Precious"* text begins:

> *It was in the vicinity of a midday July. The sun had engraved itself*
> *with a fiery needle on the many-breasted horizon. The asphalt was*
> *quivering softly, exhaling that tender, tarry odour that gives the*
> *carcinomous ideas at once puerile and corrosive about the origin of*
> *their malady. A bus in green and white livery. . . .*[13]

Many of Queneau's texts are, unfortunately for our purposes, simply switches of code: the surface text is shifted into a particular code—the distinctive style of a particular literary genre, or another "language"—philosophical, mathematical, or whatever. But Bruner pointed in a useful direction when he cited Queneau, for the really compelling variations exemplify textual changes that appear to be *produced by* and that *express a change in role.* Not merely the language but the event's ostensible meanings change. The code switches *as a result of* the change in role.

For example, Queneau offers a distinctively chauvinistic version of the event as represented by a narcissistic woman spectator who can't keep to the point. Her head is full of unrelated, "merely" personal matters:

> *Lots of clots! Today round about midday (goodness it was hot,*
> *just as well I'd put odorono† under my arms otherwise my little*

---

*Our students' term for this is "flowery."
†*Odorono:* An antiperspirant.

52

*cretonne summer dress that my little dressmaker who makes things specially cheaply for me made for me would have had it) near the Parc Monceau (it's nicer than the Luxembourg where I send my son, the idea of getting alopecia at his age) the bus came, it was full, but I made eyes at the conductor and got in. Naturally all the idiots who'd got numbered tickets made a fuss, but the bus had got going. With me in it. It couldn't have been fuller. I was terribly squashed, and not one of the men who had a seat inside dreamed of offering it to me. Ill-mannered lot . . . !*[14]

Within such a text as this, our students readily uncover the "implications of utterance." Taking in the wealth of semantic content, they simultaneously "hear" a voice and recognize that voice as representative of certain "forms of life" (to which they themselves confess!) and, indeed, as expressive of a type of person. The intimate connection here to reading, say, Dickens, is self-evident. And the recognition is a social act. The woman is speaking her part, verbalizing her role. To distinguish between mere verbal permutations and locutionary changes in text generated by changes in role is to recognize the distinctive power of role. We shall return to this question at greater length in Chapters 7 and 8. Meanwhile, Queneau's textual variations on one event—"saying the same thing" in ninety-nine different ways—lead us irresistibly to the matter of varieties of textuality.

# APPENDIX

## A Note on "Funding"

"Funding" is a term that we have appropriated from John Dewey's writings on aesthetics. He used the term often but seems never to have defined it. We use it in a sense that involves not only one's influential/formative experiences—especially those mediated by the spoken and written word—but also the meanings and values with which we retrospectively invest such experiences. It will be self-evident that members of any subculture will possess fundings that are characterized more by likeness than unlikeness. When nostalgia is expressed for the mythic "good old days" when exemplary young people spent all their leisure hours in reading good books, what seems to be involved is a regret that today's students are not appropriately funded: if only our students were funded with deep exposure to all those great works of literature . . . ! But such comminations may be malapropos.

When we explore literary instances—the formative fundings of writers
—we must clearly bear in mind Wordsworth's question:

> Who that shall point as with a wand and say
> "This portion of the river of my mind
> Came from yon fountain"?[15]

Respecting that caveat, we may nevertheless uncover an interesting
irony: the dawning of a keener sense of verbal potential, of a responsive, alert sensitivity to the possibilities of formal shaping and of
"music" or verbal expressiveness, seems to be not so much a matter of
precocious bookish *literariness* as an awareness aroused by a local,
modest, even trivial vernacular traffic—"ordinary" human discourse.
The "makers" seem to share only one common denominator in those
years of their burgeoning arousal to shaped utterance—that they have
been alerted to the tingle and *frisson* of language in their own native
soil. The crucially productive sensitizings and arousals to verbal possibility seem to have occurred, as it were, domestically, preconsciously,
precritically, tacitly; and often outside, even despite, formal schooling.

The classic exploration of such springs, the definitive affirmation,
remains Wordsworth's *Prelude*.[16] In our own century, D. H. Lawrence,
in "Hymns in a Man's Life," offers a strongly charged, even antino-
mian, case.[17] And J. L. Lowes, Denys Harding, Roman Jakobson, and
R. P. Blackmur have all severally observed/inferred similar influences
—without anxiety—in the evolution of the protean talents of Coleridge,
Jane Austen, Esenin, and T. S. Eliot, respectively.[18]

Less well known, more recent, but equally suggestive are the potent
reflexive recognitions offered by Seamus Heaney in "Singing School,"[19]
in "Reading,"[20] and in "Feeling into Words"[21]—especially this:

> I was getting my first sense of crafting words and for one reason
> or another, words as bearers of history and mystery began to invite
> me. Maybe it began very early when my mother used to recite lists
> of affixes and suffixes, and Latin roots, with their English mean-
> ings, rhymes that formed part of her schooling in the early part of
> the century. Maybe it began with the exotic listing on the wireless
> dial: Stuttgart, Leipzig, Oslo, Hilversum. Maybe it was stirred by
> the beautiful sprung rhythms of the old BBC weather forecast:
> Dogger, Rockall, Malin, Shetland, Faroes, Finisterre; or with the
> gorgeous and inane phraseology of the catechism; or with the litany
> of the Blessed Virgin that was part of the enforced poetry in our
> household: Tower of Gold, Ark of the Covenant, Gate of Heaven,
> Morning Star, Health of the Sick, Refuge of Sinners, Comforter of

*the Afflicted. None of these things were consciously savoured at the time but I think the fact that I still recall them with ease, and can delight in them as verbal music, means that they were bedding the ear with a kind of linguistic hard-core that could be built on some day.*[22]

Edwin Morgan, the celebrated Scottish poet, offers somewhat similar acknowledgments and affirmations:

*There is a poetry before poetry—that is what I seem to see if I look back to my boyhood. Ours was not a particularly bookish house, and neither of my parents was interested in poetry or the other arts, though my father had been a great theatregoer in his youth, and kept the cast-lists from old programmes pasted in an album. Nor did any poetry I learned at school leave a very strong impression until my last two years, when Keats and Tennyson suddenly took hold of me. (Modern poetry was not taught at all. I got as far as Bridges and Brooke.) But the imagination of someone who is going to write poetry can be stirred in all sorts of preparatory ways—through popular songs, through nature, through prose, through visual images, through knowledge. In this context, there are things I remember most vividly: my uncle Frank, who had a good tenor voice, sitting at the piano to sing "Pale hands I love beside the Shalimar" or "Ramona" or "Charmain," the strange longing filtering out over playing-cards, bobbed heads and cigarette-smoke; my father (who worked for a firm of iron and steel scrap merchants) describing on a long Sunday walk how steel was made, the whole process—lurid, fearsome, yet controlled, an image of power and danger—coming alive in my mind simply through the evocative force of words; looking again and again through a Victorian volume of my grandmother's filled with engravings of storms, wrecks and exotic atolls and icebergs, and stories of maritime adventure and endurance; poring with a torch under the bedclothes over sets of cigarette-cards like "Romance of the Heavens" and being equally fascinated by the "romance" and the scientific facts; discovering, on a family holiday at North Berwick, that the newly intense feelings I was having about sea and sun, and fields of poppies, and the passing of time and the seasons, were going to give me no rest or satisfaction until I had put them into my own words, sometimes in essays, sometimes in letters, sometimes in verse. At that time, while I was still at school, I was writing more prose than poetry, and took great pleasure in creating huge fantastic narratives which probably reflected my liking for Verne, Wells and Edgar Rice Burroughs. It may be that more of my "poetry" was channelled into prose tales and imaginative essays (on both of which I spent much time and energy) than into verse, though I was also beginning to explore verse expression; and this may be linked with the fact that I knew almost nothing of modern poetry till I went to university at the age of seventeen. Then I read Eliot in English, Rimbaud in French, and Mayakovsky in Russian, and a whole world, or series of worlds, of which I had not had the remotest inkling, began to explode in my mind as the novas on the cigarette-cards had done, in their own way, years before.*[23]

For our purposes, the fundings that we ask students' recognitions to draw on are rather more social and sociolinguistic—the recognition of types of discourse, tones of voice, "styles," professional jargons, cultural syntaxes. Many of these are oral rather than written, but the appeal to recognition can be applied to text as well as to utterance.

We reinforce such recognitions by providing our students with many and various texts for close reading, in order to extend their repertoire of recognizable texts and text types. This we call *short-term funding*, to distinguish it from their own long-term funding, which they bring with them, and which we elicit as part of the class's resources.

The relationship between funding and Wittgenstein's "forms of life" as interpreted by Cavell is fairly close. We can say that the ability to recognize certain "forms of life" is the result of funding—social, cognitive, and moral.

# NOTES

1. Jean L'Anselme, *The Ring Around the World*, trans. Michael Benedict (London: Rapp & Whiting, n.d.), p. 27.
2. Virginia Cary Hudson, *O Ye Jigs and Juleps!* (New York: Macmillan, 1962), p. 3.
3. Stanley Cavell, "The Availability of Wittgenstein's Later Philosophy," in *The Philosophical Investigations*, ed. George Pitcher (New York: Doubleday, 1968).
4. Helen Vendler, *The Odes of John Keats* (Cambridge, Mass.: Harvard University Press, 1984), p. 5.
5. Henry Glassie, *Passing the Time in Ballymenone* (Philadelphia: University of Pennsylvania Press, 1982), p. 38.
6. Dirk Bogarde, *A Postillion Struck by Lightning* (New York: Holt, Rinehart & Winston, 1977), p. 169.
7. Jerome Bruner, "Teaching a Native Language," in his *Toward a Theory of Instruction* (New York: Norton, 1968), p. 107.
8. Ibid., p. 109.
9. Ibid., p. 110.
10. Raymond Queneau, *Exercises in Style*, trans. Barbara Wright (London: John Calder, 1981), p. 19.
11. Ibid., p. 24.
12. Ibid., pp. 104–05.
13. Ibid., p. 192.
14. Ibid., pp. 142–43.
15. William Wordsworth, *The Prelude*, 1799, 1805, 1850, ed. Jonathan Wordsworth, M. H. Abrams, and Stephen Gill (New York: Norton, 1979), Book 2, lines 213–15.
16. On Wordsworth's own funding, see Geoffrey Summerfield, *Fantasy and Reason* (Athens: University of Georgia Press, 1985), pp. 23–71, 268–99.
17. For a comical treatment of funding, see John Barth, "Lost in the Funhouse" in *Lost in the Funhouse* (New York: Bantam Books, 1969), p. 69.
18. Summerfield, *Fantasy and Reason*, p. 293.
19. Seamus Heaney, "Singing School," in *Worlds*, ed. Geoffrey Summerfield (Harmondsworth: Penguin, 1974), pp. 92–95; reprinted as "Rhymes," in Seamus Heaney, *Preoccupations: Selected Prose 1968–1978* (London: Faber & Faber, 1980), pp. 24–27.
20. Heaney, *Preoccupations*, pp. 24–27.
21. Ibid., pp. 41–60.
22. Ibid., p. 45.
23. Edwin Morgan, untitled introduction to a selection of his poems in *Worlds*, pp. 228–29.

# CHAPTER THREE

# GENERATIVE FRAME

## *Varieties of Textuality*

*The pleasure which the mind derives from the perception of similitude in dissimilitude . . . the great spring of the activity of our minds, and their chief feeder.*
                    *Wordsworth*

# UTTERANCE AND TEXT

W hat makes a text a *text*? What are the characteristic features of textuality? How does text differ from utterance; writing from speaking? What *are* the crucial differences between utterance and text? What does text offer that utterance does not? How does an exploration of such questions inform the teaching of composition? These are some of the probings of Chapter 3, as we offer a brief outline of what we see as some of the most important characteristic features of textuality.

Our students use language in three primary modes—inner speech, utterance, and text. Quantitatively, the amount of inner speech and utterance that they produce is far greater than the amount of text. It is for these reasons that we invite them to develop an awareness of textuality. We also discuss with them the modes of inner speech and utterance. By playing these off against text, we believe they can begin to recognize and employ the textuality of texts.

Again, we aim to help them find a toehold at least in the possibilities of hypotaxis, especially in their texts. But this is not to deny (a) that some texts are appropriately paratactic or (b) that we are delighted when their utterances also perform hypotactic games.

As with variety of utterance, so with variety of textuality, our aim is to help students recognize that varied texts are "realizations" of a variety of social roles, relationships, purposes, and intentions.

Behind any text, or under it, is the echo—more or less distant—of a voice: the sounds, rhythms, intonation patterns, expressive features, of utterance. The "implication of utterance" lurks in most texts, either closely or remotely.[1]

Text loses or retains these features according to the degree to which it derives from or attempts to simulate—to create an illusion of—someone talking.

One of the options of writers is how close or how far away from "utterance" to pitch their texts. Experienced writers tend to habituate this option. Environmental determinants within the context of situation will affect such choices, even preemptively close them. Sometimes the world makes the choice for us, and we conform to a "formula": "Dear Sir. . . . "

Let us offer what seem to us some of the most interesting points on the spectrum from "total utterance" (an utterance absolutely innocent of textuality) to "total text" (a text in which virtually no trace of a speaking voice remains, and which avails itself fully of the distinctive resources of textuality).

# UTTERANCE AS TEXT

## *Mental Events Felt to Be Preverbal*

A fluid, fluctuating, kaleidoscopic sequence of images—visual, auditory, even quasi-tactile—flows haphazardly through our consciousness. We observe them without necessarily thinking about them. They "come to us" unbidden, and we find that as soon as we begin to think about them, to reflect on them, to interpret them, to explain them to ourselves, then we are using words—inner speech.

Susanne Langer has attached the term "presentational symbolism" to these floating deliquescent images, and Denys Harding, in his remarkable essay "The Hinterland of Thought," pursues these phenomena as scrupulously as anyone. Indeed, he finds a perfectly apt image in Shakespeare: "Thoughts . . . in their dumb cradles" *(Troilus and Cressida)*. Harding usefully recognizes that many of our most important mental acts are taken up not so much with problem solving as with "the recognition of our own motives, the exploring of our interests, the formulation of desires and intentions, the definition and re-definition of attitudes and preferences." For such states of being, words form "a late stage of their definition." Much of the work that we do occurs before or outside consciousness; even in sleep, our bodies can conform to the good habits that we have developed: bodily impulses are, even nocturnally, "filtered through at least some part of the array of values that constitutes the person."[2] So, most of us don't wet the bed!

Susanne Langer has remarked, Harding notes, that "Speech is, in fact, the readiest active termination of that basic process in the human brain which may be called *symbolic transformation of experiences*."[3] He further reminds us that Langer "speaks of 'presentational symbolism' to distinguish this kind of imperfectly differentiated thinking from the array of explicitly related ideas that she calls 'discursive thinking.' " Or, as he succinctly puts it, the life of one's mind is often characterized by "the partial activation of processes that could become thoughts if I stopped to think." And he brings his reading of Shakespeare felicitously to bear when he quotes *Macbeth*:

> *And pity, like a naked new-born babe,*
> *Striding the blast, or heaven's cherubin, horsed*
> *Upon the sightless couriers of the air,*
> *Shall blow the horrid deed in every eye,*
> *That tears shall drown the wind.*

and comments: "What a passage like this reveals is not disorder but a complex ordering of attitude and belief achieved a stage earlier than discursive statement."[4] It is as if Shakespeare has, with lightning speed, "captured," fixed, and represented the remarkable preverbal drama inside his own mind – a drama enacted as images, each richly funded with his culture's values.

To attempt to represent the rich hurly-burly of the mind's "presentational symbolism" in the form of text is to face an extraordinary challenge. Not only to capture the images but to convey something of the dynamic interplay between them – that is a tall order.

Visual media seem on the whole better at representing this preverbal level of consciousness than do verbal representations – that is, a *concrete* medium is more effective than the relatively abstract medium of words. We need only stress this: any text that *pretends* to represent this aspect of the life of the mind can offer the reader only an *illusion*. When we read such a text, it is *as if* we observed the odd kaleidoscope of imagery. A successful text, in this case, will create at best an illusion, a fiction of "naturalism." If it "works," it is because we are "convinced," and we are convinced only if we re-cognize.

## Inner Speech

In terms of any individual's total production of discourse, over its whole range, inner speech probably comprises a greater fraction of the whole than does any other category. Even compulsive talkers probably produce more inner speech than vocal talk.

The crucial features of inner speech were first recognized systematically by the Russian psychologist Lev Vygotsky. Before discussing his observations, however, we invite you to read this:

> *Gasworks. Whooping cough they say it cures. Good job Molly never got it. Poor children! Doubles them up black and blue in convulsions. Shame really. Got off lightly with illnesses compared. Only measles. Flaxseed tea. Scarlatina influenza, epidemics. Canvassing for death. Don't miss the chance.*[5]

You may have recognized that as a passage from Joyce's *Ulysses*. What exactly is Joyce's text doing? We cheated by decontextualizing it, especially by omitting the previous two lines, with which Joyce cues his reader and sets up his frame: Bloom engaged in conversation, but also in private rumination:

> *Mr. Bloom put his head out of the window.*
> *—The grand canal, he said.*

With fine Irish courtesy, Joyce first gives the reader a bit of situational narrative then offers a small ironic utterance, inspired by what Bloom sees out of the window. Venice's Grand Canal has palaces; this one has gasworks. And the word initiates a stretch, or strip, of inner speech. Joyce had a finely tuned, acute ear, and he didn't need Vygotsky to tell him that one of the criterial features of the syntax of inner speech is that most of its sentences consist *only of a predicate.* There is of course no need to posit the subject, because the person producing the inner speech already knows what the subject is. Joyce, in the event, walks a tightrope, balancing the needs of the reader (in Bloom's fictive situation, there is no "reader," no listener, no audience) and the claims of authenticity or "naturalism"—the presentation of a plausible illusion. Thus his first sentence "Gasworks" omits the self-evident "I now see the." His second explicitly retains its subject but registers its privateness by reversing its word order: it starts with a major part of its predicate. The third sentence omits "It's a"; and the fourth is ejaculating and therefore merely names: "Poor children!" which is an elliptical vocative form: "Oh, the poor children!"—a clamatory or deploratory form of some such utterance as "The bowels of my compassion are moved by (or, when I think of) the poor children."

As G. W. Turner, the linguist, has observed, Bloom's inner speech "though an artifact, has been widely accepted as a plausible approximation to inner speech . . . though it is of course also a controlled part of James Joyce's complex communication with his reader."[6]

Even as Joyce was writing *Ulysses,* Lev Vygotsky was teasing out many of the crucial syntactic and semantic features of inner speech:[7]

1. It is characterized by "extreme, elliptical economy" (p. 45).

2. "Inner speech is speech for oneself" (p. 131).

3. "It serves mental orientation, conscious understanding" (p. 133).

4. It possesses "traits . . . which make for inscrutability" (p. 134).

5. "It shows a tendency toward an altogether specific form of abbreviation: namely, omitting the subject of a sentence . . . while preserving the predicate. [This is] the basic syntactic form of inner speech" (p. 139).

6. "Abbreviation is not an exception but the rule" (p. 142).

7. "It is as much a law of inner speech to omit [grammatical] subjects as it is a law of written speech to contain both subjects and predicates" (p. 145).

8. "The predominance of sense over meaning, of sentence over word, and of context over sentence is the rule" (p. 147).

## *Internalized Monologue/Dialogue*

Internalized monologue/dialogue is a "displaced" social act. Without thought or conscious will, we internalize an interlocutor or an audience, which we address subvocally. Structurally, this is almost identical with *actual* speech. If we are approaching the day we have to deliver a lecture, our anticipating can at times be so intense that it is as if we were already lecturing: the inner monologue that we produce will have many of the features of lecture style. We prepare to talk by "talking."

Internalized dialogue is subtler and more obscure. Sometimes it is with another who is internalized as interlocutor. But often, especially when we are trying to solve a problem or make a decision, the two "speakers" are two aspects of the self: our sensible self and our extravagant self, a careful self and a careless self. One or other is usually dominant, and the less dominant is often in the role of consultant. The initiating self has the energy and "acts"; the consultant or confidant self reacts. (The "voice" of this latter self may well owe a great deal to an influential internalized other—for example, a parent.)

The reader-inside-the-head (primarily, a *listener* and *respondent*) has a life of its own: we don't need even to think about it in order to establish its presence; it is *already* there. It springs unbidden, in a variety of guises, according to the particular flavors of the writings' moments. For some people, this interior interlocutor, felt to be both self and not-self, makes its appearance very early in life. Edmund Gosse, for example, in *Father and Son*, remarks on an act of vandalism that he committed at the age of six that went undetected:

> But of all the thoughts which rushed upon my savage and unde-
> veloped little brain at this crisis, the most curious was that I had
> found a companion and a confidant in myself. There was a secret
> in this world and it belonged to me and to a somebody who lived
> in the same body with me. There were two of us, and we could talk
> with one another. It is difficult to define impressions so rudimen-
> tary, but it is certain that it was in this dual form that the sense
> of my individuality now suddenly descended upon me, and it is

*equally certain that it was a great solace to me to find a sympathizer in my own breast.*[8]

He subsequently connects this inner duality to his ability to be, on occasions, both participant and spectator:

*It culminated in a sort of fit of hysterics, when I lost all self-control, and sobbed with tears, and banged my head on the table. While this was proceeding, I was conscious of that dual individuality of which I have already spoken, since while one part of me gave way, and could not resist, the other part in some extraordinary sense seemed standing aloof, much impressed. I was alone with my Father when this crisis suddenly occurred, and I was interested to see that he was greatly alarmed.*[9]

Does your internalized audience, like Gosse's, not seem to possess a distinctive autonomy, a life of its own? And is this seemingly independent life not a part of your normal daily inner consciousness? so integral that its presence no longer surprises or disconcerts you? And is it not, in some guise, persistently involved in some kind of dialectical relationship with the utterance-producing part of yourself? Even as we speak of your "envisaging" it, does that verb not strike you as too deliberative, too active (rather as it is impossible to believe continuously, as you watch moment by moment, that the dummy of the really talented ventriloquist doesn't have autonomous life)?

Is this ghostly interlocutor, then, the same "person" as the reader of the text that you are composing? Or is it, rather, that this psychic interlocutor can wear a great variety of masks?

Rom Harré, in *Personal Being,* reminds us that in the medieval morality plays these various personal functions are externalized as "characters" ("Humility . . . helps the heroine Anima, the soul, against the machinations of Hypocrisy") and that they are reified as "mental organs" in cognitive psychology and Freudian psychodynamics.* "None," he argues, "can represent what is essential to a person as a psychological unity"[10] (cf. Marvell's dialogues).

Here is Barbara Herrnstein Smith's characterization of such inner dialoguing:

*We are almost continuously "saying" things to that most intimate, congenial and attentive listener whom we carry within our own*

---

*One can, in fact, go even further back and cite Prudentius's poem (c. 400 A.D.): *Psychomachy*—The Struggle (or War) Within the Soul.

*skins. Interior speech or verbal thinking is evidently a derived capacity that could not arise prior to, or independent of, one's participation, as both speaker and listener, in a linguistic community. But the functions and value of language are significantly extended by our ability to speak (and listen) to ourselves. For one thing, since one's "self" is always part of one's most immediate physical environment (as philosophers with toothaches have had occasion to observe) and also, in a sense, part of one's social environment as well (we are always our own companions) we have considerable interest in controlling and modifying its behavior; and so we take great care to feed ourselves information. Second, when we command, question, warn, and instruct the listener within, we can be, well, fairly confident of his inclination to act appropriately in serving our interests. Also, perhaps most importantly, by assuming the dual roles of speaker and listener, we are able to . . . appraise our own perceptions and responses, to expose, test, compare, and confirm or correct them. It seems clear that our capacity for interior articulation also increases our ability to discriminate and classify our experiences, and therefore enables us to make more effective use of* prior *experiences in solving problems, making plans, and generally dealing with the world as we encounter it. Interior speech certainly comprises a major part of the "activity" of all human beings, and it is likely that our sense of personal identity and, to a large extent, "consciousness" itself are products of our internalization of the linguistic transaction.*[11]

## Voiced Utterances: Monologues and Dialogues

Dialogues—conversations, discussions, quarrels, reconciliations, chatting—are a more common form of utterance than is monologue.

When he was alone, Bloom said (aloud): "The grand canal." Joyce had abandoned quotation marks, but we know that Bloom spoke aloud, for Joyce wrote, "he said." The fact that spoken utterance has received more attention than inner speech can be deduced from Joyce's unmarked "said"—not "said out loud." Thereafter Bloom, characteristically, slipped into inner speech—not even internalized monologue. It is not as if he were speaking silently to someone other than himself; he was ruminating.

The local life of many texts depends on the presence of an illusion of utterance. In novels we know this as dialogue. Well used, it *shows* style, character, mood, nature, and tone of interaction, and there is no need for the writer to fall back on what Henry James called "the platitude of statement."

One of the crucial differences between social talk—the kind of talk mostly produced—and text is that talk affords many vocal and gestural or kinetic expressive resources, whereas text affords the privileges of privacy, uninterrupted control, the power to revise. When we produce text, our readerly eyes recursively rehearse (repeat) prior strips or segments, and we can go on from what is already on the page. But the most salient difference for our purposes is between the parataxis of talk and the hypotaxis of text. (For this question, we refer you to Chapter 7.)

We believe that one of the most effective ways to help students appreciate the textuality of text is to have them incorporate utterance into their texts—that is, to have them write what appears to be a transcript of utterances, both monologue and dialogue. Similarly, we share with them texts such as those that follow—all of which involve text in the task of representing utterance.

First, here are a short (documentary) extract from Agee and a longer (fictional) one from Steinbeck, followed in each case by the kind of commentary we offer students on such texts:

> . . . *as one prominent landlord said and as many more would agree: "I don't object to nigrah education, not up through foath a fift grade maybe, but not furdern dat: I'm too strong a believah in white syewpremcy."* [12]

## Commentary

Agee is creating a sense of irony. The speaker, a prominent landlord, wishes to uphold "white supremacy"; but his way of talking—as *represented* in the eye-dialect of the text and *interpreted* by the reader—is marked by gross deviations from educated speech, deviations that the reader is to understand as a sign that the landlord himself is ignorant.

What would be the effect if Agee had written this, instead?

> I really have no objections to the education of black people, certainly not as far as fourth or, perhaps, fifth grade, but I don't believe they should be educated beyond that level: after all, I do believe passionately in the concept of white superiority, even though that may strike some people from the North as evidence of racial prejudice.

Now consider this passage by John Steinbeck:

> *For a moment a little worry came on Ma's face. "Ain't you gonna stay with us—with the family?" she asked.*

*"Well, we talked all bout it, me an' Connie. Ma, we wanna live in a town." She went on excitedly. "Connie gonna get a job in a store or maybe a fact'ry. An' he's gonna study at home, maybe radio, so he can git to be a expert an' maybe later have his own store. An' we'll go to pitchers whenever. An' Connie says I'm gonna have a doctor when the baby's born; an' he says we'll see how times is, an' maybe I'll go to a hospiddle. An' we'll have a car, little car. An' after he studies at night, why—it'll be nice, an' he tore a page outa* Western Love Stories, *an' he's gonna send off for a course, 'cause it don't cost nothin' to send off. Says right on that clipping. I seen it. An' why—they even get you a job when you take that course—radios, it is—nice clean work, and a future. An' we'll live in town an' go to pitchers whenever, an'—well, I'm gonna have a 'lectric iron, an' the baby'll have all new stuff. Connie says all new stuff—white an'—Well, you seen in the catalogue all the stuff they got for a baby. Maybe right at first while Connie's studyin' at home it won't be so easy, but—well, when the baby comes, maybe he'll be all done studyin' an' we'll have a place, little bit of a place. We don't want nothin' fancy, but we want it nice for the baby—" Her face glowed with excitement. "An' I thought— well, I thought maybe we could all go in town, an' when Connie gets his store—maybe Al could work for him."*

*Ma's eyes had never left the flushing face. Ma watched the structure grow and followed it. "We don' want you to go 'way from us," she said. "It ain't good for folks to break up."*

*Al snorted, "Me work for Connie? How about Connie comes a-workin' for me? He thinks he's the on'y son-of-a-bitch can study at night?"*[13]

## Commentary

We've made it rather difficult for you by extracting—decontextualizing —a small episode from a long novel. Everything that you might have learned about Ma, Al, and Connie, not to mention X, the unnamed speaker, is thereby withheld. Even so, because of your *present* knowledge of the general conventions of writing, and specifically of the conventions that are used to *represent* characters in fiction, we believe that you can construe a great deal about the situation and about the main speaker. For example:

1. How do you know that, in this scene, Ma has just learned for the first time that X and Connie are proposing to leave?

2. How do you know that X is *relatively* uneducated? How many *kinds* of clues can you offer?

3. How do you account for the narrator's words "She went on excitedly"? What does this sentence tell us about the limitations of *text* as a way of presenting utterance?

4. What is the effect of the repetition of "maybe"? What does it tell us about X's state of mind?

There are conspicuous moments in literature when the whole of a text is representation of utterance and sustains the enlivening illusion of hearing someone talk. Two of the most famous cases are obviously *Huckleberry Finn* and *Catcher in the Rye*. Russell Hoban's novel *Riddley Walker*, set in England after a nuclear holocaust, is an equally sustained and compelling act of impersonation. We share parts of it with our students to remind them that one of the great resources of text is to avail itself of the peculiar powers of the speaking voice. *Riddley Walker* also offers an excellent exercise in reading with the ear—a habit that few students have ever been encouraged or disposed to cultivate, more's the pity. When they read/write ineffectually, the cause is often to be traced to their indisposition to *hear* the text.

Here now is a fragment of *Riddley Walker*. Your eye may well be baffled. We hope so. Let your ear hear the voice, and all, or most, will be clear. (Hoban, expatriate American, has perfectly impersonated the nonstandard dialect of Kent, England.)

> *Walker is my name and I am the same. Riddley Walker. Walking my riddels where ever theyve took me and walking them now on this paper the same.*
>
> *I dont think it makes no diffrents where you start the telling of a thing. You never know where it begun realy. No moren you know where you begun your oan self. You myt know the place and day and time of day when you ben beartht. You myt even know the place and day and time when you ben got. That dont mean nothing tho. You stil dont know where you begun.*
>
> *Ive all ready wrote down about my naming day. It wernt no moren 3 days after that my dad got kilt in the digging at Widders Dump and I wer the loan of my name.*
>
> *Dad and me we jus come off forage rota and back on jobbing that day. The hoal we ben working we ben on it 24 days. Which Ive never liket 12 its a judgd men number innit and this ben 2 of them. Wed pernear cleart out down to the chalk and hevvy mucking it*

*ben. Nothing lef in the hoal only sortit thru muck and the smel of it and some girt big rottin iron thing some kynd of machine it wer you cudnt tel what it wer.*

*Til then any thing big we all ways bustit up in the hoal. Winch a girt big buster rock up on the crane and drop it down on what ever we wer busting. Finish up with han hammers then theywd drag the peaces to the reddy for the melting. This time tho the 1stman tol us word come down they dint want this thing bustit up we wer to get it out in tack. So we ben sturgling with the girt big thing nor the woal 20 of us cudnt shif it we cudnt even lif it jus that littl bit to get the sling unner neath of it. Up to our knees in muck we wer. Even with the drain wed dug the hoal wer mucky from the rains. And col. It wer only jus the 2nd mooning of the year and winter long in going.* [14]

Much of the compelling power of Hoban's novel resides in—is a function of—the narrating voice. The text is a consistently ingenious and sensitive registration of an adolescent boy using the dialect of his tribe. What baffles the eye—"Which Ive never liket 12 its a judgd men number innit and this ben 2 of them"—yields to the ear—"Which I've never liked; 12—it's a judgment number, isn't it? And this been (was) 2 of them (i.e., twice times 12)."

The cumulative pathos of the text—apart from the terrors, trials, and tribulations it recounts—derives from the fact that it is *not* a privileged observer's text, omniscient and safely detached, but a suffering participant's text, laced with uncertainty, tentativeness, confusion— all offered through a true voice of feeling.

## *Formal Public Utterances*

The best way to protect one's utterances and their vulnerabilities from unsympathetic arrows is to rehearse them and use all the peculiar privileges of text in order to revise, reshape, modify, have second thoughts.

The task of the text is to work effectively as a script; to offer props or crutches for the exposed monological voice; to constitute a speech, or a lecture, which, when the moment arrives, simply has to be transferred from the page onto the sound waves.

The most subtle task is, of course, to get the text, for all its carefulness, to impersonate spontaneous utterance. How many times did Kennedy rehearse the delivery of his inaugural address? Did the ritualistic formality and theatricality of the event serve to legitimate those famous unidiomatic inversions: "Ask not . . ."?

# TEXT AS TEXT

S o far, we have been looking at those forms of discourse in which text has the task of impersonating and presenting utterance. Now, we move out of utterance, as such, and look at texts that never were utterances; texts that started life as texts. We leave quotation marks behind. As with utterance as text, we shall move in an outward progression, beginning with texts meant for the self.

## *Texts for the Self*

Texts for the self are the textual equivalents of internalized monologue/dialogue. The writer and reader are both the self (cf. p. 64).

### Mathetic

Mathetic texts are those for the release of energy or tension, for reflection, for clarification, for getting something out so we can see it, for holding on to ideas, thoughts, "seeds," that would otherwise escape. Such texts are "raw" rather than "cooked." When we have written them, we can subsequently read our past representations of aspects of our lives and minds. All such texts are entirely free of the obligations and constraints of social interaction or role. For a further discussion, see page 140.

### Pragmatic

Here is an example of a pragmatic text for the self:

Phone Bill

To a spectator, this text is distinctly ambiguous. Does it mean "Pay the phone bill" or "Call William"? The ambiguity derives from the absence of context. But since the text is intended only for the writer, the context is a given, as in inner speech.

Other examples of pragmatic texts are:

1. Texts for the regulation or control of our days, such as shopping lists. Another example would be the "agenda" we prepare for work we must do next week—self-directions.

2. Initial jottings, notes, and schemes for any text that is at the drafting stage.

Such texts are often *synpractic*—that is, a verbalized part of an ongoing action.

A remarkable example of such texts, with an exploration of their uses and the needs they satisfy, is offered by Philip Roth in his novel *The Professor of Desire:* "And those lists! Those wonderful, orderly lists!"[15]

# *Texts for Others Close to the Self*

## Interpersonal/Pragmatic

Interpersonal/pragmatic texts for others close to the self are texts that renew, intensify, or sustain a bond with valued others—such as letters to friends. These texts may contain transactional elements ("Can you drop by and feed the dog while we're away?"), but their primary purpose is affective, or phatic.

## Transactional

What kind of sense do you make of the following text? Can you place it? Infer something about the context? What are the clues? Can you deduce a purpose/function for the text? Are there any parts that remain obstinately incomprehensible? Under what kinds of constraints do you think the text was written? Does the evaluative exclamation at the end strike you as incongruous or inappropriate?

> *5/5/17. Offensive patrol: twelve thousand feet. Hoidge, Melville, and self on voluntary patrol. Bad Archie over Douai. Lost Melville in cloud and afterwards attacked five red scouts. Sheered off when seven others came to their assistance. Two against twelve "no bon." We climbed west and they east, afterwards attacked them again, being joined by five Tripehounds, making the odds seven to twelve. Think I did in one, and Hoidge also did in one. Both granted by Wing.*
>
> *7/15/17. Ran into three scouts east of Cambrai. Brought one down. Meintjies dived, but his gun jammed, so I carried on and finished him. Next fired on two-seater this side lines, but could not climb up to him. Went up to Lens, saw a two-seater over Douai, dived and the others followed. Fixed him up. Afterwards this confirmed by an FE 2d, who saw him burst into flames. Tackled three two-seaters who beat it east and came home. Good day!*[16]

We hazard a few guesses about your interpretation of that text:

1. "Offensive patrol" suggests war.

2. The date 5/5/17 confirms 1.

3. "Twelve thousand feet" suggests aerial warfare.

4. "Bad Archie" is part of a private or in-group language. If the enemy occupies Douai, then "Archie" could be something that the enemy does to repel Allied planes.

5. "Red Scouts" = enemy.

6. "No bon," a bit of Anglo-French, = "no good"—the kind of polyglot language that servicemen overseas tend to invent.

7. "Tripehounds"—an *un*official name for a type of Allied aircraft.

8. "Did in" = destroyed or damaged.

9. "Both granted by Wing" ??? Who are/what is Wing? And what is being "granted"?

10. "Cambrai": like "Douai," must be a place name.

11. "Meintjies": must be the name of another pilot, on the same side as the writer.

12. "Lens" = place name. Lens is near Douai.

13. "Fixed him up" = destroyed.

14. "Confirmed by an FE 2d" = confirmed by the pilot of an aircraft, type FE 2d.

15. Penultimate sentence ambiguous. "They" beat it east; "I" came home?

16. "Good day!" expresses gratification (and gratitude?) for survival and for the victories.

Whether or not your interpretation coincided with our speculative reconstruction of it, you will doubtless agree (1) that neither you nor we were the initial audience for that text; (2) that the text is written in a kind of shorthand; (3) that its pragmatic audience was the writer himself—as pilot recording his exploits, keeping a record for some purpose, probably official—and possibly also a superior officer who could require such a record, a logbook, to be produced on demand.

Such a text—a transactional text written for the self and an intimate professional audience—has no need to take on the responsibility of making sense to a larger, exoteric audience. By the time Cecil Lewis comes to quote that extract from his 1917 logbook, in his great World

War I memoir *Sagittarius Rising,* he has already put his reader in the picture, the context has already been established. Lewis has by then familiarized his absent, unknown reader with the fact that he was a member of a squadron, which was part of a wing, and that the wing commander needed to build up a panoptic picture of the aerial war on his sector of the front, for which he depended on the testimony of all the pilots. When we read the logbook, some seventy years later, we have the eerie sense of looking over dead men's shoulders; we are outsiders who are, for a moment, being let in.

The environmental determinants—exhaustion, injury, urgency, need for economy, and so on—are sufficient to explain why Lewis's logbook was written in the manner it was. Each element of his text, both the semantic and the syntactic, can be explained in terms of the text's dominant function and of the difficult circumstances in which it was written.

## *Texts for an Unknown Audience*

### **Personal/Imaginative**

Examples of personal/imaginative texts for an unknown audience are novels, poems, drama, soap opera, vaudeville sketches. If you were to translate Cecil Lewis's logbook into a narrative or a history of aerial warfare for an unknown audience (novel readers, say, or aircraft buffs), you would have to decide which elements were "given" and which were "new"—that is, which elements your audience could reasonably be assumed to know already and which were new to them and therefore required explanation.

The predisposition to judge what your audience needs to be told in order to understand your text, and the ability to provide that information—these are *social* talents, social competences: simply the displacement of daily social tact from the context of porch or living room or telephone to the more abstracted context of the writing desk, where the addressee is absent. Awareness of absence and of its consequences is something we aim to cultivate. As soon as class members take on the role of reader of a student's text for an unknown audience, they will cheerfully display their failures to comprehend—failures that arise from the writer's failure to anticipate the reader's needs.

Syntactically, salient differences from utterance can be seen to occur. Utterances push/nudge forward, moment by moment, in *real* time, and therefore tend to produce coordinately shunted, end-on, constituents

(A, B, C, D, or A.B.C.D. or A and B and C and D)—as in a child's text, which has the primary characteristics of utterance:

> On Saturday me, Laura Jean and John went to Eastville Park. Me and Laura went in the water. Then we were playing in the mud. After, we went back in the water. Then suddenly I slipped in the water and I was wet. We were both laughing too. Then I dried myself. I had on a blue T-shirt and a summer dress. It was a warm day. After, we went to clean our feet. Then my sock fell in the water and I went in and got it. After, we went home in the camper.

Text, in contrast, is not constructed in the irreversible, pressing *real* time of face-to-face interactions; it is produced in the flexi-time of *writing*. The writer can modify, return, revise, clarify connections, rethink, reshape. The pressures of utterance are not present. The writer's control is not threatened by the interventions of an interlocutor or by the socially internalized need to "keep talking."

Thus, *consideration*—pre-meditation, meditation, post-meditation (reconsidering)—is the distinctive privilege of writing. And it's hardly surprising, therefore, that the history of writing as a cultural act has evolved its own distinctive resources—above all, the privilege of relative complexity: of superordination and subordination—in a word, hypotaxis (see Chapter 8).

## Pragmatic

It is in pragmatic texts for an unknown audience that the responsibilities and privileges of textuality can most fully be recognized. Text can make explicit all those functions and connections that most utterance leaves implicit. Since the reader is free to stop reading our book, our text, at any moment—unlike our conversational interlocutors (we rarely tell someone to whom we're listening to shut up)—we can take risks, offer redundancies, slip in definitions, give examples, explicate connections, offer readers all that they may conceivably need, even though any one individual reader may not need this or that (and can therefore skip).

Elements can be disposed at various appropriate levels of abstraction and generalization; appropriately illuminating examples can be tucked in retroactively in order to give substance to a proposition; the architectonic articulations of this section with that section can be studied, reexamined, played with; options can be laid out and tried on for size —such are some of the most telling possibilities of the autonomy of text when measuring up to its inherent constraints.

So text, fully evolved—written by someone richly funded with many and various experiences of reading previous texts—comes into its own. And if someone, invisible behind a screen, reads aloud such a text, however "spontaneously," however "informally," one's ears will recognize it as *text*. White House spokespersons read to the press from "prepared statements" (i.e., texts); and however closely a statement's writer has approximated the features of utterance as opposed to text, we will inevitably hear the voice as one that is reading aloud from a text rather than just speaking. Read, on the other hand, transcripts of the notorious Watergate tapes, and you will have no hesitation in recognizing those "texts" as a visual presentation of what is in fact utterance.

By reading aloud frequently, however briefly—generally, the point is seized quickly—we habituate our students' ears to listen for the telling characteristics of text—for example, its ability to dispose an effective array of subordinate clauses before it delivers the suspended main clause.[17]

We now offer a text—text enfranchised, text that proclaims itself as text—written for an unknown audience, disposing its parts with telling effect:

> *Acutely aware of our beings' limitations and acknowledging the infinite mystery of the a priori universe into which we are born but nevertheless searching for a conscious means of hopefully competent participation by humanity in its own evolutionary trending while employing only the unique advantages inhering exclusively to the individual who takes and maintains the economic initiative in the face of the formidable physical capital and credit advantages of the massive corporations and political states and deliberately avoiding political ties and tactics while endeavoring by experiments and explorations to excite individuals' awareness and realization of humanity's higher potentials I seek through comprehensive anticipatory design science and its reductions to physical practices to reform the environment instead of trying to reform men being intent thereby to accomplish prototyped capabilities of doing more with less whereby in turn the wealth augmenting prospects of such design science regenerations will induce their spontaneous and economically successful industrial proliferation by world around services' managements all of which chain reaction provoking events will*

*both permit and induce all humanity to realize full lasting eco-
nomic and physical success plus enjoyment of all the Earth without one individual interfering with or being advantaged at the
expense of another.*

Buckminster Fuller,
*Aboard our 1,000-miles-per-minute speeding
spaceship Earth within the outer reaches of the cosmically
spiraling and expanding Milky Way,
the Galactic Nebula.*

*Modified from 152 to 200 words at the
location on spaceship Earth where the first man-made
atomic explosion occurred: Alamogordo.*[18]

That text was Buckminster Fuller's response to a request from *Who's
Who* for an entry. Fuller's geodesic domes, to the best of our knowledge, still stand: they have not sagged or collapsed from unequal distribution of stresses and strains. But what of his hypotaxis? Has he made
excessive demands of his sentence's potentialities? Does the text cohere?
Does it make tolerable demands on a reader's short-term memory? Or
has he pushed hypotaxis too far, leaving the "natural" rhythms and
connections of utterance too far behind? Must we conclude that his text
is, like some of his inventions, ingenious but impractical?

# WHAT ALL
# "GOOD" TEXTS DO

A few years ago, we were rereading William Labov's now classic
essay "The Study of Language in Its Social Context" and were
again aroused by his remarkable observation: "When we can say *what*
is being done with a sentence, then we will be able to observe how
often speakers do it."[19]

What, then, had *we* been doing with our sentences—those that we
had been speaking and writing all those years? We found ourselves
deluged by our own answers: trying to amuse, to placate, to reassure,
to rebuke, to pacify, to forgive, to ask forgiveness, to nudge, to tease,
to deny, to gratify, to. . . . Your list, like ours, could well seem endless.

But what did our sentences have in common—what was their lowest
common denominator? We concluded that they all represented or constituted social acts and intentions: each comprised a movement toward,

with, or away from another person or other persons. The incidence of information transmission was relatively infrequent. Much more often, we seem to have been involved in influencing or modifying the conduct or attitude of another, affectively, in a subtle network of interactions and counterpointings. Later, we started to read in the area of speech act theory and discovered that speech act theorists (the practitioners of pragmatics), already had terms for these things: whenever we speak (i.e., perform a locutionary act), what the speaking *is doing*, is acting as medium for an *illocutionary* act. Our locution signifies our illocution—what is in our mind (a need, a desire, a duty, or whatever). Even apparently empty, perfunctory, or formulaic utterances carry illocutionary force. "Nice morning" or "Have a good day"—both have social meaning. The locution may strike us as banal, conventional, even tiresome, but we cannot construe it as empty of social meaning. To find genuinely vacuous, empty locutions—locutionary acts containing no illocutionary meaning—we have to turn to the glib textbooks written for basic writers, books that press students into the production of formulaic sentence patterns in which the meaning has no affective connection with the mind of the student writer. The production of such sentences is indeed a hollow and wretched ritual. We wonder that the students don't go mad, for the human purpose of any locution is to perform an illocutionary act.[20]

Henry Glassie, in *Passing the Time in Ballymenone*, observed: "To be effective, stories connect, unifying meaningfully. The structure of values shifts into visibility. To be affective, connections remain intricate and imperfect, leaving space for people to discover new and personal meanings within and between. The enactment of value remains an individual responsibility."[21] Glassie here is speaking of oral storytelling, yet the same conditions can obtain in the relationship between the student reader and the text. And the peculiar virtue of the reactive text is that it is not subordinate to the primary text but operates at the same level of discourse: it is, for example, a story as reaction to a story. And the illocutionary energies of the student in role as participant make for a strong text: naive, sometimes; crude, even inchoate, on occasions; but strongly impelled, energized, and informed by illocutionary heft or clout.

# NOTES

1. Cf. Michael Halliday, *Language as Social Semiotic* (London: Arnold, 1979), p. 133.
2. See Denys Harding, *Experience into Words* (London: Cambridge University Press, 1982), pp. 175–97.
3. Susanne Langer, *Philosophy in a New Key* (Cambridge, Mass.: Harvard University Press, 1976), cited in ibid., p. 180.
4. Harding, *Experience into Words*, p. 182.
5. James Joyce, *Ulysses* (New York: Vintage Books, 1961), p. 90.
6. G. W. Turner, *Stylistics* (Harmondsworth: Penguin, 1973), p. 201.
7. The page references that follow are to Lev Vygotsky, *Thought and Language* (Cambridge, Mass.: M.I.T. Press, 1962).
8. Edmund Gosse, *Father and Son: A Study of Two Temperaments* (Harmondsworth: Penguin, 1979), p. 34.
9. Ibid.
10. Rom Harré, *Personal Being* (Cambridge, Mass.: Harvard University Press, 1984), p. 10.
11. Barbara Herrnstein Smith, *On the Margins of Discourse* (Chicago: University of Chicago Press, 1983), p. 92.
12. James Agee, *Let Us Now Praise Famous Men* (New York: Ballantine Books, 1970), p. 270.
13. John Steinbeck, *The Grapes of Wrath* (New York: Penguin, 1976), p. 144.
14. Russell Hoban, *Riddley Walker* (London: Picador, 1982), p. 8.
15. Philip Roth, *The Professor of Desire* (New York: Farrar, Straus and Giroux, 1977), pp. 152ff.
16. Cecil Lewis, *Sagittarius Rising* (Harmondsworth: Penguin, 1977), p. 143.
17. A handy repertoire of interesting cases is offered by Virginia Tufte, *Grammar as Style* (New York: Holt, Rinehart and Winston, 1971), Chapter 16.
18. Buckminster Fuller, entry for *Who's Who*, from *Saturday Review*, March 2, 1968.
19. William Labov, *Sociolinguistic Patterns* (Philadelphia: University of Pennsylvania Press, 1972), p. 258.
20. Cf. Halliday: "Anyone who formalizes natural language does so at the cost of idealizing it to such an extent that it is hardly recognizable as language any more." *Language as Social Semiotic*, p. 203.
21. Henry Glassie, *Passing the Time in Ballymenone* (Philadelphia: University of Pennsylvania Press, 1982), p. 180.

# CHAPTER FOUR

# APPLICATIONS
## Syntax as a Notch on the Evolutionary Ladder

*. . . One was . . . to fly backward, the other could not help being carried forward.*

*Edmund Gosse*

# "WODWO" AS A PRIMARY TEXT

E very text ever written can conceivably be used as a primary text, to provide the short-term intensive funding that results in the making of a reactive text.

On some occasions we use a poem—not because it is poetry as such but because it happens to display especially strong textual characteristics.

We invite you to read the following poem, first aloud, quite quickly; then silently and slowly; then aloud again, in a manner that is appropriate to what you will by now have discovered in the text. We would merely explain that a wodwo is a forest spirit, a wild man of the woods; people in Europe believed in wodwos without question for millennia, well into modern times.

### WODWO

*What am I? Nosing here, turning leaves over*
*following a faint stain on the air to the river's edge*
*I enter water. What am I to split*
*the glassy grain of water looking upward I see the bed*
*of the river above me upside down very clear*      5
*what am I doing here in mid-air? Why do I find*
*this frog so interesting as I inspect its most secret*
*interior and make it my own? Do these weeds*
*know me and name me to each other have they*
*seen me before, do I fit in their world? I seem*      10
*separate from the ground and not rooted but dropped*
*out of nothing casually I've no threads*
*fastening me to anything I can go anywhere*
*I seem to have been given the freedom*
*of this place what am I then? And picking*      15
*bits of bark off this rotten stump gives me*
*no pleasure and it's no use so why do I do it*
*me and doing that have coincided very queerly*
*But what shall I be called am I the first*
*have I an owner what shape am I what*      20
*shape am I am I huge if I go*
*to the end on this way past these trees and past these trees*
*till I get tired that's touching one wall of me*
*for the moment if I sit still how everything*
*stops to watch me I suppose I am the exact centre*      25

> *but there's all this what is it roots*
> *roots roots roots and here's the water*
> *again very queer but I'll go on looking*[1]

Ted Hughes's poem "Wodwo" is a text that we read with our students during the earlier phases of our work together. It has just the right balance of clarity and obscurity to serve as a compelling representation of an attempt to make sense of an experience even as it is happening. Structurally, it is a paratactic series, its constituent parts accompanying and commenting on actions, mostly exploratory in nature—both in the sense of exploring a new world and also in the sense of trying to make sense of the facts of perception. The *ur*-man's uncertainties are clearly enacted by the very syntax itself: his relative inability to "make sentences" is a function and an expression of his inability to "make sense" of his senses and of what they register.[2]

Wodwo is a paratactic language user in search of hypotaxis. At a more basic level, he is groping toward, reaching for, "transitivity." With the benefit of hindsight, we can observe that it's going to require some evolutionary-cum-cultural shifts, leaps forward, before his world can be construed hypotactically, as a complex whole, with subordination and superordinations putting things "where they belong." Hughes's poem can, then, be read as a parable about syntax and about the meanings of syntax.* Complex sentences are representations of a view of experience that is inherently complex, and—more emphatically—characterized by connectedness, interrelatedness, conditionality, causality, concessiveness, contradictions, and so on. It is experience, furthermore, of which some part is felt, at some moment, to be more important than other parts (i.e., it is a world of foregrounds and backgrounds). What happens to these utterances when we nudge Wodwo two or three rungs up or down the evolutionary or developmental ladder? To put it another way, what happens when we deprive Wodwo of any notion, however slight, of hypotaxis? And conversely, what happens if we transform his "state of mind" into one that has the full range of hypotaxis at its disposal?

What syntactic resources does Hughes give Wodwo at this stage, the stage represented by Hughes's text? Well, "What am I?" is a clear enough question!—even though we would probably be inclined to ask the less useful form of the question: "Who am I?" The main clause of the next sentence is clearly: "I enter water," and the only symptom of

---

*So can William Golding's novel *The Inheritors*, in which stages in the early cultural evolution of humans are *realized* in the languages that Golding attributes (fictively) to the various stages.

his possessing less than perfect equipment is to be found in the inconsistency with which he separates off (or fails so to separate) participial phrases from main clause. Clearly, part of the pleasurable fiction of this poem is that Wodwo himself is in charge of the graphological conventions that go into its being printed as text: text representing utterance. (Cf. Raymond Queneau's "Awkward" on p. 52 and Russell Hoban's *Riddley Walker* on pp. 69–70.) The third sentence "What am I . . ." plunges us into deep water—both literally and syntactically!

We can go with "What (who) am I (to presume, to be asked), to split . . . water?" Or we can hear a stronger ejaculation: "What? Am *I* (to be expected) to split . . . ?" Our syntax of subject and predicate, especially when the subject is signified by the first person singular pronoun, is a representation of the relationship between self and not-self. Our syntax is also active and passive, and so allows us to be seen to *do* or to be done to. Wodwo plays precisely and delicately with this grammar of epistemology, this epistemological grammar. The focus and climax of this strand in the poem seems to occur at "me and doing that have coincided very queerly"; the syntax of a simple declarative, for example, "I do this," is itself seen as inherently unavailable. The very structure of subject: verb, or subject: predicate—the basic structure whereby we make verbal sense—is not yet securely available to Wodwo. When we apply Erich Auerbach's observations on the strengths of the paratactic to this text, we discover that Hughes has offered us a perfect example of parataxis at the very moment when it is about to shift, to burgeon into hypotaxis. We note, for example, the emergence of subordination in lines 17, 21, and 24; and his questions also seem likely to yield hypotactic answers: "If I do this, then. . . ."

# STUDENTS' OPTIONS IN WRITING A REACTIVE TEXT ON "WODWO"

With "Wodwo" as a primary text, then, what do we ask our students to write? Their options are these:

1. To move Wodwo even further *down* the scale of mental evolution, and to produce a text that represents the utterances he would then produce, given the same environmental determinants

2. To move him *up* the scale of mental evolution and do the same

3. To take on the role of either of the following spectators:
   a. A naive child stumbling on Wodwo in the woods; the text to represent the child's inner speech, or the child's conversation with a second person
   b. An anthropologist, speaking from a prepared script; the text to represent a voice-over commentary for a television documentary on the wodwo.

# PARTICIPANT TEXTS ON "WODWO"

Let us now look at some students' attempts to exercise options 1 or 2: attempts to shift the text (i.e., Wodwo's state of mind) down a few notches, in the direction of some kind of ultimate parataxis, or upward, in the direction of hypotaxis. We wish to stress that students wrote these as participant texts—that is, the focus of their attention was *being* a wodwo at a particular stage of its development. At no time were they briefed to work specifically for either a simple or a complex structure and lexicon; we were interested in having these emerge in the text as a consequence of the student's choice of evolutionary (developmental) level. The assignment was so couched as to de-emphasize the syntactic elements we were specifically interested in.

Dean Zarcone's (Q) comment on Hughes's text included the following:

> Seems like the first being on earth. He is free, has no threads attached, doesn't seem to know where he came from, doesn't know why he's here. He isn't a little kid because no one that small has thoughts that big. . . .

Barbara Schmitt (Q) moved Wodwo up a few notches:

> I am the only one of my kind that I know of. I share my world with the beasts that walk on four legs. I hunt and live as they do. Still, I'm not like them. I have seen something in the water that appears to be me—it does what I do when I

do it. Its glassy surface holds the sky and as I glide through its surface I feel as I imagine a bird would, as it glides through the sky.

Occasionally, my world is disrupted by "Others" who with their beasts, which they have some strange control over, hunt in my world. I resemble them in some ways. But why? I walk as they do, on two legs, and I have other features of theirs, but I am not the same. They hunt differently and control animals, but the animals in my world fear them—so I do. If I am like them, why do I fear them?

Note that Barbara's creature achieves not only a clear control of transitivity but also a degree of hypotactic structuring. Dean, too, moved Wodwo a few notches up the developmental ladder:

Here I am in the forest, taking a nice quiet walk. I should really start to go home, because it's getting cold out here. I should have eaten something before I left because I'm starting to get hungry. I think I'll get some water from the stream. Maybe I'll get water from upstream because I see a frog sitting on the rock who just came out of the water, and this stream doesn't seem too appetizing now. . . .

Sakura Khan (Q) chose to place Wodwo a few notches down on the evolutionary ladder. We have selected her text on account of its artful simplicity—the art that conceals art.

## A Microreading of
## One Student's Participant Text

Here is Sakura's text; you will note that it concentrates on sustenance:

Smell water. Near. Water! Cold, cold again. Cold before, cold now.

Up, down. Up, down. It moves. Go in, go in, in my mouth. Down, go down.

They don't move. Big ones don't move. Small ones don't move. They were there before, they are there now. That big one. Nuts, many nuts before. Many nuts now. No, no nuts. They moved. Where?

In pushing Wodwo a few notches down on the evolutionary ladder, Sakura nudged her text toward extreme parataxis, fashioning a kind of *ur*-utterance. Paring away the higher reaches of thought, she allows Wodwo only those mental operations (as evidenced by utterance) that are directly concerned with the same acts of perceiving as Itard observed in the case of the celebrated Wild Child of Aveyron.[3] So we remark the primacy of sensation—smell, touch, and sight; the fundamental binary frames of permanence/impermanence; and the satisfying of needs or appetites—questions of survival.

For us as readers (spectators), the text possesses a distinctive naive charm; but for Wodwo, the participant, every act, every utterance is intently concerned with survival. The frog—for which Wodwo has no conventional name—is seen through a semantic shift, not as bearing an identifying name but adverbially ("up" and "down") and in terms of the repeated rhythmic form ("up, down"). The act of seizure is left implicit; Wodwo's record is not of the self so much as of that which will perhaps serve the needs of the self. Characteristically, this utterance offered as text is perfectly indifferent to its audience; there is absolutely no attempt to put the reader in the picture. The absence of other as audience is, indeed, one of the freedoms, perhaps the quintessential freedom, of inner speech, releasing it from the duty of contextualizing, which is clearly a social act resting on the recognition of a social obligation, the duty of meeting the needs of an other.

Assume for the moment that Sakura's text (with its withholding of in-text context clues) were removed from the supportive context of this, our text. Suppose her text to be words found on a scrap of paper picked up casually, out of idle curiosity. How then would you read it, interpret it? Would you draw on your funding of cultural codes and thereby move to conclude that it was a transcript of a child's speech, synpractic speech? And would you support this assumption by assuming further that fond parents had actually gone to the trouble of transcribing it? If not, then how would you interpret it so as to generate a meaning you could be comfortable with? As a reader, you are entitled to require satisfaction.

Before one can interpret, one must first read. What does one have to read? Words, yes. And also a set of signs that help to make meaning, signs called punctuation—one of the most interesting of our culture's sign systems. (What a pity, incidentally, that so few students are made aware and appreciative of that system's resources, as meanings. A brief glance at David Crystal and Derek Davey's *Concerning English Style*, with its fascinating bits of talk, is a reminder that a reasonable, informative transcript of talk requires a very rich battery of such signs.) Sakura, however, is not transcribing utterance. She may *seem* to be doing so, but if we accept that seeming at its face value, we shall then leap onto the stage at the theater and try to pull Othello away from Desdemona, before he can strangle her! Sakura has created a little fiction, an artifact, depending on a make-believe kind of actuality; and her pointing, her way of disposing her commas and so on, is part of her text. The question we now wish to offer is simple enough: Is Sakura's punctuation entirely successful? Does it show signs of mastery? of control? Where might she have used colons or dashes? On a larger scale, how effective is her paragraphing? And conversely, is a subtler means of pointing, something with finer nuances, appropriate to so "primal" a text?

It seems to us that there are in the text some nice distinctions: "Smell water" ends with a period; but when Wodwo actually finds the water, she allows him an exclamation mark. Why "Cold, cold again" rather than, say, "Cold. Cold. Again!"? Playing with a sense of both continuity and discontinuity, she has made her choices.

And such choices must presumably involve, implicate, the ghost of the voice that is more or less hovering within most texts; for one reads with the inner ear as well as with the eye. Indeed, it's probable that whereas the eyes constitute the means, the end has rather more to do with the ear, with hearing the ghostly echo of the voice, which lingers in print. "Smell water. Near." seems to signal expectation, whereas "Water!" is the gratification of arrival. The repetition of "Up, down" seems to establish through mimesis the presence of an action that is repeated, and an action that is in itself perceived as a marriage of binaries. How, then, is the frog, the unnamed amphibian with its amphibious adverbs, seen to move? After doing its little hop ("Up, down"), it comes to rest on a period. And the duration of time it is "up," at the top of its jump, is rather brief; the modesty of the comma is an acknowledgment of the power of gravity.

Let us force a distinction. Is Sakura's punctuation primarily syntactical, confirming and pointing up the relationships between the parts? Or is it primarily dramatic, miming the act represented? a way of realizing rhythm, the rhythm of action and of a synpractic voice that moves in tandem with the activity it comments on? an activity that explores and finds, a voice that does likewise?

A close reading of Sakura's text involves the reader in a variety of interpretative acts, which must be framed by the reader's sense of the rules or conventions required of texts in our culture. We know, for instance, because it's "our way of doing things," that when the third paragraph begins with a pronoun, something is being withheld; namely the identity of the pronoun's antecedent. Is that because Sakura grew up in Japan, using English as her second language? Is it something to be cured, corrected? Let's suspend judgment and see what happens. The referents of "they" are subdivided into two sub-categories: "big ones" and "small ones." The contrast of "big" and "small" will probably, in the absence of other markers, lead us to expect something like this: "Big ones don't move. Small ones *do* (move)"— assuming a silent, implied, "but." But her text denies this expectation; it surprises one with that jolt of sheer (mere) repetition. The action simulated by the text then comes to focus on *"That* big one" (our emphasis), to the exclusion of all the small ones. And it was in that big one, that Wodwo had previously discovered nuts. On a first reading, "Many nuts now" is probably read as a certainty, a statement of fact; but this reading, like Wodwo's expectation, is frustrated, denied, and the pararhyme of "now. No . . ." is like a dying fall, a cadence, a falling-off. "No, no nuts": the duration of the repetition of "no" (and we don't deny that the second "no" cannot mean *exactly* the same as the first "no"), the duration of those *no*'s offers us an illusion of the time taken to discover and confirm the absence of food; and "No, no . . ." is like a shake of the head—for we never shake our heads to one side only. Then, with "They moved," the echo seems to tell us that the paragraph has come full circle. But it is not so. On the contrary, it started positively and ends almost negatively. And there is the additional paradox that the initial "They don't move," with its apparent negative, is in fact positive; while the penultimate "They moved," which seems to be positive indicative, carries a negative force.

So Wodwo's relationship with his world has changed. Something has happened. And we come to feel something akin to Samuel Beckett's Maddie Rooney in *All That Fall*: "Will it hold up?" To which the likely answer is, "It will not."

Sakura's tripartite paragraphing offers something such as:

1.  World as predictable, constant, dependable

2.  World as sustaining, physically

3.  World as undependable

Hence the whole text can appropriately end not with an affirmation but with an interrogation. The world of her Wodwo is a question not yet answered.

One last general point seems called for before we leave Sakura's text. Sakura is a student writer, not a student of, say, psycholinguistics or any other kind of linguistics. If there is, in our work with her, any place for "theory," it must be as an ancillary succedaneum, a provisional frame, a set of constructs that helps her to write better—that is, with richer awareness of what is entailed in the making of texts. If we over-power her with theory, our influence on her as a writer will probably prove to be counterproductive. She may, nevertheless, be interested to learn of some of the interesting connections between her texts and the remarks on language offered by good readers.

And indeed she was interested. When we outlined Vygotsky's char-acterization of inner speech (see p. 63), she was delighted to discover that he had "anticipated" her text and that she had unwittingly fol-lowed his findings, never having met them before!

Replacing the subjects, we find that her text yields this:

(I) smell water. (It) [is] near. (I) [have reached the] water. (It) [is] cold, cold again. (It) [was] cold before, (it) [is] Cold now.

(This frog) [goes] up [and] down. (It) [goes] up [and] down. *It* moves. (You) go in, go in, in my mouth. (You) [go] down, go down.

*They* don't move. *Big ones* don't move. *Small ones* don't move. *They* were there before, *they* are there now. (They) [are] [on / in] that big one (i.e., tree?). (I) [found] nuts, many nuts before. (I) [will find] many nuts now. [But] (I) [find] no, no nuts. *They* moved. (They) [have gone] where?

Sentence 3 of the second paragraph and sentences 1–4 of the third paragraph seem to break the rules. But do they? Sakura presumably felt a need to present the subjects of these sentences explicitly—but why? Is it a function of her act? (Vygotsky's item 3: it helps us to regulate and clarify our actions; see p. 63.)

One of the paradoxes of our work lies in this: Language, whether as utterance or text, is our primary form of mediation—a symbolic system that represents and presents something other than itself. The corollary of this paradox involves the relationship between the roles of partici-pant and spectator. One of the most useful discussions of this subject is to be found in Helen Vendler's *The Odes of Keats*, in her chapter on "Ode on a Grecian Urn," where she teases out the way in which Keats moves as on a pendulum between (a) vicarious or virtual participa-tion in the life represented on the urn, and (b) the more detached and reflective, generalizing and evaluative role of spectator. "Beauty is Truth" is the participant's claim; "Truth is Beauty," the spectator's. And that, says Keats, is all you will ever know—what you can come to know in your role of either participant or spectator—there is nothing else.

When the poet participates in the fictive life of the urn, he can no longer consider the characteristics of the medium; when, conversely, he reflects on the nature of the medium, as a spectator, he can no longer enjoy/feel/experience the compelling illusion of participation.

Let us consider a simpler case. When someone shouts "Stop!" to prevent us from walking carelessly into a moving car, we do not pause to judge the felicity or otherwise of the utterance. Streets are for pragmatic participants. It is enough that we stop, and so preserve the integrity of our bones.

Similarly, when we write fluently, moving energetically with the full flow of the syntagmatic, we rarely need to pause to consider our paradigmatic options: the very nature of fluency is that our "automatic pilot" doesn't experience the dilemmas of paradigmatic choice. Raymond Williams has contended that in a happy communicative act, the attention is on that which is to be communicated rather than on the medium of communication. The medium is invisible, transparent. We see through it to that which is to be represented and presented.

But this is only part of the truth. An experienced storyteller may well have, moment by moment, an intense awareness of his or her medium and of its momentary word-by-word potential for going this way or that. And Henry Glassie and Theodore Rosengarten have shown how a fluid dynamic awareness of, and responsiveness to, various audiences for the same story will reshape the utterance (see Chapter 5, p. 106).

Pedagogically, we need to recognize the nature of these discrete options, subsumed in the making of any discourse, and to separate them out in ways that will enable our students to enjoy appropriate states of mind—ways of disposing their attention—at any given stage of their composing. When constructing her ostensibly simple text, Sakura *thought* for a whole day, on and off; and she wrote five versions of her text within two hours. Her "final" text still failed to satisfy her. The frog episode, she felt, lacked "power." Her thinking hours were committed to an effort to find a plausible form/appropriate "cultural syntax" (see Chapter 9, pp. 199–201, for more on this) for her fictive speaker. She thus found herself engaged in a fairly philosophical series of reflections on the relationship between mental development and discourse, between the epistemic and the verbal. As her text began to come into focus, she wrote down her tentative words. These were manifests of bits of thinking/perceiving. They were also, in themselves, something for her to reflect on. So she became caught up in a fascinating kind of dialectic, between her options in terms of *what* was to be represented, and her options in terms of the verbal representation. In the process, she discovered the intimate nature of the relationship between thought and language. Each of her four subsequent texts involved deliberate choice, local and small in scope but related to her sense of the whole text as it evolved. The medium itself became the focus of speculation, consideration, and criticism.

Quantitatively, her text is modest. But qualitatively it seems to us impressive—not only because of the intensity and strenuousness of the thinking that went into it but also because of the scrupulous economy of the words on the page, the tip of her iceberg. Before we leave Sakura, here are her own comments on her Wodwo.

### Reflections

"Cold before, cold now": he doesn't take it for granted now, but he will be able to, later.

"Cold, cold again." The first "cold" is him touching the water; the second is his comment on what he feels.

"Up, down. Up, down." At first, I had a comma after the first "down." Then I changed it to a period, because of the rhythm of his motion.

"Go in, go in, . . ." Wodwo is having some difficulty getting the slippery struggling frog into his mouth.

"They" (para. 3, first word): refers to all green things, both trees and grasses.

"That big one": he chooses a particular tree.

"Many nuts now. No, no nuts.": it's between "now" and "No" that he has to admit that he's failed to find them.

*General comments:* I was thinking about it all the time; I wanted a language for him that would be a minimum language but powerful. I had trouble with how he would have constructed his sentences. I decided I had to put his thoughts in some version of our language. I didn't feel satisfied at the end; some words still don't "click"; the frog part isn't as powerful as I'd like.

I had to lose vocabulary and grammar to find a language that seemed to suit him. So I gave him fragments.

I shouldn't have used any of these words, but I had to use some words!

# SPECTATOR TEXTS ON "WODWO"

Finally, here are some texts by students who chose option 3b (see p. 85)—the anthropologist spectator, speaking from a prepared script.

## OBSERVING THE WODWO
### (expert voice-over commentary)

Among the most crafty of the Upper Lowland marsh animals of Finland is the Anglo-Saxon, or Nordic Wodwo. This gentle giant of the marsh, so misunderstood by early man, proves to be one of the more intelligent species of mammals in the region. The Wodwo is very adept at hunting and fishing in the wild. . . . As seen here, the Wodwo often catches fish with his bare hands in shallow streams. He is sometimes seen using a large and rather crude club as a means for capturing larger fish by striking blows to the head. The Wodwo is very skillful at hunting on land as well. . . .

Shown here on exclusive footage, a Wodwo has no problem in slaying an elk that has wandered from the herd. Although elk are plentiful here in the Lowland marshes of Finland, the Wodwo's diet mainly consists of small mammals, fish, and the various native plants of the area. . . .

This little fellow is experiencing one of his first encounters with native marine life. He appears to be uncertain as to what is happening in the pond. Young Wodwos are often left alone during their first experiences at fishing, so that they can gain self-confidence in future hunting. A watchful sibling pays close attention to the young Wodwo to prevent any unfortunate occurrences. Although seemingly hidden, many larger animals sense the presence of Wodwos in the area and will not drink from the pond until the young Wodwo has left. . . . Well, it appears that our young friend still has a lot to learn about fishing; so far, he has only caught two frogs. He is now looking into a hollowed section of a nearby tree, known to contain nuts deposited there by some small mammals within the area. Much to his disappointment, the Wodwo finds no nuts. . . . His lesson for the day is now finished. . . .

Wodwos were once being killed by the thousands by the Finns, for fear that they would raid the villages and attack the people. Such uneducated activity had continued throughout Finland's Lowland Marsh area until the turn of the century, when the hunting of Wodwos was prohibited. Today, only a few hundred Wodwos survive in the wild. Zoos throughout the world maintain only a few score of them; indeed, the breeding of Wodwos in captivity has proven to be very unsuccessful. In conclusion, we see that the protection of Wodwos will have to continue if future generations of man are to be able to appreciate their extraordinary beauty.

Peter Mazzola (Q)

## HOMO ERECTUS

*Homo erectus* is a species that dates from the Mid-Pleistocene in Africa, about two million years ago. They are fully bipedal, omnivorous, tool-using hominids. Some *Homo erectus* bones are found in caves, suggesting the use of more or less permanent home bases. Besides animal bones and stone tools, some of the caves contain heaps of charcoal and charred bones, showing that fire had been domesticated and brought indoors by this time. Presumably, this habit originated in the use of natural fires to keep warm, cook food, or split stones.

This stage in human evolution is correlated with the colonization of other colder areas by emigrants from Africa. Their anatomical or physiological adaptations alone will not permit human beings to survive winters as cold as those of central Europe and China; behavioral adaptation or technological expertise is necessary. Plainly, the prehuman brain had developed to the point where *Homo erectus* could produce social and technological solutions—such as fire, clothing, stored food, and communal living in caves—to the problems of surviving cold winters. These solutions probably led to the development of some of the most important features of *Homo sapiens.*

Today we journey to the southern plains of Asia, in search of Wodwo, our long lost relative.

Preserved for over two million years in the glacial ice that passed over Asia, Wodwo is man's oldest living relative. A Wodwo was captured six months ago by this man [a man appears on the screen], Dean Smith. He caught the Wodwo while it was raiding his farm. The game wardens then built a fence two miles in diameter, around his home in order to observe him.

The film you are watching was taken one month ago, just when the Wodwo had become comfortable with its surroundings.

There is the Wodwo. It stands about 5 feet tall with a 28-inch reach. It seems to favor roaming about without clothing.

The Wodwo has made its home in this shallow cave. Right now it is going to its favorite stream for a drink and a bite to eat. As you can see, it prefers to eat its meat raw. Lastly, we gave it a small problem to solve. The day before, it was picking nuts, and it piled them all next to a tree. We came and took them. As you can see, the Wodwo is slightly puzzled. But after a while it will forget and write it off as history.

Through this relative of man, we hope to discover a lot more about man's past and man's destiny. The Wodwo can provide us with the means to understand ourselves.

Ulric Ortiz (Q)


This is Quebec, Canada, the largest province in Canada. About two thousand miles north of Montreal, a hundred miles northeast of Quebec City, the provincial capital, lie the Laurentian Mountains. Covering nearly 800,000 square miles and composed entirely of virgin forest, the Laurentian range is one of Canada's best-preserved forests.

The forest also retains one of the rarest and most intriguing creatures alive: the *Laurentianus Manilogicus,* more commonly known as Snowman.

First spotted by forest rangers nearly a decade ago, these creatures have evaded scientific research until recent years, when anthropologist Janet Sinclair observed one for a year, living in a concealed tree house.

As you can see, the Snowman is not really a man but a mountain goat with a human head, human arms, and a slightly more enlarged intellectual capacity than goats. This peaceful and gentle creature of the wild combines the advantages of the sure-footed mountain goat with nimble human movements, to escape danger and defend itself.

The chief diet of the Snowman is leaves. The forest floor is rich with young shoots that have very little chance of growing into fully fledged trees and the Snowman finds this its favorite diet. It also eats fruits and even nuts, as seen here, using stones to break them.

Its movements are controlled by the distribution of the weight of its upper torso. To move forward, it pushes its chest forward, and to move backwards, it straightens its chest and moves its legs sideways.

The mental aptitude of these creatures has never been properly assessed. The only evidence to prove its superior intellect is the various actions that untrained animals could never perform, but that are performed breezily by the Snowman. Here we see a Snowman counting the number of nuts it has collected and then storing them in a box made of leaves.

The Snowman is a solitary creature. Not more than five have been sighted in a decade. Their numbers seem to be in the teens, and the chances of conceiving offspring are nearly zero, according to zoologist, David Attenborough. Though they live to a ripe old age of nearly two hundred years, the era of the Snowman is surely coming to an end.

What can we do to save these amazing creatures from becoming extinct? The question, which has created an uproar between certain environmentalist groups which support natural extinction and those who demand action to save the Snowman, is a very difficult one to answer. At least, one thing that is clear is that these creatures, these harmless wonders of creation, will always continue to excite our imagination, as time and history will prove.

Fillmore Apeadu (Q)

Thus inventing contrastive states of mind (the meanings are in the differences)—states of mind derived from a simplified view of evolution—calls forth contrastive texts. The virtue of the texts representing primal levels of consciousness lies not so much in the evocation of a pastoral innocence or simplicity as in an economy of verbal means, shaping a text out of minimal resources, a text in which each detail, each word, each comma, is carefully judged in order to yield the required semantic force. The converse virtue of the sophisticated voice-over spectator-texts is to be found in the move toward a more richly orchestrated syntax, a polyphony; an awareness of the audience's needs and the appropriate use of devices, such as contextualization, to meet those needs.

# NOTES

1. Ted Hughes, *Wodwo* (London: Faber & Faber, 1971), p. 183.
2. Hughes is playing with the code of conventional syntax and with how one can be expected to interpret deviations from that code. Cf. Virginia Tufte, *Grammar as Style* (New York: Holt, Rinehart and Winston, 1971), Chapter 16: "Syntactic Symbolism: Grammar as Analogue." An instructive complement to "Wodwo" is provided by John Barth's story, "Title," in which the post-modernist narrator expresses nostalgia for the good old days when the grammar of prose fiction was simple because the world was simple, and vice versa.
3. See Roger Shattuck, *The Forbidden Experiment* (New York: Washington Square Press, 1981).

# CHAPTER FIVE

# GENERATIVE FRAME

## The Possibilities of Narrative

> *Tell me a story, great-aunt,*
> *so that I can sleep.*
> *Tell me a story, Scheherezade,*
> *so that you can live.*
> *Tell me a story, my soul, animula,*
> *vagula, blandula,*
> *little Being-Towards-Death,*
> *for the word's the beginning of being*
> *if not the middle or the end.*
> Ursula le Guin

# NARRATIVE AND SOCIAL INTERACTION

W e trade in stories of our own lives and in stories of the lives of others—others we actually know, and of those we know, virtually, through the news, through the fabric of our histories, through literature. Story is the stock in trade of our social lives. "What's new?" we ask, on coming home after a day's work, and we catch up on the day's events. We tune in to the "what happened" of our intimates by sharing the day's stories. To those whom we know, we offer continuations: "Mary is doing much better today; she should be home next week." We don't need to contextualize—to explain who Mary is; what her operation had been; what hospital she is in; where her home is. These are the givens in our close relationships. We share common knowledge, common information with those who form the immediate circles of our lives. "You know what Lauren did today?" we ask. Our partner knows immediately who Lauren is and what she *might* have done *today*. Given our shared awareness of what she usually does, we can abbreviate, cut verbal corners. When the partners know "what's going on," says Lev Vygotsky, we find a "simplified syntax, condensation, and a greatly reduced number of words." Intimates often don't even need words, he says, pointing to a tender scene between Kitty and Levin in *Anna Karenina*:

> *Now Levin was used to expressing his thought fully without troubling to put it into exact words: He knew that his wife, in such moments filled with love, as this one, would understand what he wanted to say from a mere hint, and she did.*[1]

Narratives play a crucial, fundamental role in social interactions. Every day has its stories, made up of those *actual events*—the what happened, that we turn into *experiences*, the events that we *make our own* in the telling and in the listening. In the social fabric of our daily lives, every story has a teller and a listener. The listener may be a self that listens, inwardly, as we recount a past event or rehearse a plan for the future. But the listener is just as commonly an other: an intimate, with whom we share the day's happenings, or a stranger (say, on a long plane ride) to whom we suddenly find ourselves spilling our life's story.

"It is hard to take more than a step," says the literary critic, Barbara Hardy, "without narrating":

*Before we sleep each night we tell over to ourselves what we may also have told to others, the story of the past day. We mingle truths and falsehoods, not always quite knowing where one blends into the other. As we sleep we dream dreams from which we wake to remember, half-remember and almost remember, in forms that may be dislocated, dilapidated or deviant but are recognizably narrative. We begin the day by narrating to ourselves and probably to others our expectations, plans, desires, fantasies and intentions. The action in which the day is passed coexists with a reverie composed of the narrative revision and rehearsals of past and future, and in this narrative too it is usually hard to make the distinction between realism and fantasy which we make confidently in our judgements of literary narratives. We meet our colleagues, family, friends, intimates, acquaintances, strangers, and exchange stories, overtly and covertly. We may try to tell all, in true confession, or tell half-truths or lies, or refuse to do more than tell the story of the weather, the car, or the food. We may exchange speaking silences or marvellous jokes. And all the time the environment beckons and assaults with its narratives. Walls, papers, mass-media, vehicles, entertainments, libraries, talks, slogans, politicians, prophets and Job's comforters persuade, encourage, depress, solicit, comfort and commiserate in narrative forms. Even when we try to escape narrative, as when we listen to music or do mathematics, we tend to lapse. Even logicians tell stories. Humankind cannot bear very much abstraction or discursive reasoning. The stories of our days and the stories in our days are joined in that autobiography we are all engaged in making and remaking, as long as we live, which we never complete, though we all know how it is going to end.*[2]

Stories infuse and inform our lives to such an extent that we generally take them for granted because they are simply there, like the air we breathe. Narrative is ever-present; as Roland Barthes says, "narrative is international, transhistorical, transcultural; it is simply there, like life itself."[3]

# NARRATIVE AND LITERATURE

In the teaching of composition, we have tended to bypass narrative, to relegate it to a step along the way to more complex forms, particularly to exposition. Narrative is generally seen as a "simple" mode that embodies chronology, the setting down of events as they happened. When textbooks consider narrative at all, they generally assume that narrative simply writes itself: all one need do is begin at "the beginning" and end at "the end."

But what about the stories we call "literature"? They are worthy of study, research, scholarship. Critics spend their lives interpreting and reinterpreting "fictive" stories: the stories of Odysseus, Don Quixote, Stephen Dedalus, Molly Bloom, Sister Carrie. The chasm between "our" own lives and those of the literary characters we study in graduate school and read about in literary journals—that chasm is wide and deep. There is student writing/nonliterature on the one side, with story relegated to the "merely" personal, the simple, the easy; and there is "literature"—novels, short stories, epic poetry, autobiography, biography—on the other side. The one is worthy of attention, the other not.

The British educator, Harold Rosen, sums up the paradox very well:

> There is a persistent message of our society and in particular our educational system: stories are for children, the gullible, the naive. We have other kinds of discourse for the serious business of society. "We may start by telling stories but we must end by telling the truth," including the truth about stories which we call literary criticism or even narratology. In the literature of language education it is often proposed that the ultimate goal for the teaching of composition is academic prose, objective exposition or some such. No one tells us why language development should not include as a central component getting better at telling and responding to stories of many different kinds.[4]

And yet, in other disciplines—in history, philosophy, psychology, anthropology, art history, linguistics, sociolinguistics, folklore studies, literary criticism, literature, and a new discipline called *narratology*—the study of narrative has taken a quantum leap. To W. J. T. Mitchell, at the University of Chicago Symposium on Narrative in 1979, "The study of narrative is no longer the province of literary specialists or folklorists borrowing their terms from psychology and linguistics but has now become a positive source of insight for all the branches of human and natural science."[5]

It is from these scholars—particularly those who quarrel with the arbitrary distinctions between "nonliterary" and "literary" language—that we, in teaching composition, can benefit. For too long has literature been separated from, cordoned off from "ordinary language." And once we begin to look to nonliterary discourse, assumptions about literature as a language in opposition to "ordinary language" collapse. It is from "the world," the social contexts in which we live, and not from literature that we need to build our theories and practice of composition. For too long has "life" been separated from "art." Particularly in the teaching of English, students have been made to feel like outsiders, allowed occasionally to peek into the mysteries of an image, a metaphor, an allusion, into what Frank Kermode calls the "secrets" that "overreaders" read into literary texts. Reading literature has been exclusionary; students have felt themselves and their own "mundane" lives and language removed from that other world. The literary/nonliterary dichotomy damages and inhibits and separates. Students who, generally, feel themselves alienated from the heights of "literature" need to experience themselves as users of language within a social context—one that is accessible, manageable, and attainable.

Let us examine those features of narrative that can make what we do every day accessible, manageable, reachable to our students of composition, as they are invited to reflect on stories—the powers and possibilities of narrative.

# NARRATIVE AS COMPOSITION

A story is, first of all, a composition, a construct. It is a way of ordering, shaping, interpreting events. Stories do not happen "out there"; we shape stories as a means of representing the world to ourselves and to others. In this sense, all narratives are fictions; there is no one true story. Think for a moment of William James's oft-quoted phrase: "buzzing, booming mass" of things whirling and swirling about us—colors, voices, faces, sounds, textures, millions of sensations per moment that enter us, at times overload us. Human beings have fortunately devised ways of ordering that which is out there, of making sense of it. As humans, we *represent* to ourselves what our world is like—each of us differently but each rooted in the social, ideological culture that we inherit. Each of us, says psychologist George Kelly, has a *construct* system. Constructs are transparent patterns or "templets" that we lay on apprehendable "reality"; we "phrase" an experience in the same way that the musician sets off a sequence of notes in a piece of music. Says Kelly,

> *The substance that a person construes is itself a process—just as the living person is a process. It represents itself from the beginning*

*as an unending and undifferentiated process. Only when man attunes his ear to recurrent themes in the monotonous flow does his universe begin to make sense to him. Like a musician, he must phrase his experience in order to make sense out of it. The phrases are distinguished events. The separation of events is what man produces for himself when he decides to chop up time into manageable lengths. Within these limited segments, which are based on recurrent themes, man begins to discover the bases for likenesses and differences.*[6]

Many of our phrasings are stories; our constructs, beginnings and endings. As Frank Kermode says, we begin life in the middle:

*Men, like poets, rush "into the middest," in medias res, when they are born; they also die in* mediis rebus, *and to make sense of their span they need fictive concords with origins and ends, such as give meaning to lives and to poems.*[7]

The story is the flesh that reveals our constructions, our compositions. It is a narrative sequencing that we lay on the undifferentiated. We *construct* beginnings and endings; we *see* conflict and resolution; we *select* dialogue and character; and we *interpret*, we *evaluate*. The data of our lives, the events out there, according to Kelly, constitute the "concrete." Our perceptions and conceptions are abstractions that make up construing, and construing is a process of abstracting. To understand events, then, we concretize them. In the words of Kelly, "To make sense out of concrete events we thread them through with constructs, and to make sense of the constructs we must point them at events." A dialectical play, then, is our most frequent, habitual game: out of the concrete, we abstract generalizations; to "support" the generalizations, to make sense of our interpretations, we supply the concrete. We tell stories, says Joan Didion, "in order to live," in order to make sense of our world, in order to live with what she calls the "shifting phantasmagoria." And we would add: we tell stories in order to live with ourselves and with others, in order to understand the past and anticipate and prepare for the future.

Stories are Janus-like: they look back and forward. We anticipate events on the basis of what we have sorted out from the past: we frame the world out of hypotheses we have drawn from past experiences; and we submit our hypotheses to the test of actuality and modify our predictive apparatus in the light of what happens. What happens today is seen in the light of what happened yesterday and last year, and in the light of what we *expect* to happen tomorrow. Stories are not set; they are retellings and reconstructions of events that have happened. But each time we tell it, the story is *new:* the situation is new, the audience is new, the moment is new. And we construe the telling in light both of the present moment and of our present needs or intentions or purposes—to enlighten, to delight, to terrify, to frighten, to warn our listeners.

Students need to know that stories are *constructs:* the stories we tell to ourselves are representations of what happened, they are not the event itself. And when we offer a presentation of a representation, that too is a construct, given the social context in which we are at the moment. A story, then, is a text—open for shaping and reshaping, selecting and reselecting, ordering and reordering.

# BELATEDNESS

Freud's concept of *Nachträglichkeit,* translated as "deferred action" or "belatedness," is crucial here. It embodies the notion that "the past or indeed any object of memory or language . . . comes into being only after the fact, as a function of the place language or memory requires it to hold."[8] Students are often under the misconception that they can/should capture events exactly as they happened (a kind of *total* literal truth), from "the beginning" to "the end," with accuracy, faithfulness, sincerity, and honesty. Thus when we have asked them to write of a childhood experience, no wonder they've often been stuck. They believe they must adhere to the "facts" and nothing but the facts. But how many facts do they actually remember? What do our memories yield to us five minutes after an event? Five years? Fifteen years?

We recall a student who, after reading Richard Wright's *Black Boy,* blurted out in class one day: "I hate Richard Wright." When invited to say why, he said, "Because he remembers *everything* from when he was four years old, and I can't remember *anything* from when I was twelve, and that's only six years ago." What he hadn't realized, what he hadn't been told, is that that kind of memory is a rarity, and that the ordinary, the "normal," the usual is, fortunately, *not* to remember everything. We are reminded of a case, described by the Russian psychologist Alexander Luria, of a man whose memory "seemed to have no limit, a mnemonist whose mind was so extraordinary that Luria wrote of him in terms reserved for the mentally ill. He could commit to memory in a couple of minutes a table of fifty numbers, which he could recall in every minute detail many years later. His greatest difficulty was in learning how to forget the endless trivia that cluttered his mind."[9] The neurologist Colin Blakemore reminds us to remember the "importance of forgetting": "The selection process that lets us store in long-term only a tiny fraction of the running contents of short-term memory is essential if the brain is to use particular instances to derive general principles, by a process of inference."[10]

The powers of memory, then, allow us to select and choose, order and interpret, particularize and generalize. In all this, language is the great mediator. And every representation is a fiction, a text that, when rendered powerfully, gives the listener or reader the illusion of being actually there. We are not, but such is the power of language that even our most perceptive students need to be let in on the secret; and once they are, the possibilities of textuality begin to open before them.

# FLUIDITY AND STABILITY

The writing moment merges with the past moment to create/construct a text—a representation of the what happened—that we present to another, that we share with others as they share with us. Virginia Woolf knew this keenly when she sat down, two years before her death, to write an autobiography. She talked of the "*I now*" merging with the "*I then*" and knew very well that what she wrote today would be different from what she attempted next week or next year:

> It would be interesting to make the two people, I now, I then, come out in contrast. And further, this past is much affected by the present moment. What I write today I should not write in a year's time.[11]

Each time we relate a story, then, it is both old and new: there are the events we draw from our lives that we construct into a text and there is the new: our angle of vision, our selection, our memory, our interpretation, our age, the moment of writing, the social context, the listener or the absent reader. Theodore Rosengarten, biographer of Nate Cobb, noted that Cobb had different versions of the "same" story for different listeners:

> The teller in his native setting does not intend the same tale, told exactly the same way for every listener. I heard Ned Cobb tell a particular story five or six times to different people. He would vary a mood, add or omit a detail, shift himself from foreground to background, to produce the effect he wanted. He had one version for his family, one for the neighbors, one for traveling salesmen,

*and one for me—and they were all the same story, each told with
the personality of the listener in mind.*[12]

Students need to know that we *construct* beginnings and endings,
we resolve tensions, we clarify the uncertain, we make room for the
new, within the context of the old—we are continually involved in
that balancing act, reaching for equilibrium. A story fundamentally
reflects a jolt to the equilibrium. And in its resolution of tension,
we often find a change, a new pronouncement of equilibrium—for
that moment. The story allows us to hold on, to retain, to shape, to
form, to tease out levels of significance, as we are impelled toward
interpretation, toward making meaning, toward what William Labov
calls *evaluation*. The story is a way of fixing, of steadying, of stabiliz-
ing. "Fixing" is a useful image—not in the sense of making repairs,
but in the sense of making stable, firm, secure; of fastening, setting
firmly in place, in the sense that we fix our eyes on an object—a face,
a chair, a tree, a painting—as we direct our eyes steadily to that object.
When we reconstruct a past event, we direct our minds to it, re-present
it to ourselves, arrange it "properly" in our minds so that we can set
it in order, understand. In chemistry, the notion of fixing involves
making solid or nonvolatile. In photography, the act of fixing makes a
slide permanent, prevents it from fading. When we re-present to ourselves something that has happened to us, something that we have
made happen, we are fixing it in that sense, so that it is ordered, comprehensible, acceptable; so that it doesn't fade; perhaps so that we
don't explode—from the tension.

For story is resolution of tension: a problem arises, a question is
raised; the story is resolution, answer. As we turn over the events of the
day, as we turn them into experiences by interpreting them, by making sense of them, as we reconstruct, represent them to ourselves, as
we make beginnings and endings, we, as well, review the solutions and
the answers. Some are satisfying, some are not. How many of us have
taken an event that has left us unsettled, and as we reconstructed it,
allowed ourselves to be a more satisfying character, a more daring person, one who came out with the right answer, an answer that dazzled
those about us. One who was able to overcome the enemy—the boss
who refused to listen, the friend with whom we quarrelled. We allow
ourselves to play a different role; in our reconstructions, our representations, we come out better in the story than we did in "real life." Story
impels us toward spectatorship: when we are *in* actual events as they
are happening, we are participants. Once we step out of the event—five
minutes later or five days later or five years later—once we represent the
event and turn it into experience, something that happened to *us*—we

become spectators, able to reflect on the past, to make sense of it all, from a distance. (See Chapter 6.)

# EVALUATION

S tory impels us toward *evaluation*—toward interpreting, valuing, making meaning, making sense, weighing and measuring, figuring out, coming to terms with, resolving, considering, unifying—all those acts of mind that are involved in trying to understand. When we ask students of composition to write a thesis statement, we are reducing a pluralistic, multifaceted play of mind that we engage in in our daily lives to a one-dimensional static choice: What's your thesis statement? And when we separate narrative from exposition, we fail to see the exposition that inheres within narrative. For no narrative is merely a retelling of what happened. Students of narrative generally agree that two features are basic to every narrative: the narrative core—the "and then, and then, and then"—a sequence of actions in time, a "once"—and evaluation—the attempt to make sense of the narrative core or, as William Labov says, the implicit or explicit answer to the question "So what?" Barbara Herrnstein Smith puts it this way:

> It is, I think, quite possible that every "story," fictional or non-fictional, has what could be called a kernel theme or indeed a "generating" principle, in accord with which its elements have been selected from all the possible things the narrator could at that moment have said or written: something quite close to what, with regard to a conversational anecdote or news-story, we speak of as its "point," and which could also be seen as its motive or, most simply, the reason why it was told. If, as I suggested earlier, the basic or minimal plot of every story (change, reversal of fortune, or peripeteia, as structuralists from Aristotle to Barthes have maintained) can be reduced to the assertion "something happened," then its basic theme or generating principle would seem to constitute the reply-in-advance to the listener's always potential question, "So what?"; and both basic plot structure and basic theme could be seen as indeed universals of narrative, grounded in the recurrent occasions, contexts, dynamics, functions, and motives of one of the most universal of all forms of verbal behavior (or "speech-acts"), namely telling.
>
> In ordinary verbal transactions, we do not tell stories (for example, relate personal anecdotes, repeat news events) merely to inform our listeners that something happened: things are always

*happening, but there is not always any reason to tell them to someone. One reason we do sometimes tell them is that the fortunes of those involved in the story (for example, the speaker himself) are presumably of some independent interest to the listener. If that is not the case (and of course it is usually not the case in fictional narratives), the story is usually told because it exemplifies or indicates (or apparently contradicts) some general proposition—again, one that is presumably of some interest to the listener—which may or may not be explicitly stated.*[13]

The generating principle, the point, the story's raison d'être, the theme—all this in narrative is *atemporal* or *achronological* and makes itself felt explicitly and implicitly in every story we tell or read. Labov, in his essay "The Transformation of Experience in Narrative Syntax," categorizes explicit and implicit evaluators, and insists that embedded evaluators make for the *best* story: they leave the listener or reader something to chew on.[14] We know this in our daily lives: how often do we bristle at didacticism or overt telling; we want to be "shown" and then given the opportunity to make up our own minds. We ask our students: What constitutes a *good* story? Our own research tells us that students know, as tellers and readers, that implicit evaluation scores higher than explicit.

Take two well-known short stories, O. Henry's "The Gift of the Magi" and de Maupassant's "The Diamond Necklace." O. Henry is not willing to let the reader make up his or her own mind about the *meanings* of his tale; he elaborately *tells* at the end what he thinks of his characters:

*The magi, as you know, were wise men—wonderfully wise men—who brought gifts to the Babe in the manger. They invented the art of giving Christmas presents. Being wise, their gifts were no doubt wise ones, possibly bearing the privilege of exchange in case of duplication. And here I have lamely related to you the uneventful chronicle of two foolish children in a flat who most unwisely sacrificed for each other the greatest treasures of their house. But in a last word to the wise of these days let it be said that of all who give gifts these two were the wisest. Of all who give and receive gifts, such as these are the wisest. Everywhere they are wisest. They are the magi.*[15]

De Maupassant, on the other hand, leaves us gasping at the end of the story, with Mathilde's shock that the diamond necklace had been fake. He leaves us, still, at the end, *in media res,* and we are left wondering, imagining, speculating on all sorts of things. What happened next? (Incidentally, we have found "The Diamond Necklace" to be a powerful generative story for producing reactive texts, and the pair, O. Henry and de Maupassant together, a productive opportunity for showing varieties and powers and differences of endings.)

Evaluation, meanings, authority, the wisdom of the tribe—all are transferred in stories. We find Henry Glassie, the folklorist, talking of the "authority" of stories:

> *Stories properly transfer authority. Adults tell their peers stories they learned from other adults, but they tell their children stories they learned from their parents or got from print. Properly set, they are important moral lessons. Children who hear about sick deer will grow into ceilers [storytellers and storylisteners] obliged to visit and accept hospitality. They must learn to be aware of the repercussions of their own best intentions.*
>
> *Fireside tales and examples are contained, named entities, asserted by dint of implicit authority. A parental figure has the right to instruct. But ceilis are made of equals, so their stories do not propose conclusions but raise problems. Ceili tales reverse tales for children: their moral is unformed and implicit, their authority is often explicit. The narrator entertains us and then leaves us to find the messages in his stories—their warnings and information.*[16]

The story, then, offers us a chance to trade values. "Evaluative devices," states Labov, "say to us: this was terrifying, dangerous, weird, wild, crazy; or amusing, hilarious and wonderful; more generally, that it was strange, uncommon, or unusual—that is, worth reporting."[17] And it is our system of values—what we thought to be worth reporting or tellable—that binds or separates teller and listener. If we tell you a story and evaluate it by saying "He got what he deserved" and you agree, then we stand together; we recognize, for the moment, perhaps for longer, where we stand. If we are at the beginning of a relationship and you disagree, we are hesitant, wary, cautious. Stories are ways of testing the waters of our systems of values; and we are involved in such social probings all our lives.

# OPEN-ENDEDNESS

The most valuable stories always offer us opportunity to encourage reading and rereading, interpretation and reinterpretation—keeping a text open and not closing it down: we need only look to the great stories—those that still invite, impel us toward interpretation and reinterpretation. Ted Hughes calls a story a "unit of imagination":

> *A child takes possession of a story as what might be called a unit of imagination. A story which engages, say, earth and the underworld is a unit correspondingly flexible. It contains not merely the space and in some form or other the contents of those two places; it reconciles their contradictions in a workable fashion and holds open the way between them. The child can re-enter the story at will, look around him, find all those things and consider them at his leisure. In attending to the world of such a story there is the beginning of imaginative and mental control. There is the beginning of a form of contemplation. And to begin with, each story is separate from every other story. Each unit of imagination is like a whole separate imagination, no matter how many the head holds.*[18]

The story of Christ, of the Holocaust, Grimms' fairy tales, stories of fiction and fact "not only think for themselves, once we know them," says Hughes. "They not only attract and light up everything relevant in our own experience, they are also in continual private meditation, as it were, on their own implications. They are little factories of understanding. New revelations of meaning open out of their images and patterns continually, stirred into reach by our own growth and changing circumstances." And he goes on: "History is really no older than that new-born baby. And every story is still the original cauldron of wisdom, full of new vision and new life."[19] Hughes argues powerfully for the place of stories in education—in the growth of understanding and consciousness. We agree—and we bring to our classrooms the stories of others and the stories of ourselves.

# BREAKING THE HOLD OF CHRONOLOGY: A STORY

Our students, in thinking about their own stories, are often tied to chronology, to the telling of A and then B and then C, in the order in which the events occurred. It is up to us to bring to them the possibilities of narrative, the varieties of textuality open to narrative. Elementary school teachers with whom we have worked tell us of a phenomenon we discover in our college classrooms: When children are asked to tell or write a story, they often offer a "bed-to-bed" story: "I woke up this morning at 7:15, and then I ate breakfast (Rice Krispies with milk) and then caught the school bus at 8:03 [The digital watch encourages accuracy!] . . . and then at 9:30 [P.M.] I went to bed." In the meantime, the weary listener is yawning. The *good* story keeps us listening and asking for more. Tellers and listeners, writers and readers alike, know what constitutes a good story: the one that keeps others listening, the one that keeps others turning the page. We offer you, now, a story of one of our students, Stanley Panek (Q), as he worked through a number of texts to arrive at one that satisfied him and gave him pleasure.

We begin at the beginning of an advanced freshman composition course. Students are invited to begin writing in their journals in response to a variety of questions:

If you were to begin *a* story of your life, where would you begin?

Why do you suppose we said *a* story of your life?

Isn't there only *one* story of a life? Why? Why not?

Begin a story of your life today. Next week, begin another story of your life. How do they differ? *Where* did you begin?

If you were to *tell* a story of your life to someone, where might you begin? What does the telling offer you that the text does not? And vice versa?

What is your earliest memory?

*How* do you generally remember? Images? Voices? Scenes?

We then "sit around the fire," imagining that we are keeping ourselves warm on a cold, blustery night, in a world without TV or "The Walkman," that through the fire and our words, we will keep ourselves warm and our minds safe from the terrors of the dark. We remind ourselves of *reasons* for telling stories. Here is Barbara Hardy's accounting of reasons:

> *trying to keep your head on your shoulders,*
> *passing the time in inns, on the road, and*
> *on your death-bed, making sense out of*
> *confusion, covering up the naked truth,*
> *introducing yourself, or soothing your child.*[20]

And here is Ursula le Guin's:

*Tell me a story, great-aunt,*
*so that I can sleep.*
*Tell me a story, Scheherezade,*
*so that you can live.*
*Tell me a story, my soul, animula,*
*    vagula, blandula,*
*little Being-Towards-Death,*
*for the word's the beginning of being*
*if not the middle or the end.*[21]

We are all tellers and listeners, introducing ourselves by sharing each other's stories, and we become, remarkably quickly, a community— what Glassie calls a *ceili.*

Tellers now become writers: "On demand," they take ten minutes of class time to begin writing *a* story of their lives. The bell rings. They take their texts home and the following week offer them to a group of readers. Tellers and listeners become writers and readers. The writing act grows out of the speech act.

Stanley offers his first text. He is a tall, lanky 20-year-old, an accounting major who is relieved that English 120 is his final English requirement. Never again will he have to take another English course. He doesn't see himself as a writer or as a reader. He is certain that the end of this long road of English courses—through twelve years of elementary and secondary schooling and three years of college—is, happily, in sight. Here is Stanley's first text (February 1, 1984). He had construed the writing of *a* story of his life to mean the writing of his autobiography, and so he writes a "bed-to-bed" story, this one beginning with his parents emigrating to America from Poland in 1961, and ending with the "present moment"—his reaching his twentieth birthday. In between he *covers* his childhood, elementary school, high school, part-time work, exploring New York City, entering college—all in 4 pages! We note that his title is simply "Stanley Panek."

### *STANLEY PANEK*

In 1961 Joseph and Bernice Panek came to America from Poland with a three-month-old baby named Mary. The three of them resided at 250 Metropolitan Avenue in Williamsburgh, Brooklyn. Although having been issued a legal permanent alien status, they were not sure if they would stay very long in America. You could just imagine the difficulties they had not having any money and not knowing the language.

Two years later, Christina was born and the four of them moved to a bigger apartment on the south side of Williamsburgh. Being that now there was another mouth to feed, Bernice had to go to work. She found a part-time job working in a girdle factory six blocks away from home. Most of her friends, who were also mothers, worked in that factory part-time. But Bernice didn't work very long because she was pregnant again. About a year after Christina was born, on May 20th, Bernice gave birth to a baby boy. They named him Stanley.

I was a finicky child. My mother had to trick me and play games with me in order to feed me. But before you knew it, I was feeding myself.

I don't remember very much about my childhood. The earliest memory that I can recall is going food shopping to the supermarket with my whole family. I remember sitting in the shopping cart with my sister Christina. My father would usually push us while my mother would pick the groceries off the shelves. My other sister would always run around the whole store, taking things that she wanted but couldn't have, such as candy, icicles, marshmallows, and cookies. Most of those things my mother would put back while she wasn't looking.

I also remember the checkout clerk. She was a nice middle-aged lady. My mother would usually go to her lane. She always gave us lollypops. She always had a smile on her face. I can still remember her face and her voice. I wonder if she still works there. For that matter, I wonder if the store still exists.

When I reached the age of five, I went to kindergarten. I remember crying because I didn't want my mother to leave. Most of the other kids were crying also. But once I got to know everybody, I liked it. I started to hate school when I was in about the second or third grade. I hated doing homework and sitting in a hot classroom when it was nice outside. I couldn't wait for recess in order to go out and play. When I was in the fourth grade, we moved to the north side of Williamsburgh. There we had a basement and a backyard where we could play safely.

Time went by fast and in 1978 I was already starting high school. I went to St. Agnes in New York City. I decided to go there because most of my friends went there and it was only a half hour away from my house by train. In my sophomore year, my parents decided to move out of Brooklyn. We moved to Floral Park, a town on the outskirts of Queens. It would now take me over an hour to get to school. I would have to take a bus and a train. I considered this to be a real hassle. I got so fed up with the traveling that I wanted to transfer to Saint Francis Prep. But that would also take about an hour to get to, so I decided to stay at Saint Agnes.

Now I was a teen-ager. I wanted to be more independent and responsible, so I got a job working in a law firm as a file clerk only one block away from school. I stayed with that job for two years. That was a fun job, I learned a lot working in that place. It taught me how to "play the game."

Sometimes when there wasn't much work to be done, I was sent out on errands. I didn't mind that at all because I got out of the office, and I was able to explore the city. Some of the buildings that I visited were the Chrysler Building, Pan Am, Empire State Building, Twin Towers, City Corp, Rockefeller Center, City Hall, and many many more that are not as famous but just as nice.

In the summer I would go by foot if the destination wasn't too far. One time while running an errand, I had seen a movie being filmed. It was a scene with Dustin Hoffman and Dan Ackroyd. This was being filmed for the movie *Tootsie*. My friends didn't believe me, but when they saw the movie and the scene that I described to them, they believed me. There were other interesting things that I saw on the streets of New York City such as magic acts, three-card monte games, people playing musical instruments ranging from a one-man band, flute act, to a big band with various instruments.

In 1982 I graduated from Saint Agnes and in the fall I quit the job at the law firm and went to Queens College. The college environment was very different from that of a high school. It took time to get used to. But by the time the spring semester appeared, I felt like I had been going to college for years. And now I am in my fourth semester and I am still not definitely sure of what I want to do with my life.

I remember when I was a freshman in high school and I would say to myself, that I can't wait to go to college when I get older. But now as I approach my 20th birthday, I wish that I were back in high school, or even in grammar school for that matter. But I know that I cannot do this. I must start to take things more seriously. I must start acting my age in that cruel world out there, or else I might not make it.

Stanley, along with the rest of the class, brought this first version to class. At the beginning of that session, students were asked to write for ten minutes on what they had hoped to accomplish in the text, what they saw as the strengths of the piece, what questions remained with them now at this rereading, and what questions they would have for the reader. Here are Stanley's comments:

> In this piece, I intended to give the reader a short over-view of my life from birth to the age that I am right now. I didn't want to go into much detail because that would make it really long and possibly boring.
> Basicly [sic], I discussed a childhood memory which would take care of my first ten years. And then I discussed something else from my teen-age years.
>
> Questions:
> 1. Did my paper make any sense?
> 2. Is the reader going to understand what I mean?
> 3. Is my grammar, punctuation, and spelling proper?
> 4. Did I accomplish what I set out to do?
> 5. Is it interesting?
>
> Strengths:
> 1. I didn't go into much detail.

In that same session, students then broke up into groups of four and had the opportunity for their peers to react to their texts, focusing on the same aspects: strengths, questions, and what they saw the writer trying to accomplish. Stanley heard four such readings.

Now each student handed in a copy of his or her text, along with his or her written response and the written responses of peers. The students had been told that this first version was to be considered as a *proposal* for a longer, fuller work, and that we would act as editors: we would underscore what we thought were the strengths; we would question and probe and query, as editors do, and we would get back to them. Fortunately, Stanley saved these responses; so that when he turnd in his folder of work for the semester, we were able to reread our own texts. (A curious sensation, is it not, to come upon our own responses to student writing? How different would the response be a month down the road? a year? These teacher texts are sometimes brutal reflections of an impatient self, a bored self, a near-sighted self!) We, therefore, humbly offer you our comments—knowing full well there could be other versions.

2/25/84

Dear Stanley,

I would accept this "proposal" for your autobiography on the basis of the first page of this essay. The opening with your parents' emigration and the shift from the birth of Stanley to "I" is brilliant: what an eye-catcher. I want to read further to find out how you fared, how you learned to "feed" yourself. It seems to me that there are several themes running through the essay. One is the theme of learning to *feed* yourself. I suggest this: think about strengthening that thematic thread; think about how and in what ways you have learned to "feed" yourself—your mind, your body, etc.

I always look to beginnings and endings, how they relate to each other: you begin with your parents and end with your talking about making it in a cruel world. Are there connections between the beginning and the ending? I wonder.

I find the recollection of your shopping with your family in the supermarket exhilarating; I urge you to think of other episodes—that scene is much more vivid for me than your saying that you saw many "nice" buildings in Manhattan. Again, if you think in terms of "feeding" yourself, then you might home in on what matters.

You felt the need to run through your whole life: I wonder why? The essay could be an elaboration of one or two memories, their significance, rather than an excursion through your whole life.

You are a strong writer—I'd like to see you think about this first essay, particularly about the form—and what you ultimately want to say.

I suggest then: (1) think about developing themes (2) pulling out a few more episodes (3) reflect upon what you say in the end—that it is a cruel world. That, for me, is a surprise; I'm curious to know what you mean.

Your editor

Why is it a *strength* that you didn't go into much detail?

At the next session, students were invited to produce *reactive texts*, to enter into their own texts by trying these exercises:

1. Try three new beginnings. Compare them with your original.

2. Allow a character other than yourself to speak. How do the "voices" differ?

3. Set up a dialogue between two characters within the text. Where are the tensions?

4. Recast a scene from another character's point of view. Does this point of view allow the narrator to see things differently?

5. Represent an actual event as if it is happening to you while you are a participant; represent the same scene as a spectator —removed by time from the event. What are the differences?

6. Try another ending.

Here now are several of Stanley's reactive texts. First, a new beginning:

> I often wonder what Stanislaw Panek would be doing now. Would he be a soldier in the army, a country boy who would some day take his father's job working in the wheat fields, or would he be working in a steel factory in America and sending what he earned back to his wife in Poland. I wonder. He might even be in a prison camp or maybe even dead, killed by some communist because he didn't obey him.

Next, a representation of conversations between him and his father, where he protests that he is *not* his father:

> My father tells me the same old story. I must have heard it about sixty times.
> When I was young, I was only able to finish the fourth grade because of the war. And after the war it was too late to go back to school. I didn't have the same chance as you do. If I were in your shoes I would be studying day and night.
> And then I interrupt him and tell him that if he were in my shoes, he wouldn't be studying all day and night. I try to explain to him that the American educational system is different from that of the Polish. Therefore the students' study habits are different. But he doesn't understand.

When I was starting college my father couldn't understand why I didn't know what my major was. So now I tell him that I am majoring in Computer Science when I actually switched my major to accounting. He just doesn't understand that I am Stanley Panek and not Stanislaw Panek.

On May 15, 1984, Stanley handed in his final folder, and in it we found this piece.

## WHO AM I?

On the birth certificate it clearly states my name, Stanislaw Panek. But what does that tell me or you, or anybody else for that matter, about me, about who I am?

He was born in Saint Catherine's Hospital in Brooklyn, New York. His parents immigrated from Poland in 1961. He has two older sisters. One of them was born in Poland in 1961 and the other was born in the United States in 1963.

Now what does this information tell you about Stanislaw? It doesn't tell you anything about me. But it does tell you something about my parents, Joseph and Bernice.

They were foreigners in a vast and complex city. They didn't know the language or understand the culture of the country. This would mean that Joseph would have a hard time getting around as well as finding a job. But somehow, somewhere, he would have to find a job. Bernice also had to seek employment because they were not able to make ends meet. Except there was one problem if Bernice would go to work. Who would take care of her children while she and her husband were working? Apparently there would only be one solution. Either Bernice or Joseph would have to work in the morning and the other one would have to work at night. And that is what they did. Joseph worked in the A.M. and Bernice worked in the P.M.

What a change this must have been for my father. Imagine having to go from working in a big open field to a cluttered old factory. And for my mother, from milking cows and feeding pigs and chickens to working in a huge and crowded factory, sewing pieces of material which at the end of this mass production line would result in being a dress or a shirt.

Could you imagine a dress made out of pieces of material that previously were balls of cotton? I find it incredible and so did my parents. My parents worked very hard; they also gave up a lot of things in order to feed and educate me and my sisters. They did this so that someday we could be strong, healthy, and educated adults.

Today Stanislaw Panek has become Stanley Panek, or should I say Stanley Stanislaw Panek? Yes, I think that's more appropriate. You see, if I were born in Poland, and if my parents didn't come to America, then my name would have strictly been Stanislaw Panek and most likely I would be wearing my father's shoes when I grew up. The reason being that shoes are not that easy to come across in Poland. If you are lucky to come across any in a store all you would have to choose from would be one or two different styles. You definitely wouldn't find any imported designer shoes like Pierre Cardin's from Paris, France, or Capezzio's from Italy. Those types of shoes are unheard of in Poland.

If I were Stanislaw I would most likely be a farmer just like my father was. If I wasn't a full-time farmer, then that would mean that I had gotten a different pair of shoes, my own, and I would most likely be a factory worker in a nearby city. Except somehow I doubt that very much.

I wonder if Stanislaw would have a brother. It's very possible because in Poland one more child wouldn't present a difficulty. It isn't like it is here in America. One mouth is just about as hard to feed as four; that is, of course, if you live on a farm.

I also wonder if I would take my father's shoes off and come to the United States. To the land of opportunity and wealth. And if I did, I wonder if I would prefer it to Poland.

Well anyway, I wasn't born in Poland so I am not Stanislaw even though that is my name on my birth certificate. Instead I am Stanley. I live in America and I walk in my own shoes. So if someone walks up to me and asks my name, I will tell them Stanley.

Between February 1 and May 15, *something happened* that allowed Stanley to uncover the tensions in his earlier draft, to throw away and begin again, to see patterns in his own life-in-text that he could explore, to break out of the bed-to-bed telling that had constituted his first version, which covered his entire life. As one of our colleagues said on reading Stanley's text: he "masters time by reading his life thematically." He does so by disclosing a question that nags at him, by exploring the question "Who am I?" through two frames: through his name—

his Polish name and his American name—and through the image of shoes—his father's shoes and his own shoes. And for the moment, he insists, he is Stanley and not Stanislaw. He is participant and spectator, he is reflective, interpretative, evaluative of his life, as he constructs a text—which, incidentally, is shorter than the first version written three months before.

We try, as much as is humanly and institutionally possible, to keep texts "open" as long as we can throughout the artificial limits of a writing course in a semester. So often, in writing courses, we expect students to write "on demand," to "finish" a text, to begin and end within a week, two weeks, three weeks. And yet, as those of us who write know, there are some texts that we keep working on, sometimes for years. As instructors, we try to set up constraints that are not so rigid. If we had insisted that this text be "finished" by February 28, it would presumably have been a very different text, probably not so powerful, satisfying, or thoughtful. Keeping texts open—giving students time— can be problematic. We take a chance. Students, who are generally not accustomed to this kind of flexibility, can put off and put off, and then, in a mad rush at the end of term, try to finish off their unfinished texts. We take the chance. As a matter of fact, we feared that Stanley might be one to let it slide. We met with him in conference to talk about this text and others. Occasionally, in class, we would ask him how things were going, as any interested editor would do. In the meantime, he got on with his other work, writing other texts. But this one he kept on hold.

The end of the story? On the last day of class, Stanley walked up to the desk and asked about "this course called Literature and Psychology"—an elective. He said he was thinking about taking another English course. *He* seemed surprised at himself. In his evaluation of the course, he wrote, "I've learned to read with my eyes and my ears." We thought: "This is a good ending, and a good beginning."

# NOTES

1. Cited in Lev Vygotsky, *Thought and Language* (Cambridge, Mass.: M.I.T. Press, 1962), pp. 140–41.
2. Barbara Hardy, *Tellers and Listeners: The Narrative Imagination* (London: Athlone Press, 1975), pp. 4–5.
3. Roland Barthes, "Introduction to the Structural Analysis of Narrative," in his *Music, Image, Text,* trans. Stephen Heath (New York: Hill and Wang, 1977), p. 79.
4. Harold Rosen, "The Nurture of Narrative," paper presented at the IRA Convention, Chicago, April 1982.
5. W. J. T. Mitchell, "Editor's Note: On Narrative," *Critical Inquiry* 7, no. 1 (1980), p. 1. (The essays included in this issue of *Critical Inquiry* are a product of the symposium on "Narrative: The Illusion of Sequence," held at the University of Chicago, October 26–28, 1979.)
6. George Kelly, *A Theory of Personality* (New York: Norton, 1963), p. 52.
7. Frank Kermode, *The Sense of an Ending: Studies in the Theory of Fiction* (London: Oxford University Press, 1967), p. 7.
8. Perry Meisel (ed.), *Freud: A Collection of Critical Essays* (Englewood Cliffs, N.J.: Prentice-Hall, 1981), p. 25.
9. Colin Blakemore, *Mechanics of the Mind* (London: Cambridge University Press, 1977), p. 109.
10. Ibid., p. 110.
11. Virginia Woolf, *Moments of Being: Unpublished Autobiographical Writings,* ed. Jeanne Schulkind (New York: Harcourt Brace Jovanovich, 1978), p. 75.
12. Theodore Rosengarten, "Stepping over Cockleburs: Conversations with Nate Cobb," in *Telling Lives: The Biographer's Art,* ed. Marc Pachter (Ithaca, N.Y.: Cornell University Press, 1979), p. 117.
13. Barbara Herrnstein Smith, *On the Margins of Discourse* (Chicago: University of Chicago Press, 1983), pp. 194–95.
14. William Labov, "The Transformation of Experience into Narrative Text," in his *Language in the Inner City* (Philadelphia: University of Pennsylvania Press, 1972).
15. O. Henry, *41 Stories* (New York: New American Library, 1984), p. 65.
16. Henry Glassie, *Passing the Time in Ballymenone* (Philadelphia: University of Pennsylvania Press, 1982), p. 79.
17. Labov, *Language in the Inner City,* p. 371.
18. Ted Hughes, "Myth and Education," in *Writers, Critics, and Children,* ed. G. Fox et al. (London: Heinemann, 1976), p. 80.
19. Ibid.
20. Hardy, *Tellers and Listeners,* p. 9.
21. Ursula K. le Guin, "It Was a Dark and Stormy Night; or, Why Are We Huddling About the Campfire?" *Critical Inquiry* 7, no. 1 (1980), p. 192.

# CHAPTER SIX

# GENERATIVE FRAME

## Being a Participant, Being a Spectator

**All ye need to know**
**John Keats**

# SPECTATOR AND PARTICIPANT: SOME REFLECTIONS

L et's start with some reflections from the notebook of one of our students:

Spectator versus participant. The interesting question is whether one may *fully* be both at the same time. I'm sure one can *be* both. Last Sunday, for instance, when I was painting, Gerald stood behind me for a few minutes, watching. Obviously, he was spectator and I was actor. But I became spectator, too. His being there made me aware of what I was doing. I carefully rolled each stroke, still making sure to leave each spot covered with paint. My attention to task didn't waver— maybe became stronger. And yet I watched myself do it, too. I was aware of how my performance looked from behind, because I was watching. So I *was* both watcher and doer. But only a moment before, I had been only doer. *All* my attention was then on the paint, the roller, the wall. Does that mean I had split that attention in two? divided my faculties? In that case, I was not fully doer or observer, but only half of each—or some other percentage (70–30?). Yet I don't remember feeling really distracted, nor do I recall feeling that more attention was on one or the other. Perhaps there are two separate faculties for performer and observer: the one was fully engaged in painting, but the other lay dormant until Gerald's presence called it out to work. Why not? It's so seldom we really need both at the same time that we could easily go through life using one, then the other—or using one more than the other—and assume that the same brain is alternating functions when, actually, we are alternating which part of the brain functions. Is it a question for neurologists? or for philosophers? Or does it need an answer at all? I don't know. Perhaps by week's end I'll know whether it should matter to me as a writer.

Judy Lord (U)

You might care to reflect on recent moments in your own life when you have been (a) a completely absorbed participant, (b) a detached spectator, or (c) something of both, simultaneously, with the two frames held in a state of momentary equilibrium.

Hold those reflections, those recognitions, in the back of your mind while we return to Helen Vendler's essay on Keats's "Ode on a Grecian Urn." She discovers in the poem a complex and subtle interplay of empathy and detachment. She sees Keats as moving between empathic participation in the lives represented on the urn, on the one hand, and a cooler detachment, contemplating the urn as a work of art, a representation, on the other.* There is the act of "entering into the existence of other beings" – a "journey outward from habitual self into some other" – and, conversely, the reflectiveness of "the philosophic mind."[1] She relates this particular case, usefully, to the development of Keats's mind as revealed in his letters: Sensation/Beauty on the one hand; Thought/Truth on the other.[2] And she sees Keats as finding an "equilibrium of feeling" as the urn is seen as offering "its paradoxical union of stimuli to sensation and thought alike." The empathizer, entering the virtual world of the urn's scenes, discovers and affirms that "Beauty is Truth"; the reflective mind, conscious of and appraising the artefact as art, concludes that "Truth is Beauty." For Keats, then, "the dialectic between empathy and reflection [is] an ineluctable process of consciousness."[3] In a fascinating note, Vendler recognizes that "It is a matter of dispute whether one can maintain consciousness of matter and medium at once – can weep for the heroine, so to speak, while admiring the zoom shot." She herself sides with Keats and concludes that "As soon as intellectual consideration of medium comes into play, the fiction of the construct lapses." Her intention here is not to evaluate but rather to characterize. Indeed, she argues of stanza 4 that "the reflective position of aesthetic response is shown to be as 'immediate' and full of feeling as the sensory response itself is."[4]

Keats, in his relationship with the lives represented on the urn, offers us the complementary modes of what we propose to call *participation* and *spectatorship*. Vis-à-vis the urn, he enters the role of participant and the role of spectator. Our case is that what is true of the urn is universally true: "that is all/Ye know on earth, and all ye need to know" – all one can ever know must be known as either participant or spectator, there is simply no other option available. But fortunately what one *can* know, in sum – both as participant and as spectator – is, in the event, all one *needs* to know.

It is on the basis of these two fundamental frames of relationship – discourse that represents knowing as participant (pragmatic) and

*Cf. Halliday's distinction between "pragmatic" and "mathetic," pp. 28 and 31.

discourse that represents knowing as spectator (mathetic)—that a coherent schema for composition can, we believe, be founded. And when we talk of participation and spectatorship, we refer not merely to the experience of art—a painting, novel, or movie—but to every moment of our lives, and especially to every moment of our *social* lives.

# THE SHIFT FROM PARTICIPANT TO SPECTATOR

SPECTATOR              PARTICIPANT

To represent these roles as opposing, contrasted, discrete, or polarized is to deny the experiential fact that our energies generally ebb and flow, imperceptibly, moment by moment, between some degree of spectatorship and some degree of participation.

Synchronously, at any moment, we can both participate in a relaxed conversation and withdraw to some degree inside our heads, stand back (metaphorically) and enjoy some measure of detachment or, as Goffman puts it, "half-tune out."[5] In a fierce quarrel, on the other hand, the privilege of distance is simply not available: one is committed to a seemingly total act of participation.

Diachronically, time bears actualities back into our past. They vanish. We are no longer "there," no longer "then." We are now *absent* from the actual, in time or place, or both. Then, we were participants; now we enjoy the human privilege of being spectators of our present representation—in words and images—of *that* experience of participation. As spectators, after the event, we are cooler, wiser, more knowing, more clever, more astute, than we were as participants— hence the French idiom *pensées de l'escalier*\*—the brilliant ideas we have as we leave a room and a situation, moving out of the pressures of participation.

Much of the material, the data, of our spectatorship is in fact our own past, available to us as memory. Occasionally, disconcertingly, we recall a moment of acute embarrassment or failure as if we were once again participants, and we wince or blush, involuntarily.

As spectators of our own past, we can observe and make representations of that past which serve to establish, for our satisfaction, a sense of its meaning, its significance. In a word, we can evaluate. As we do

---

\*Literally, "thoughts of the staircase."

this, privately, inside our own minds, our inner speech conforms to those characteristics identified by Vygotsky: we do not contextualize, we do not articulate the "subject" of a "sentence." We have no need to. But when we engage in our normal social life, one of our primary satisfactions is to present those representations to others. We are, say, not quite sure what to make of it or we are angry or amused, so we answer our social need: we share with someone else. What then happens? In the first place, our representation is quick to offer *contextualization*, to put the other person in the picture. Second, we offer a tentative effort at *evaluation*, either explicit or implicit. Our interlocutor's task is to react: he or she has to satisfy our needs by confirming, modifying, responding in some recognizably useful way to our presentation—not only by accepting our representation but also by recognizing its "meaning." If the "meaning" is different from ours, then we can remind ourselves that "To be real, a community exists divided."[6] If the meaning is the same, then we are in some sense reassured.

It is worth noting that no one can serve as a "useful" spectator of our own representation unless that person has been funded with past occasions for participation in experiences similar to those we are representing. The interlocutor's ability to recognize the "meaning" of our representation will depend on such funding. (We don't turn to 18-year-olds for advice about marriage.)

# CAVEAT SPECTATOR

## *William James on a Certain Blindness*

To emphasize the centrality of these two frames—spectatorship and participation—we invoke William James's essay "On a Certain Blindness in Human Beings." James admits to his own failure—as an urban, cosmopolitan intellectual—to appreciate that the clearings in the woods of North Carolina, which he perceived to be the result of vandalism, a failure to respect nature, were to the local settlers a sign of remarkable, hard-won progress, the basis for a decent rural economy and domestic comfort. He had felt impelled to ask his driver, a local man, what kind of people would possibly do such things. The answer was, "All of us. Why, we ain't happy here unless we are getting one of these coves under cultivation." James continues:

> *I instantly felt that I had been losing the whole inward signifi-*
> *cance of the situation. Because to me the clearings spoke of naught*

*but denudation, I thought that to those whose sturdy arms and obedient axes had made them they could tell no other story. But, when they looked on the hideous stumps, what they thought of was personal victory. The chips, the girdled trees, and the vile split rails spoke of honest sweat, persistent toil and final reward. The cabin was a warrant of safety for self and wife and babes. In short, the clearing, which to me was a mere ugly picture on the retina, was to them a symbol redolent with moral memories and sang a very paean of duty, struggle, and success.*

*I had been as blind to the peculiar ideality of their conditions as they certainly would also have been to the ideality of mine, had they had a peep at my strange indoor academic ways of life at Cambridge.*

*Wherever a process of life communicates an eagerness to him who lives it, there the life becomes genuinely significant. Sometimes the eagerness is more knit up with the motor activities, sometimes with the perceptions, sometimes with the imagination, sometimes with reflective thought. But, wherever it is found, there is the zest, the tingle, the excitement of reality; and there is "importance" in the only real and positive sense in which importance ever anywhere can be.*[7]

Earlier in the paper, he had argued:

*The spectator's judgment is sure to miss the root of the matter, and to possess no truth. The subject judged knows a part of the world of reality which the judging spectator fails to see, knows more while the spectator knows less; and, wherever there is conflict of opinion and difference of vision, we are bound to believe that the truer side is the side that feels the more, and not the side that feels the less.*[8]

It was to illustrate this argument that he introduced the *exemplum* of his encounter with the clearings in North Carolina.

James's position—"The spectator's judgment is sure . . . to possess no truth"—is categorical; absolute enough to stop us in our tracks. "Truth . . . reality . . . the truer side . . . feels the more." Irresistibly, we are reminded of Keats's Grecian urn. And the fine and delicate equilibrium of Keats's achievement nudges us to say to William James: "Just a minute! Hold it!" The pause allows us time to recognize that James is offering a moment of interaction between two "worlds," two cultures: the "world" of the Boston Brahmin, for whom "unspoiled" nature is a valued spectacle, a luxury; and the "world" of those who have to fell trees in order to scratch a living from the land. The one can stand back and savor the earth as a manifestation of a Burkean "sublime"; the other rolls up his sleeves and grabs his axe. Each of these "worlds," as James elsewhere acknowledged, has "its own special and separate style of existence." And "each world, *whilst it is attended to*, is real after its own fashion; only the reality lapses with the attention."[9] But as Erving Goffman has observed, James's "crucial device . . . was a rather scandalous play on the word 'world' (or 'reality'). What he meant was not *the* world but a particular person's current world—and, in fact, . . . not even that. There was no good reason to use such billowy words. James opened a door; it let in wind as well as light."[10]

## Henry Glassie on Context

Modern ethnographers such as Henry Glassie and Hugh Brody are alert to the possibility of precisely such misunderstandings. Their commitment to their work, whether we call it social anthropology or folklore studies, seems to rest on the conviction that the spectator— the outsider—*can* come to know and possess some useful kind of truth. But it is noteworthy that both Glassie, in *Passing the Time in Ballymenone*, and Brody, in *Maps and Dreams*, are scrupulously aware of the problems involved in such interpretation, such "making sense." Hence while neither falls prey to an excess of methodological self-consciousness, each is at pains to lay his procedural cards on the table. Here, for example, is Glassie, warning his readers to tread delicately and not be seduced by glibly facile usage:

> *Encouraged, its way cleared of distracting exceptions, my thought became direct. Common days break into light and dark. While the sun shines, they work. When night falls, they assemble in the kitchen and talk. The nighttime gathering of neighbors is called a ceili (pronounced kaylee). Its center is held by stories.*
>
> *I had not come to Ireland to record stories, nor had I concentrated on them during my first visit, but the more I considered my experience and read through my notes, the more stories consolidated their centrality. It is not the folktale as a category of oral literature that claims such significance, but those stories adults who know one another tie into the conversation when they face the long night together. As I thought about stories, life began to arrange itself around them as context.*
>
> *Context is not a difficult notion. But loose colloquial use can trick us into employing "context" to mean no more than situation.*

*Then the power of the idea evaporates, and studying context we enlarge and complicate the object we describe but come little closer to understanding than we did when we folklorists recorded texts in isolation. Context is not in the eye of the beholder, but in the mind of the creator. Some of context is drawn in from the immediate situation, but more is drawn from memory. It is present, but invisible, inaudible. Contexts are mental associations woven around texts during performance to shape and complete them, to give them meaning.*

*Meaning is a difficult concept, for it means too much. Meaning begins in the correspondence of sensate form to invisible idea, logically links intention and response, then expands through private association to join all a thing is with all it can be in the minds of its creators and perceivers. Finally, meaning carries through the shared experience of form and idea to philosophical bedrock. Most crucially, meaning is that which joins people through things, transforming forms into values, values into forms. Understanding values is the purpose of study.*

*The tale in the ceili is central, situationally, contextually, philosophically. It emerges in the middle of the nighttime's conversations. It draws widely from life to make itself meaningful. Its meanings lead into confrontation with fundamental values.*

*When I went to Ireland next, in June 1977, I felt I had located the culture's key texts, and stories were our topic. I came to stories from ceilis, from their situation, rather than the other way around, and that was good, for I knew how they fit their scene, and I knew I was dealing with tales that were alive and throbbing with importance. They could lead me into the culture.*[11]

## D. W. Harding on the Role of the Onlooker

"Is it a question for neurologists? or for philosophers?" asked Judy Lord in her reflections (see p. 124). Doubtless both, we are inclined to answer; and it was also a question for D. W. Harding, literary critic, social psychologist, and coeditor of *Scrutiny*. In 1937, he tackled it bravely and elegantly in his celebrated essay "The Role of the Onlooker."[12]

What, Harding asked, is the nature of our *activity* when we see a play or read a novel? He wittily conceded, or appeared to concede, that such a question is "perversely naive"; and we know that it doesn't have to be either perverse or naive: witness Keats relating to the urn, or Vendler relating to Keats's poem.

Harding proposes four "modes of activity":

1. The "operative response" — actually doing things: for example, mowing the lawn, as a working response to the height of the grass.

2. The "intellectual comprehension of things and events around us."

3. Looking or listening, not in order to use the things one perceives or to understand them intellectually but simply "for the sake of experiencing them and organizing them at the level of perception."

4. "Detached evaluation": it is "in this that the role of spectator typically consists."

Each of these four modes of experiencing, Harding insists, embraces both relatively trivial, superficial occupations and also "the most significant undertakings we are capable of, . . . highly developed and complex forms of activity."[13]

He proceeds to examine each mode in some detail and observes:

> *What, then, is the nature of the bond between the onlooker and the event? And — the corollary of this question — in what sense is the onlooker detached? . . .*
>
> *In the first place a scene may secure the onlooker's interest because it discloses or makes more vivid to him certain of the possibilities of his surroundings, possibilities which, although not directly involving him at the moment, must yet affect his expectations. Our hopes and anxieties for ourselves and other people very largely depend upon what we have learnt, as spectators, of the possibilities that surround us. Our interest in these possibilities extends beyond the desire to comprehend them intellectually. They are relevant to our other desires and values: we not only comprehend them, we are glad or sorry about them on account of the significance they have for ourselves, for our friends or perhaps for people in general.*
>
> *But besides this it may safely be said that no event would secure our attention as spectators unless we were bound by some sentiment or ideal, however slight and weak, to the people or things which were directly involved. One factor governing the strength of our concern, therefore, will be the intensity of the sentiment that binds us to the participant; and just as the strength of our sentiments and ideals varies by imperceptible degrees so does the extent of our detachment or involvement when looking on at an event.*

> *The adversities and the good fortune of a very close friend may affect the spectator even more than they would have done if they had happened to himself; those of a slight acquaintance or a stranger make him somewhat concerned or rather pleased. . . .*
>
> *The intensity of the attitudes evoked in us as spectators therefore depends on two things: the strength of the sentiment that binds us to the participant, and the importance of the event in the light of our own values.*[14]

Harding is scrupulously careful to insist on a crucial distinction: the condition of being a "typical spectator," for his purposes, must be distinguished from those cases where bouts or moments of "standing back," to see more clearly, occur in the process of a participatory activity; and also from these:

> *. . . [T]he typical role of spectator is not found in situations where we wish to participate and are unable to. The thwarting of an operative response gives rise to such experiences as grief, envy, helpless fury, resignation, rebellious disappointment, or remorse. These emotions arise on occasions when our evaluation is clearly preparatory to action but the action is either unsuccessful or has to be inhibited. We are in the physical position of the spectator without having his detachment. And in everyday speech we are then said not to be "merely looking on" but to be "looking on helplessly."*
>
> *Nor is the typical spectator the man who neglects to make an operative response that is expected of him, the man whom we accuse of "looking on indifferently."*[15]

What then of detached evaluative responses? These, Harding claims,

> *tend to be more widely comprehensive than the evaluation which precedes participation. One views the event in a more distant perspective and relates it to a more extensive system of information, beliefs and values. And this detached evaluative response undoubtedly possesses the utmost importance in building up, confirming and modifying all but the very simplest of our values. It is as onlookers from a distance that we can most readily endure the penetration of general principles among our sentiments. . . .*
>
> *The event we look on at from a distance affects us, but it is set in a wider context than the urgencies of participating relationships usually permit us to call up around events. And for this reason, if we could obliterate the effects on a man of all the occasions when he was "merely a spectator" it would be profoundly to alter his character and outlook.*[16]

In childhood, we move easily and unself-consciously between the role of participant—"playing doctor," say—and the role of spectator: children switch easily from "being a doctor" to being a child playing a game of make-believe. In such make-believe play,

> *all who take part have combined in themselves the roles of both entertainer and audience: they are representing possibilities of experience—for instance of being teachers and children, hosts and guests, tradesmen and customers—and simultaneously, in their role of audience, they are evaluating them.*[17]

As adults, we no longer indulge in social make-believe. What do we do that is analogous to such play? Harding's answer is that adults gossip:

> *Gossip is the second method through which the possibilities of experience—reported or imagined—may be communicated and evaluated. Here the roles of entertainer and audience have been differentiated, and we can observe a faint approach towards formal entertainment (especially when a social group extrudes a recognized raconteur or wit). Gossip still differs from formal entertainment, however, in two ways. For one thing the roles of entertainer and audience are passed backwards and forwards from one person to another. And, further, the audience's attitude—of agreement, emphatic or qualified, or of disagreement—may be expressed directly and promptly to the speaker. But the essential fact in gossip as in entertainment is that the speaker who raises a topic is presenting what he takes to be an interesting situation—actual or possible—in what he regards as an appropriate light. He expects his hearers to agree on the interest of the situation and the fittingness of his attitude.*[18]

Finally, Harding produces his trump card:

> *The playwright, the novelist, the song-writer and the film-producing team are all doing the same thing as the gossip, however innocent they may be of witting propagandist intentions. Each invites his audience to agree that the experience he portrays is possible and interesting, and that his attitude to it, implicit in his portrayal, is fitting. In the less developed levels of entertainment the process is chiefly one of reinforcing commonplace values in a trivially varied array of situations. In the representational arts, most obviously in literature, the author invites his audience to share in an exploration, an extension and refinement, of his and*

*their common interests; and, as a corollary, to refine or modify their value judgments.*[19]

Twenty-five years later, Harding extended his argument, proposing that

*the events at which we are "mere onlookers" come to have, cumulatively, a deep and extensive influence on our systems of value. They may in certain ways be even more formative than events in which we take part. Detached and distanced evaluation is sometimes sharper for avoiding the blurrings and bufferings that participant action brings, and the spectator often sees the event in a broader context than the participant can tolerate. To obliterate the effects on a man of the occasions on which he was only an onlooker would be profoundly to change his outlook and values.*[20]

Then in 1966, at the Anglo-American Seminar on the Teaching of English (The Dartmouth Seminar), Harding and James Britton worked together and discovered that they had come to very similar conclusions by independent routes; and Britton subsequently remarked, "I think it is no distortion of Harding's account to suggest that as participants we APPLY our value systems, but as spectators we GENERATE AND REFINE the system itself."[21] Britton and his colleagues in London then formulated the following schema:

*[In discourse there are] three major categories of function: transactional, expressive, and poetic. TRANSACTIONAL is the form of discourse that most fully meets the demands of a participant in events (using language to get things done, to carry out a verbal transaction). EXPRESSIVE is the form of discourse in which the distinction between participant and spectator is a shadowy one. And POETIC discourse is the form that most fully meets the demands associated with the role of spectator—demands that are met, we suggested, by MAKING something with language rather than DOING something with it.*[22]

The concept of the "expressive" function owes something to the pioneering work of Edward Sapir. But Britton found closely related, even synonymous, terms in the work of Roman Jakobson (Jakobson's "emotive" being "a direct expression of the speaker's attitude toward what he is speaking about"), of Dell Hymes, and of William Labov (who sees the expressive mode as "the role of language as self-identification").*

# SPECTATOR/PARTICIPANT ROLES AS FRAMES FOR COMPOSING

Our own interest, in recent years, has been in exploring the usefulness of the spectator/participant roles as offering a way of unifying our students' work both as readers of literature and as writers of texts. We have concluded that they offer a viable and clarifying schema within which to organize our students' activities, and that they can most usefully be applied in three major ways: as frames for writing in role, as frames of alternation, and as illuminating frames.

## As Frames for Writing in Role

The roles can serve as complementary frames for the student writer making texts, in role, as either spectator or participant—an aspect that is explored in detail in Chapters 7 and 8.

## As Frames of Alternation

The roles can also serve as a frame for the alternation of activity (writing texts) and reflection (writing about the text that has been made), an ebb and flow. Student writers participate in the making of texts; afterward they become spectators of their own texts. When we stand back to become spectators of our own work in progress, the frame is different in important respects from that which applies to our contemplation of someone else's finished text; our own texts never feel *finished* to us. Becoming a spectator of one's own work in progress involves the sense of further action, revision, etc. The text is *open;* there is an element of continuing intention, of reconsidering, and of

---

*The interested reader may care to compare these three categories of function with the six that Michael Halliday posits, and of which he argues, "the mastery of all of them— with the possible exception of the last—[is] a necessary and sufficient condition for the transition to the adult system." In order, they are: Instrumental, Regulatory, Interactional, Personal, Heuristic, Imaginative, and Informative (*Learning How to Mean*, p. 37).

reevaluation, in such moments of detachment; they point forward to the next reentry. As with Britton's description of the "expressive," the distinctions here between participant and spectator are "shadowy."

An exemplary use of this paradigm of complementarity and shaping:

action → reflection → action → reflection

is to be found in the work of Dorothy Heathcote.[23] She has her drama students generate roles and "become" them; when the action reaches an impasse—uncertainty, confusion, overload, or a sense of closure—she nudges them out of the vicarious role and back into the role of student thinking about and evaluating what he/she has just produced. Because they have "had an experience," because "something has happened to them" the students have rich material to reflect on, to consider, to evaluate. As T. S. Eliot wrote, "Those to whom nothing has ever happened cannot know the unimportance of events."[24] Cognitively, a mass of vivid particularities within the action participated in, yields up cohering generalizations, findings, conclusions, and guidelines for the next phase of the action.

This ebb and flow, the alternation of activity (writing) and reflection (writing about texts), is exemplified at various places in this text, when we show students reflecting on their texts.

## As Illuminating Frames

Finally, the spectator/participant roles can serve as illuminating frames through which to understand more fully both a literary text and also the activity of the reader. We offer four examples: *Hamlet*, Henry James, Richard Wright's *Black Boy*, and the postmodernist novel.

### Hamlet

The prince of Denmark is a spectator who feels a moral obligation to become a participant. The play is characterized by an unusually strong foregrounding of soliloquy. Many people remember it as "the play with the soliloquies," and the most frequent visual representation of the play is of Hamlet alone. We suggest that this is so because one of the major themes of the play is the weighing of the relative moral and existential claims of participation and detachment, and because the soliloquy is, par excellence, the characteristic mode of discourse for the detached spectator. Look again at Hamlet's soliloquies, and you may confirm our view that their primary functions are (1) the clarification of values in the service of a possible, possibly effective, entry into participation and (2) a way of justifying nonparticipation.

## Henry James

Critics such as Barbara Hardy attend to the subtle sensibilities of James's narrators. Says Hardy:

> *Henry James likes to show the working of sensibility and intelligence in the present happening, but since he so often centres the interest in a spectator he can show and exploit a slight but subtle and important gap between happening and interpretation: the narrative contains a narrative of what happens counterpointed on a narrative of what seems to be happening, or what the spectator tells himself is happening. The gap is also present—on an enormous scale and with vast irony—in* Tom Jones *and* Wuthering Heights. *One of James's great achievements is to narrow the gap so that some readers never see it at all and the rest have to work uncomfortably hard to see it. Amongst his major themes is the relation between what occurred and what was reported, expected, believed, dreamed, and falsified.* [25]

## Richard Wright's *Black Boy*

Wright's autobiography is an interplay between the participant and the spectator. Throughout the entire work, Wright offers us, first, the participant's account: he makes us feel *as if* we are there with him, when he is four years old, *living through* events as they are happening —so much so that we have found students disconcerted that Wright can "remember" so much (see p. 105). But the memories are counterpointed by the distanced narrator, who looks back on events and comments, interprets, makes sense of, evaluates. Once students unlock the *structure* of Wright's autobiography—the interplay between participant and spectator—they see that an entire work can rest on a conceptual frame that is a dialectic between then and now, far and near, close and distant, inside and outside.

## The Postmodernist Novel

The postmodernist novel often achieves its most striking effects by playing games with the reader's role. We settle into a vicarious, empathizing participation, then turn the page only to be reminded that we are spectators. "Look," says the text, "you're reading a novel!" (Examples are Italo Calvino's *If on a Winter's Night a Traveller* and John Barth's *Sabbatical*.)

We now turn to a closer examination of texts written in the role of vicarious participant (Chapter 7) and of texts written in the role of spectator (Chapter 8).

# NOTES

1. Helen Vendler, *The Odes of John Keats* (Cambridge, Mass.: Harvard University Press, 1984), p. 131.
2. Ibid., pp. 146–48.
3. Ibid., p. 132.
4. Ibid., p. 311.
5. Erving Goffman, *Frame Analysis: An Essay on the Organization of Experience* (New York: Harper & Row, 1974), p. 502.
6. Henry Glassie, *Irish Folk History* (Philadelphia: University of Pennsylvania Press, 1982), p. 9.
7. William James, "On a Certain Blindness in Human Beings," in his *Talks to Teachers* (New York: Norton, 1958), p. 151.
8. Ibid., p. 150.
9. William James, *Principles of Psychology*, vol. 2 (New York: Dover Publications, 1950), pp. 291–93.
10. Goffman, *Frame Analysis*, p. 3.
11. Henry Glassie, *Passing the Time in Ballymenone* (Philadelphia: University of Pennsylvania Press, 1982), p. 33.
12. D. W. Harding, "The Role of the Onlooker," *Scrutiny* 6 (1937), p. 247.
13. Ibid.
14. Ibid., pp. 251–52.
15. Ibid., pp. 250–51.
16. Ibid., p. 252.
17. Ibid., pp. 256–57.
18. Ibid., p. 257.
19. Ibid., pp. 257–58.
20. D. W. Harding, "Psychological Processes in the Reading of Fiction," *British Journal of Aesthetics* 2, no. 2 (1962).
21. James N. Britton, *Prospect and Retrospect* (Montclair, N.J.: Boynton/Cook, 1982), p. 51.
22. Ibid., p. 53.
23. See Dorothy Heathcote, *Collected Writings on Education and Drama*, ed. L. Johnson and C. O'Neill (London: Hutchinson, 1984).
24. T. S. Eliot, *The Family Reunion* (London: Faber & Faber, 1960).
25. Barbara Hardy, *Tellers and Listeners: The Narrative Imagination* (London: Athlone Press, 1975), p. 20.

# CHAPTER SEVEN

# APPLICATIONS
## *Writers as Participants*

*a movement, that now*
*And again now, and now, and now . . .*
*Ted Hughes*

*Everything actual must be transformed by imagination into something purely experiential; that is the principle of* poesis.
Susanne Langer, Feeling and Form

# SOME DISTINCTIVE FEATURES OF PARTICIPANT TEXTS

Participant texts tend to be characterized by certain distinctive features, of which the most striking are parataxis, the absence of contextual clues, implicitness, and synpraxis.

## Parataxis

A participant text is marked by *synchronicity:* the action it describes is happening "now," even as the participant is speaking. It is utterance represented by text. There is an illusion of simultaneity. Since the mind that is producing the utterance doesn't appear to know *what will happen next*, the utterance is nudged along moment by moment, and there is little or no confident anticipation of the outcome, of "how it will end."

A participant text is also marked by a *lack of connections;* connections that would be obvious to a spectator are not available to the participant. (The effect is similar to when one watches someone else doing something and perhaps making mistakes; as a spectator one can see more than the participant can see, and one feels an impulse to intervene.)

The result of these two factors—utterance at the moment of experience (synchronicity of experiencing and uttering) and the inability to see connections—is that when those utterances are represented in text, the text will be mostly, if not entirely, paratactic. (For more on parataxis, see pages 147–169.)

## The Absence of Contextual Clues

Since—like inner speech—most participant utterance is self-directed, it displays little or no awareness of audience. No attempt is made to put the reader in the picture. The utterance is predicated on the simple fiction that there is *no* audience.

### *Implicitness*

When Ted Hughes wrote "Wodwo," he did not spell out explicitly the frames and states of mind that characterized his version of a wodwo. Rather, he presented those frames and states in the very language itself: the syntax is "semantic": it carries meaning, it is a "cultural syntax." It is for the reader, then, to observe the language and to draw—from the fact that it is as it is and not otherwise—the appropriate inferences. The reader must tease out the implication—that which is "folded in." The dominance of implicitness over explicitness is again a sign of the absence of awareness of audience, of the absence of any audience other than the "speaker." In mature writers, this apparent indifference to the needs of the reader is, of course, a fiction.

### *Synpraxis*

Many participant texts are textual representations of synpractic utterance—the jabber-jabber (often inner speech) that we produce as an accompaniment, guide, regulator, explicator of whatever action we happen to be performing. Wodwo's utterances are clearly of this order: he verbalizes in order to act more effectively. Such synpractic verbalizing often comprises speculation, pausing, considering, and focusing.

# RUSHING HEADLONG AS A PARTICIPANT: RUSHDIE AS A PRIMARY TEXT

Participant texts often read like a riddle. One of the virtues, for us, of the participant texts that we share with our students is that they, as readers, have to do a lot of work. Many participant texts are conspicuously private, and they have to be deprivatized—the reader has to construct a public or social meaning.

Consider, for example, the following prose passage, which we have deliberately decontextualized in order to reinforce our point. First read it silently. Then read it out loud.

> *No colours except green and black the walls are green the sky is*
> *black (there is no roof) the stars are green the Widow is green but*
> *her hair is black as black. The Widow sits on a high high chair*

*the chair is green the seat is black the Widow's hair has a centre-parting it is green on the left and on the right black. High as the sky the chair is green the seat is black the Widow's arm is long as death its skin is green the fingernails are long and sharp and black. Between the walls the children green the walls are green the Widow's arm comes snaking down the snake is green the children scream the fingernails are black they scratch the Widow's arm is hunting see the children run and scream the Widow's hand curls round them green and black. Now one by one the children mmff are stifled quiet the Widow's hand is lifting one by one the children green their blood is black unloosed by cutting fingernails it splashes black on walls (of green) as one by one the curling hand lifts children high as sky the sky is black there are no stars the Widow laughs her tongue is green but see her teeth are black. And children torn in two in Widow hands which rolling rolling halves of children roll them into little balls the balls are green the night is black. And little balls fly into night between the walls the children shriek as one by one the Widow's hand. And in a corner the Monkey and I (the walls are green the shadows black) cowering crawling wide high walls green fading into black there is no roof and Widow's hand comes onebyone the children scream and mmff and little balls and hand and scream and mmff and splashing stains of black. Now only she and I and no more screams the Widow's hand comes hunting hunting the skin is green the nails are black towards the corner hunting hunting while we shrink closer into the corner our skin is green our fear is black and now the Hand comes reaching reaching and she my sister pushes me out out of the corner while she stays cowering staring the hand the nails are curling scream and mmff and splash of black and up into the high as sky and laughing Widow tearing I am rolling into little balls the balls are green and out into the night the night is black . . .*[1]

We now invite you to consider the following questions. Consider them not primarily in terms of coming up with answers but rather as occasions for thinking, speculating, surmising.

1. When you were reading the text out loud, what did you *hear* that you had not noticed when you read it silently?

2. Why do we call that passage a text?

3. What do you think the text is representing?

4. What features of the text would you point to in support of your answer to question 3?

5. What problems do you have as a reader meeting that text for the first time?

6. Are those problems intriguing, provocative, teasing, irritating, frustrating? How else would you characterize them?

7. In the context from which we have removed it, that passage is followed by a sentence that is as unlike the passage as one could imagine, both in its meaning and in its structure. Construct your own suggestion for that sentence.

8. Compose a title for the passage. What sorts of thing do you have to do in order to do this?

9. See if you can relate the following terms to your reading of the passage:
   mimesis    enactment    expressiveness    immediacy
   repetition    voice    incoherence

10. Roman Jakobson assigned six functions to human utterances: emotive, referential, poetic, phatic, metalingual, and conative. He claimed that in any given situation, one of the six will be dominant.[2] Which of the six functions seems to you to be dominant in that text? Which of Halliday's? (See p. 135.)

11. Jakobson also claimed that "The verbal structure depends primarily on the dominant function." How does the verbal structure of that passage seem to depend on its function?

The passage that you have just been considering—from Salman Rushdie's novel *Midnight's Children*—is one that we find students in freshman composition courses come to enjoy and appreciate very much, once they have had the opportunity to think about it and to recover from their initial reactions of perplexity, frustration, even revulsion—which are not all bad, since they are better than indifference or apathy. The questions are such as we offer to our students. Given such questions to focus on, the students then have a three-part set of constraints or supports: the text, their initial responses, and their answers to the questions. It is in allowing for, even provoking, tensions between any two of these that energy is educed.

Question 1 is a way of bringing students to discover the importance of readings with the *ear*.[3] Certain features of the text, features that the eye will overlook—for example, repetitions—are thereby thrown into relief. Conversely, to be able to *see* the text is to be in a position to examine some of its distinctive features in a way that would not occur if the text were merely read aloud.

Since the words are on the page and not merely in the air, we say that they comprise a text. But we have a slight hesitation in claiming that it is a text, because it is so emphatically a representation of utterance, of words "spoken"—even going so far as to include the pre-verbal "mmff."

Since the utterances represented by the text offer no kind of context within which, against which, the reader can "place" them and derive clues with which to make sense of them, these utterances appear to have virtually no awareness of audience; they are not trying to present their representation to someone other than the one who produces it. Some degree of confusion or uncertainty in the eavesdropping reader would therefore appear to be in order. Again, since the dominant function is not explicit, the reader has to use whatever the text provides to infer such a function; and the only clues are those to be found in the "verbal structure," for that is all the reader has.

As readers, then, we are likely to read the text not only in a linear fashion, following it as it unfolds, but also recursively, darting our eyes and minds back and forth in our efforts to make sense. As we do so, drawing also on what we have observed through hearing the words, we begin to notice certain features of the text—such as syntactic uncertainty, repetitiousness, pell-mell onrushing rhythms—which are reinforced by the nature of the images offered. The "meaning" offered by most student readers centers on such notions as hallucination, nightmare, and madness. The disorder, the overwhelmedness of the images —these are also present in the sheer form, or formlessness, of the sentence patterns.

The text, then, appears to be expressive of mental or perceptual disorder. The repetitions are of images that the person constructing the text seems unable to control. The text does not allow us to stand back and see what's going on from a more distant, generalizing vantage point. The text offers an illusion of vivid immediacy; its disjointed, staccato rhythms convey an intense sense of something being enacted at this very moment, rather than of an experience "recollected in tranquillity." This effect is reinforced by the use of the present tense: it is happening, so it seems, even as the words are being uttered.

As for the segment of text that follows that extract (see question 7), the clues suggest that it will have to do with peace as opposed to disturbance, with sanity rather than insanity, with health as distinct from disease, and that the segment will be coherently ordered, its very syntax and structure representing control or tranquillity.

In fact, the next paragraph begins with the words "The fever broke today." And our case is that the reassurance offered by that simple sentence is to be derived as much from its brevity, its coherent grammar, its sheer order, as from what it is saying.

Our great privilege as readers is that we can now reconstrue the "crazy" text at leisure. Reassured by the fevered one's recovery, we can go over the chaos and the terror, picking our way calmly through all those awful images, no longer overwhelmed, no longer oppressed. One simple sentence of four words has placed the fever at a safe distance. And now that we know "what it was," we can enjoy the artifice whereby the writer had us up to our necks inside his feverish terror. In a word, we can move from a vicarious or virtual participant role to a spectator role.

# THE RESPECTIVE STRENGTHS OF PARATAXIS AND HYPOTAXIS

Daumier, the great nineteenth-century graphic artist, has a cartoon in which a man is learning to swim by straddling a chair in his living room, rather than by getting into real water.

Being in water produces, we hope, those movements, more or less controlled, called swimming. And our case is that composition teachers have to get student writers into the water—that is, into the determining environment.

Our case is that convincing patterns of prose arise from an internally felt, inwardly realized, act or condition, either actual or vicarious. Our first task, then, is to project our students into such discourse-provoking situations as will inescapably give rise to, provoke, inspire, an appropriate range and variety of types of discourse, both spoken and written, both utterance and text. As we proceed, our students can learn to recognize the distinguishing features of various kinds of discourse. And such knowledge as they acquire will be gained through the complementary activities of reading/writing, talking/listening. Such knowledge may at times be tentative, uncertain, speculative, inchoate. The important thing is to have something interesting to work on, to care about, to be affected by. In these matters, any categorical separation of the cognitive and the affective spells disaster.

When we ask our students to generate a text, we want them to acquire among other things a writerly and readerly sense of structural resourcefulness. Put crudely, *we want to help them appreciate the respective strengths of parataxis and hypotaxis,* where parataxis achieves an effect of unmeditated and unmediated directness but does precious little work to help its audience, whereas hypotaxis represents the speaker/

writer's performance as a realization of an obligation to offer the audience explicit connections, controlled levels of significance, adequate contextualization, and an appropriate evaluation.

We believe that a persisting, recurrent stress on the crucial differences between parataxis and hypotaxis is of use to students precisely because they are, first, talkers and, second, writers: they talk far more than they write. And although utterance is generally dialogical and text monological, students often tend to transfer the paratactic features of utterance, where they may be said properly to belong, to the quite other context of *text*, where the persistence of parataxis can involve a failure to seize and exploit, experiment with and enjoy, the infinite possibilities of hypotaxis in the making of text. Our appeal is not to *logic:* there is a great deal of loose, illogical writing about the illogicality of weak student texts. This is a misnomer, a misdiagnosis. The connections whose absence is construed as illogicality are not so much logical connections as *social* connections. "Logic" is a feeble and mostly inappropriate term in such matters.

When we say or write, "Although it was raining, I decided to go for a walk," the text offers (through its concessive conjunction), a recognition that, in general, people don't choose to walk in the rain. The function of the subordinate clause is not to express "logic" but rather to recognize what is expected or unexpected, normal or abnormal, unremarkable or remarkable. Similarly, when we say or write, "I'm going to try it because I want to," we are engaged in a social act—a recognition of our audience's right to be given an explanation. The function of subordinating conjunctions must not be confused with the symbolic force or intent of the signs characteristic of mathematics or formal logic. Subordinating conjunctions are, rather, a recognition of our audience's need for something by way of legitimation, context, explanation. And the use of subordinate clauses is a social act that generates effects in the audience/reader. When we "consider," we discover the need for such clauses; when we offer our considerations to others, as text, the evidence of our having considered is there *in the hypotaxis.* We have internalized/anticipated and have tried to satisfy the appropriate and relevant needs of someone else.

The formative models for hypotactic structures are to be found *not* in grammar exercises or sentence-combining drills but in our arguments with ourselves (internalized dialogue) and in our reading of texts; and that act of reading is not a *conscious search* for hypotactic structures but a matter of making *meanings*—meanings that are shaped by and embodied in such embedding structures. We attend to the meanings, and in the process we assimilate (mostly outside awareness) the structures.

To press the distinctions between parataxis and hypotaxis is to help students recognize some of the criterial characteristics of both utterance and text. For students who tend to write as they talk, that is a useful bit of enlightenment.

Parataxis is the name given to structures of discourse where the relationship between the parts is one of parity, where all the meanings appear to operate at the same level of significance, without foregrounding or backgrounding. The structure is one of piecemeal horizontal linearity. Few connectives occur, and these are merely coordinating, with "and"—as we would expect—the most persistent: "I'm going home, and I see this man, and he's like a wino, and he smiles at me, and I don't know whether to smile back, and he. . . ."

Characteristically, parataxis is a feature of much spoken discourse, of utterance, where we make it up as we go along, composing utterance at the point of experiencing, to a considerable degree. Historically and culturally, parataxis is seen as being characteristic of oral cultures. In our society, it is found most frequently in the texts of immature writers, and especially of writers who have not yet discovered the resourcefulness of "text" through extensive reading.

The only relationship between parts that parataxis usually offers is the temporal relationship—*time* moves the utterance from one moment to the next—and this is manifest in the use of simple apposition or juxtaposition. One of the most recent discussions of this matter is to be found in Thomas Farrell's provocative paper "I.Q. and Standard English."[4] Farrell quotes the Oxford classicist M. L. West to this effect: "A series of thoughts ABC, where A and B or B and C make a coherent sequence, but ABC taken as a whole seem to lack all cohesion, is characteristic of archaic Greek literature."[5] And he cites James Notopoulos to the effect that "Parataxis is first of all a state of mind."[6]

The most brilliant account of parataxis, however, Farrell surprisingly does not mention, and that is in Eric Auerbach's *Mimesis* (subtitled *The Representation of Reality in Western Literature*). Auerbach remains, for all the methodological shifts of recent years, one of the great *readers*. And in his reading of Augustine's *Confessions*, he not only traces a rich connection between Augustine's prose and that of the Bible—both of which exploit the distinctive strength of parataxis—but helps us to recognize and identify that strength: Augustine chooses on occasions not to avail himself of the complex hypotactic resources of classical Latin and instead uses the more "primitive" forms of parataxis. The point we wish to seize on here is Auerbach's contention that "In English it is more dramatically effective to say: He opened his eyes and was struck . . . than: When he opened his eyes, or: Upon opening his eyes, he was struck."[7] It is also worth noting that paratactic forms tend to coexist

147

with a tone that "has something urgently impulsive, something human and dramatic" to convey.[8] Later, in his reading of the *Chanson de Roland*, Auerbach makes another remark that is especially pregnant for us: "The poet explains nothing; and yet the things which happen are stated with a paratactic bluntness which says that everything must happen as it does happen, it could not be otherwise, and there is no need for explanatory connectives."[9]

# TWO MORE PRIMARY TEXTS

## *A Paratactic Text from Beckett*

Let us stay with Auerbach's contention that parataxis is an effective way of conveying the sense that "everything must happen as it does happen, it could not be otherwise." Hold that in mind while reading the following passage from Samuel Beckett's *Watt*, preferably aloud:

> *Personally of course I regret everything. Not a word, not a deed, not a thought, not a need, not a grief, not a joy, not a girl, not a boy, not a doubt, nor a trust, not a scorn, not a lust, not a hope, not a fear, not a smile, not a tear, not a name, not a face, no time, no place, that I do not regret, exceedingly. An ordure, from beginning to end. And yet, when I sat for Fellowship, but for the boil on my bottom . . . The rest, an ordure. The Tuesday scowls, the Wednesday growls, the Thursday curses, the Friday howls, the Saturday snores, the Sunday yawns, the Monday morns, the Monday morns. The whacks, the moans, the cracks, the groans, the welts, the squeaks, the belts, the shrieks, the pricks, the prayers, the kicks, the tears, the skelps, and the yelps. And the poor old lousy old earth, my earth and my father's and my mother's and my father's father's and my mother's mother's and my father's mother's and my mother's father's and my father's mother's father's and my mother's father's mother's and my father's mother's mother's and my mother's father's father's and my father's father's mother's and my mother's mother's father's and my father's father's father's and my mother's mother's mother's and other people's fathers' and mothers' and fathers' fathers' and mothers' mothers' and fathers' mothers' and mothers' fathers' and fathers' mothers' fathers' and mothers' fathers' mothers' and fathers' mothers' mothers' and mothers' fathers' fathers' and fathers' fathers' mothers' and mothers'*

*mothers' fathers' and fathers' fathers' fathers' and mothers' mothers' mothers'. An excrement. The crocuses and the larch turning green every year a week before the others and the pastures red with uneaten sheep's placentas and the long summer days and the new-mown hay and the wood-pigeon in the morning and the cuckoo in the afternoon and the corncrake in the evening and the wasps in the jam and the smell of the gorse and the look of the gorse and the apples falling and the children walking in the dead leaves and the larch turning brown a week before the others and the chestnuts falling and the howling winds and the sea breaking over the pier and the first fires and the hooves on the road and the consumptive postman whistling* The Roses Are Blooming in Picardy *and the standard oillamp and of course the snow and to be sure the sleet and bless your heart the slush and every fourth year the February débacle and the endless April showers and the crocuses and then the whole bloody business starting all over again. A turd. And if I could begin it all over again, knowing what I know now, the result would be the same. And if I could begin again a third time, knowing what I would know then, the result would be the same. And if I could begin it all over again a hundred times, knowing each time a little more than the time before, the result would always be the same, and the hundredth life as the first, and the hundred lives as one. A cat's flux. But at this rate we shall be here all night.*[10]

After the ironic surprise of the first sentence's last word, one guesses one is in for trouble, or fun, or a mixture of both. And when the passage is read out loud, sure enough what most students *hear* is not so much a melancholy or a pessimism as a paradox: Watt enumerates so fully that the very fulness of his enumeration works against the ostensible semantic meaning of his utterance. There is something absurdly contradictory about being so richly positive about your negations.

As for the structure, the repetitiveness is more apparent than real. The ear *hears* accumulations, climaxes, pregnant pauses, neat little summations, expressive images, and detects both the persistence and the patterning. There is a subordinate clause early on, at "when I sat . . ."; and there are subordinate clauses at the end: "And if I could. . . . And if. . . . And if. . . ." The rest of the text is entirely paratactic. And the effects of such unrelieved parataxis are very striking: each groan is equivalent to all others; all aspects of life are *equally* regrettable; and this is the way the world *is*—no explanations, no concessions, no conditionals; "everything must happen as it does happen."

149

## A Paratactic Text from Mailer in Role As . . .

Consider now this extract from a professional writer's work: read it aloud, and listen to the kind of "voice" the text represents and enforces. See if you can characterize the "speaker":

> We got into Bobby's car, and drove across Bel Air into Beverly Hills, and in one of the houses off Rodeo Drive was where she lived. It was dark, and there were no cars outside, and the garage was locked, so Bobby and I went to the back of the house. He found the wire to the burglar alarm and cut it and cracked the latch on the window. There we were standing in her kitchen. He looked in the rack for a carving knife and found one. Then we went up the stairs to her bedroom. I remember it was on the side that would have a view of the hills above Beverly Hills, and all the while he was doing this, despite the benzedrine in my blood, I never felt more calm as if, ha ha, I was on This Is Your Life, and they were talking about me looking for the woman's door. I even held Bobby's hand, the one that did not have the knife.[11]

Mailer's own text reminds us that in certain situations the reader-in-the-writer actually knows more, and must know more, than the ostensible writer! The prose was written by Mailer, but it is not Mailer's "voice" that we are listening to. Whose, then, is it? The short answer is: nobody's. It's a fiction. But a more interesting answer is that it is Mailer's, not *in propria persona,* as himself, but as Marilyn Monroe; not, indeed, as Marilyn Monroe, but as Mailer's conception, his imagining, of Monroe in a specially wild and manic moment of her life. What, then, is the nature of Mailer's achievement here? Let's look at the syntax: "We . . . and . . . and. . . . It was . . . and . . . and. . . ." The conjunctions are *primitive.* The only explicit connection between the segments of this experience is the primal connection of chronological sequence; in a word, the representation of the event is "childish." If this is the "voice" of an adult, then the adult has either never grown up or is now regressing. The effect is one of breathless haste — entirely appropriate to the escapade in question; but it's also one of a kind of terrible innocence, a foolish innocence. No adult should be this innocent!

Where is any awareness of consequence of acts (a normal criterial feature of adult minds)? The point of the syntax is exactly that: the mood, the temper of the actor in this crazy action is precisely one of feckless inconsequentiality. The meaning is *in* the "childish" sentence structure. Your intuition, as an adult reader, will have told you that this prose is in some sense off-center, abnormal; it doesn't match up to your expectations of what normal adult narrative prose is like or should be like. And you are right. Mailer, the complicated, knowing adult writer, is offering a *persona;* he is offering someone else, through the voice of a first-person narrative, which seems to come exclusively and consistently out of a particular sensibility. The voice's style *is the characterization.* So through the use of memory, ear, and social insight, Mailer has created a voice that says, implicitly: "I am Marilyn Monroe." And we guess that in order to do this, Mailer, the concurrent and recursive reader of his text as it evolves, is on guard for signs of any slipping back into the more complex voice that he himself as a person possesses. Mailer is, after all, a lover of complex sentences, a connoisseur of hypotaxis. Mailer as a reader had to know more than Mailer as a writer could ever know as long as he sustained the illusion of *being* Marilyn Monroe. Mailer has here created a *participant* text, with Monroe as the participant. The profit of reading such a text then, is to be found in attending to the ways in which Mailer's prose works to sustain his impersonation.

# REPRESENTING THE EXTREME SITUATION

A brief glance at the traditional folk stories of any community will confirm the impression that the function of any cultural tradition is precisely to offer the contrastive frames of the ordinary (what is usual) and of the odd (the unexpected, the exceptional). It is a question of the difference between the routine of dailiness and the crisis of the extreme situation.*

Here now is a student text dealing with an extreme situation.

> So warm and dark. I feel so comfortable. No need for anything. Just dark warmthness. There are walls. Suspended between them, I stay here dark and warm. What is this sound in the walls and up above as if something moves through the wall and pounds overhead. What could it be?

---

*Cf. Peter Berger and Thomas Luckman's account of casual conversation: "conversation that can *afford to be* casual precisely because it refers to the routine of a taken-for-granted world. The loss of casualness signals a break in the routines and, at least, potentially a threat to the taken-for-granted reality" (*The Social Construction of Reality,* Doubleday, 1967, p. 172).

Are there others like me through the walls? I try to break the wall, but it yields to my force, then rebounds back in place. What is out there? I'll stay dark and warm, forever? What? Moving now? Turning and turning. Pressure all around. Am I to be crushed? Greater and greater, the pressure builds. The floor is now the ceiling or is it the walls? What is happening? Pressure building. New sounds. Sounds of fear and pain. Pressure building now, four fold building, crushing, building, crushing, then gone, as my atmosphere drains away from me through a hole in the ceiling or floor or is it one of the walls? I feel I shall never know. The walls moving now, getting closer, pressing against me, crushing, squeezing. The hole now opens and begins to engulf me, the walls crushing me, pushing into this hole, into the throat of some great beast. Being swallowed whole. What will I find at the end of this throat? Moving, crushing, why? Then I break free. The light, painful and blinding—am I to be burned by this light? No, too cold, so very cold—am I to freeze? But then comes the pain and I gasp for air and I AM ALIVE!

Eric Capponi (Q)

Within the broad category of "extreme situation," Eric has chosen birth. His text sets up a teasing relationship with its reader, somewhat like a riddle. The "narrator" is generating a moment-by-moment narrative, a text whose emergence, segment by segment, offers itself as *simultaneous with the events it records.* His text is, in effect, a transcript of utterances: unvoiced utterances that move, so to speak, through darkness, asking a lot of questions. The effect is of a text that, from moment to moment, does not know what it is going to be next. It is as if Eric is responding to John Donne's "In the wombe wee have eyes and see not, eares and heare not."[12]

The purpose of a traditional text would be to offer a *typical* representation of what generally happens when people are born in a more or less normal fashion. The purpose of Eric's text is rather to dramatize the experience of one particular birth, and to do it within a participant frame.

A spectator's (or participant-spectator's) account of a birth would assume a responsibility to offer not only a representation of the event but also a "gloss" or evaluation of it—that is, to represent the event as being either typical or atypical, taking its place in our continuously growing sense of what is usual and what is unusual. Think only of Sterne's *Tristram Shandy.* But the participant account has no such responsibility. The purpose of a participant text is simply to offer a specific or particular representation, without contextualization, without evaluation, without explanation.

In keeping with the nature of a participant's point of view, the participant text offers the reader or audience no help at all; for it is, in effect, unaware of audience. It is as if the "speaker" is not in any way concerned to be understood! Hence the text's riddle-like nature. A great deal that any interlocutor in a dialogue would legitimately ask for is simply withheld. For the strategy of the participant text is both to give and to withhold, especially to withhold. The pleasure in reading a text such as Eric's, then, is very similar to that in being given a riddle to solve; it involves a pleasurable degree of uncertainty, of solving, of a slow, teasing penny-dropping; it is the pleasure of actively interpreting, of completing the text, of filling in the tantalizing silences, and overall, of making some kind of coherent sense of the total experience. Did you feel that pleasure as you read it?

# REPRESENTING EXTREME STATES

As Rushdie's text exemplified, "extreme" states—fever, hallucination, nightmare—can legitimately give rise to, find expression in, "extreme" texts; conversely, states of peace, tranquillity, control, can most appropriately be verbalized in texts that are themselves peaceful, tranquil, under control.

We find that we can best help our students to recognize the features of a coherent text by looking at incoherent texts—the meaning lies in the differences. We now present six student texts, all of which represent "deviant" states of mind. Later, in Chapter 8, we will present the hypotactic texts that are companion to these—written by the same students. Meanwhile, see if you can decide how much defensible meaning, sense of context, state of mind, tone, or whatever you can infer from them.

> I don't know. I think. Think I saw it. I think I saw it the other day. It is over there. Don't ask me any more questions about it! I already told you what I know! Last time. Last time I saw it, it was over there. Maybe. Maybe, somebody moved it. Can it be? Since it is no longer there. Perhaps. Perhaps,

she took it with her. Could be. But. But why? Why would she do that? She doesn't. She doesn't have a need for it. I don't think. I don't think she took it. Could it have been? Could it have been moved? To where? To where has it been moved? Somebody could have hid it. Hid it behind there. Why hide it? Why hide it over there. Maybe they didn't want. Want anyone else to use it. Why? I don't know. Leave me. Leave me alone.

Lynn Horn (Q)

Jesus, I am so cold. I can't believe it's morning already. Just went to sleep, damn it. This is the hardest time of the day, and look at these hands tremble, like an old man's. Another chance not to make good. At least John dragged his butt out of here already, I can get in a little wallowing before breakfast. I can't think, that test is going to be a disaster, a humiliation, and it's so fucking easy, what would you have done with this garbage in your better years, ace that shit in a coma, that's right. I got an hour, come on, try and read that book. I really don't want to, don't know if I can, don't know why I can't. God, am I grim, I feel badly most all the time now and I don't know why. Probably fed up with my own laziness. Delancey St. here I come, come hell or high water, there'll always be windshields to clean, be my own boss, go as far as my squeegee can take me. Wonder how I'd look in dreadlocks. Hmm!!

My eyes betray me, I can't read this, I itch all over. I mean I'd like to concentrate, but when I make an effort, every cell in my body clamors for attention, first one, then they all pick up the chorus, and my heart starts to resound like Methodist bells. Only an hour, that's enough. Christ, I didn't even realize I was raising my voice. Feel pretty good as a matter of fact. Aristotle, the theory of the household, all right let's start this brain up. This stuff is so dry, but I'm getting there. Does the boy still have it? Could be, though it's a pale reminder of the past. Yes, it does differ from political authority, old Aristotle's quite right; of course, it wouldn't buy lunch at Chock Full O' Nuts but a valid point just the same.

What do you know, all done, and in thirty minutes, not bad even by my old standards. God no, it just hit me, somehow I hoped it wouldn't. I can't go, don't torture yourself, you know you're not going, if I'm going to ruin my life I'd rather be decisive about it. I feel that pressure seeping away. I won't be unhappy, I'll pull out of this soon, that will be so sweet. Now I've got the whole day, alone, I think I'll try to sleep now, though I know better.

Marc Kieselstein (Q)

Feel weak. My head is ringing. Am unstable. Must try to prevent it from happening again. Oh no! Going to happen! Too late . . . Where am I? At my house. Oh . . . look! There are my parents. I am riding my bicycle. Talking to my friends. Happy. Not with my friends. I am . . . Where am I? I am, wait! Am I back? Oh yes, I am back . . . oh no! Now know where I am. C'mon . . . what is taking so long? Just a matter of time, now. As soon as I can open my eyes. Be rid of this dilemma. Can't wait! Feel the blood rushing back to my head. Can now open my eyes. Can see. Oh yes, the teacher's looking at me. Am lying on the floor. Now fully conscious, though I do feel dizzy. Some students are helping me back to my seat.

Peter Mazzola (Q)

Deer are invisible in a forest covered with snow. The glowing eyes are piercing the night as a pearl. The night is a night of a dancing ball in the forest. The ball is draped with white lace. The deer's masks are invisible in the silent night. The snow is falling silently on the forest encroaching a narrow road. The road becomes a road vanishing at the end of the forest covered with snow. The snow is brightening the cold night. The forest is a breathing creature hiding the invisible deer. The snow is dancing a waltz with an audible rhythm—un, deux, trois, un, deux, trois. The forest orchestrates the waltz echoing in the crisp air—un, deux, trois, un, deux, trois. The deer are dancing the waltz in the forest covered with snow. The deer are merrymakers of the merrymaking in the forest covered with snow. The night is a merriment full of snow. The deer become visible in the forest covered with snow. The snow is falling, falling in the night. The night is glowing in the brightened night. The deer become invisible again. Again the deer are invisible in a forest covered with snow: falling, falling, and falling. . . .

Masaru Matsumoto (Q)

Wow! Imagine right here . . . check it out. . . . It's only us three . . . nice beach. . . . No one else but us three. Is it real? So many, I never saw so many, well actually I never saw any before. But real battleships. It's weird. They're so nice and big and only us three. No one else left. . . . It's like a World War II movie. How can it be? So real! All of them. . . . Wow this is some trip, it feels so real . . . I want to tell them will they know what I mean? What are they thinking of? Is it my eyes? Am I seeing things? Why are there so many right here in the Atlantic Beach Bay? There's the bridge: everything, so desolate, only us three left, what will we do for women? What a trip! It can't be for real! But imagine if it was. Only us three. . . . They don't even know what I'm thinking, they'll think I'm crazy if I tell them. . . . But they're there, right there. (Said slow). How long have I been like this? Haven't said a word for hours . . . was it hours? What time is it? How long have I been here? It started at Joe's house at about nine. I couldn't believe those Snoopys. I never knew it would look like that, just a stamp. Amazing! They think I've freaked. . . . Haven't spoken for so long. I know how my face looks, it must be a face with no expression. Why? They keep asking me what's wrong. . . . How should I know? But I don't know what to say. . . . So I say nothing. . . . Why am I so confused?

. Look at them, look at the bugs . . . I can't keep my eyes off them. . . . They are so many . . . all over . . . so many all over. . . . I feel disgusted. . . . So many under my feet. Everywhere I look, bugs—so many—get them away—you can't even kill them. Stop looking . . . I can't. They're there, all over. I told Joe and Stu. . . . They agree, but why? Are they being nice. . . . They seem to be with me, but somehow it's as though I'm in it alone. Did they take their Snoopys . . . or do they only want to see my reactions. . . .

Taking LSD never done that before. . . . Only once . . . should I have? Got to try everything once. Hey! Freud took it. . . . It opens the mind. I wonder what a shrink would say about my thoughts. . . . What does it all mean? Will these things come back to me in a few years? On TV. . . . In the Movie with the boy and his father. . . . It never left him. . . . The kid always had his trips even though he stopped taking LSD. . . . I hope that won't happen to me. . . . I never seen battleships before. . . . They were there, I know it. It'll be funny when I tell people. . . . They really were there. . . . It really wasn't my bad eyes. . . . Don't forget the aircraft carrier. . . . Are the battleships still in the bay? I can't see from here, in this forest. . . . You can only see trees and all those very ugly bugs. . . .

Where to? following the tread marks . . . where to? Just follow the high-tops. . . . His feet will direct his body. . . . He doesn't even know it. . . . His feet move while he goes, it carries him . . . just follow Stu's feet. Where to? Why here? Wow! what's he doing? Playing golf. . . . Now four. . . . He's old. . . . But Joe keeps faking it. . . . Speak up. . . . Why not? Why don't I say anything? What can I say . . . ?

So boxed in will I ever get out . . . ?

In my hand. . . . It's been through a lot. From the fields, to a factory, to a distributor, and then a local store, where I bought him. . . . Imagine all the places he's been and seen. . . . Even after he will be burnt up, after I've used him, there will still be a part of him left. It's seen what I've seen, it's been with me, close to me while I've tripped. Where is its destiny? He's traveled a lot and when I throw him away, where will he go? Who else will know him? Maybe he will stay here, maybe he will be taken away, without even a word said, no explanation given. All the way from Virginia to N.Y. (via highway 95), and of course, into my hands. He's been through a lot, and his trip is still going. What will be of my cigarette? Will he stay? How many people will know him? . . . Bye. . . . All boxed in like my cigarette was, at least here there are no bugs. . . . Only grass, glorious, beautiful grass, long beautiful hills of grass leading to water. I love water. . . . Should I jump in? . . . It's too far. . . . Everything is too far. . . .

Still the Dead. . . . Okay I can handle it, but, I can't tell one song from the next. . . . It just goes on and on. . . . Wait!!! The music stopped. . . . So has my mind. . . . It's no longer drifting, it also stopped with the music. . . . Music stops trips. . . . The music's back, same Dead, but no trips. . . . Why did the music have to stop? That feels stupid. . . . I can't go back to the way it was, for it isn't the way it was. . . . It is now side II, not side I. . . .

Don Winter (Q)

Ouch! Feel like I'm gonna pass out . . . legs feel weak. Going up these stairs NEVER tired me out before—I'm almost winded! I *must* be sick! Hope I make it home today. Maybe if I eat a little something I won't feel so lousy— where's my orange? Let the car warm up while I'm peeling it—that's all I'd need now, have the car stall out and get rear-ended by someone then bye-bye license.

On the road again . . . stop being silly now and drive! So many trucks on the LIE all the time! Back off! Don't hit me— just because you're bigger gives you no right to pick on me— besides I'm new at this. Exit here. Only sixteen more miles. Why the hell are my palms sweating? Oh yea—the fever. Southern State—hate this curve. Oh, no! Not the buzzing again! There go the legs! Quit shaking! Wow! Feels like I'm on an amusement park ride! Yes, here I am playing with my life on the Southern State—world's largest bumper car ride! Should I get off here and go to the shop! No, they'll only ask questions. If he finds out I drove the car like this he'd get another nervous attack—I don't want to (and can't) deal with that now. I should find out what they want for dinner . . . why'd she have to go now!? Renate doesn't need her there to have a kid anyway! To hell with them, they're big boys now— they can fend for themselves—I'm going to bed! That guy behind me must hate me—I practically cut him off—too bad.

Home. Throw this junk inside and relax. Smells nice, tu-lips are all out, hyacinths are dying—get outside dog! When will they learn to wash dishes?! TEA!!—peppermint—save that one, Earl Grey—yuck! camomile—tonight, mellow-mint —makes me nauseous . . . don't need help in that depart-ment. Get rid of this damn fever with peppermint tea— sweat it out!

It's so nice out, hate to sit around inside. Walk the dog— get fresh air. Can't make it, hate to turn back though. I'm beat—getting that jittery feeling again. Wish Chris were here—feel better when he's around—probably wouldn't do him a hell of a lot of good to see me moping around. Feel like I'm melting from inside out . . . tired too. Why not?! So stupid! Eyes are almost asleep, brain's dead too, hand's next . . . beautiful clouds. . . .

Barbara Schmitt (Q)

# THE STRANGE PARATAXIS OF SHERWOOD ANDERSON

N ow, to end this chapter, we offer an extract from a letter written by Sherwood Anderson, March 1931, to his friend Charles

Bockler. We invite you to read it, to consider how it works on you, for you, and then to compare your reading with our commentary:

*Dear Charles:*

*It is a day when I feel very small. There are days when I am afraid of people. This is one of them. It is cold and bleak outside. I went to the P.O. hoping no one would speak to me. The sky seemed big and the buildings and all the people.*

*I suppose that is why we want women, days like this. We become frightened children again. Women should learn more from their lovers than they do. They should learn from their lovers what children are like.*

*Yesterday was cold and bleak. I went walking with a man here. It was bitter cold. We came to an old brick yard. They had taken the fire from a kiln the day before but it was still hot. We huddled against it out of the cold.*

*A man came along the road, chewing tobacco and spitting. The man told me about him. He is a white man and some years ago married a young white girl of sixteen. Then he went about selling her to Negroes and whites. He lived by selling her. They were both arrested.*

*In court she began pointing out this man and that man. "He sold me to that one, and that one, and that one."*

*All the men in the court room got scared. "She might point at me," they thought, even though they had not been with her. They remembered things they had done. . . .*

*I hope you do not have queer lost days like this but I guess you do have. It is a good thing I guess that women do not get onto us. We are not brave. We are only sometimes bold.*

*I am sure you are like me in that you have such times when you feel yourself just a lost thing floating in some queer kind of emptiness.—S.A.* [13]

## Commentary

We find this letter *oddly* disturbing, *oddly* powerful. When we consider how it is that the text affects us in this way, we conclude that it has a great deal to do with the way the text proceeds, moves forward. The bleakness of what it says—"very small," "afraid of people," "cold and bleak outside," for example—this bleakness is reinforced by the skeletal nature of the text's structures. The "queer kind of emptiness" that Anderson is concerned to express finds its analogue in the silences between the sentences. In those silences there is a void, created by the absence of conjunctions and other connectives. There is a striking antifluency in the disconnectedness, almost a sense of paralysis, of impotence. (Cf. Eliot's "I can connect nothing with nothing" and Forster's "Only connect. . . .") The result is a strong effect of vulnerability, of the writer as "patient" (i.e., as suffering). Hypotaxis would have affirmed, implicitly, a coherent and managerial, even magisterial, sense of a person who can *control* difficult contradictions, getting on top of experience that challenges the self. We are disconcerted because we expect to meet the typical features of a spectator-text, but Anderson *limits* himself to the inherent constraints, perceptual and linguistic, of a participant.

# NOTES

1. Salman Rushdie, *Midnight's Children* (New York: Bard/Avon Books, 1980), p. 249.
2. Roman Jakobson, "Concluding Statement: Linguistics and Poetics," in ed. Thomas A. Sebeok, *Style in Language* (Cambridge, Mass.: M.I.T. Press, 1960). See especially pp. 354–57.
3. On the inherent limitations of the eye in reading, see Walter J. Ong, S.J., *Interfaces of the Word* (Ithaca, N.Y.: Cornell University Press, 1982), Chapter 5; and John Barth, *Lost in the Funhouse* (New York: Bantam Books, 1969). [Authors' Note]
4. Thomas Farrell, "I.Q. and Standard English," *CCC* 34 (December 1983).
5. M. L. West, *Hesiod* (Oxford: Clarendon Press, 1966), p. 186.
6. James Notopoulos, "Parataxis in Homer," *Transactions of the American Philological Association* 80 (1949), p. 1.
7. Eric Auerbach, *Mimesis: The Representation of Reality in Western Literature*, trans. Willard R. Trask (Princeton, N.J.: Princeton University Press, 1974), p. 71.
8. Ibid., p. 70.
9. Ibid., p. 101.
10. Samuel Beckett, *Watt* (New York: Grove Press, 1981), pp. 46–47.
11. Norman Mailer, *Of Women and Their Elegance* (New York: Tor Books, 1981), p. 158.
12. John Donne, *Death's Duell*, sermon preached at White-Hall, Lent, 1630.

    In *Lost in the Funhouse*, John Barth pushed the fiction of utterance even further back in time, and "Night-Sea Journey" is, so to speak, the transcript of the utterance of a sperm on its perilous voyage toward the egg. This is clearly a journey that intrigues Barth, for he returns to it in *Sabbatical* with some dazzling statistics that suggest that part of its fascination for him lies in the way the odds are stacked against success for any individual voyager. The fiction of offering the utterance of a solitary sperm was clearly so difficult for many readers to grasp in 1968 that many reviewers, Barth noted later, insisted on identifying the narrator as a fish!

13. Sherwood Anderson, *Selected Letters*, ed. C. E. Modlin (Knoxville: University of Tennessee Press, 1984).

# CHAPTER EIGHT

# APPLICATIONS
## Writers as Spectators

*Look, stranger, on this. . . .*
*W. H. Auden*

# A SPECTATOR IN ROLE: MALOUF AS A PRIMARY TEXT

Consider, if you will, this extract from David Malouf's novel *An Imaginary Life*, based on what few historical facts are known of the later years of the poet Ovid. After he had offended the emperor, Ovid was exiled to a remote province of the empire, where the natives spoke their own language and knew no Latin. Ovid was lodged with a family, under the keen observation of the father, who may well have been given instructions to kill the exile at a convenient moment.

Ovid is forced to go hunting with the men of the tribe, and one day they capture a feral child, a wild child, reared in the wilderness by animals. The child is brought back to the village, and Ovid is made responsible for his care. The "I" is Ovid.

*Looking at him on occasions, I have a clear glimpse of what he is doing. He is dreaming himself out into the winter countryside. I see him, briefly, moving over the soft snow among the birch trees, chewing strips of bark, kneeling to tear up lichen. I touch his shoulder, and he feels nothing. The black eyes, sunk deep in their sockets, stare through me, to dazzling fields of ice under the wind. When he quickens to a change of weather, it is, I realize now, to the change that comes over a landscape he is moving through in his head. If I thought we might find him again in the spring, I would let him go. But that is impossible. Having brought him in among us there is no way back. Already, in the warmth of the room, he is losing his capacity to withstand cold. For weeks now he has wrapped himself, like the rest of us, in a blanket of hide. Out there he would freeze. Whatever his secret was, I have taken it from him. He is as vulnerable now as anyone of us, and in that at least—even if the old woman does not see it—he shows himself human at last.*

*As if to prove what I have just perceived, the Child has a fever. Sitting as he does with his knees drawn up, staring, he suddenly pitches over and lies in a faint, but when I move to cover him, he wakes, and almost immediately begins shivering. Huge beads of sweat break out on his brow, his hair drips with it, his whole body streams. And in between the periods of burning, he freezes. I think he has never known before what it is to be cold. His whole body clenches on it, this new feeling, this discovery within himself of what winter means, what it is to be snow and ice, to feel oneself enter the realm of absolute cold, that polar world at the body's limits. He draws his knees up, closing upon himself. Every muscle in his limbs, his shoulders, his neck, goes rigid, his fists clench, his jaws tighten. He looms terrified, and when the convulsions begin I have to hold him, forcing a knife handle between his teeth, while he jerks, stiffens, goes through a whole series of spasms, and then sinks exhausted into a kind of nerveless sleep. Then again, the sweating. As I raise him in my arms and try to force a few drops of water between his lips, I am reminded of my brother, and realize what he means to me this Child, what it might mean to lose him.*

*The old woman watches from across the room. I know what she is thinking. This is no ordinary fever. The Child is wrestling with his demon, the animal spirit who protected him out there in the forest, and is fighting now to get back. When I appeal to her for some sort of medicine, some of the herbs she gathers and makes potions of, she shakes her head and turns her thumb down, spitting. I have to watch the Child day and night. If she thought for even a moment that the spirit might triumph and enter the Child's body again, she would cut his throat. I know it.*

*But the younger woman, who has a child of her own and is soft-hearted, cannot bear to see the boy writhe as he does, and sweat, and shiver, and jerk about under the rugs. Secretly she brings me food for him and a bowl of clean water.*

*I hear the old woman arguing with her, and I know what she is saying. What if the Child gave up the struggle, and we found ourselves shut up here with the giant white wolf who is his familiar, and who might at any moment succeed in filling the Child's body and then breaking out of it. The fever, she believes, is part of the painful transformation. The Child's blood boils and freezes, as drop by drop it is being changed. The Child's belly cringes for the raw meat that is the wolf's diet. His limbs strain to grow claws. His jaw clenches against the growing there of fangs. And what if it isn't a wolf after all? But some other beast? Larger, more terrible than even she can imagine.*

*The young woman quails. And I see a new doubt has been sown in her mind. What if the beast, finding the Child too difficult to conquer, chose the body of her own son instead? It would be so easy. While we are all sleeping, our bodies empty in the dark, the Child's spirit slips out, crosses the room, enters her son's body—and there, it is done!*

*For two whole days the young woman refuses to come near us. She watches the Child, she watches her son, she keeps the boy as far from our corner of the room as possible, while the old woman whispers and flaps about between us.*

*But in the dead of night, when the Child's fever is at its crisis, and I am forced to call for help, it is the younger woman who stirs in the dark, wraps herself in her cloak, and comes with water. I am desperately tired and through sheer exhaustion, after nearly five days of watching, seem always on the edge of tears. My hand shakes so much that I cannot lift the bowl to the Child's lips.*

*She takes it from me. Kneels. Lifts the boy's head, letting him gulp at the coolness, and when she has laid his head back on the pile of rags I have contrived for a pillow, sits fanning him, while I rest for a moment against the wall and sleep. When I start awake again she is still there, her face just visible in the folds of the cloak. She sits perfectly upright, her hand moving back and forth to make a breeze. She nods, indicating that I may sleep again, and immediately I fall back into my body's depths.*

*In the early morning light that seeps in through the window cracks, I wake to find her holding the Child in one of his fits. She looks frightened, and I know that this is the real moment of crisis. I know too what it is she fears.*

*The Child's body jerks, loosens, his limbs fly about, . . .*[1]

Malouf's text is an ideal complement to that of Rushdie on pages 141–142. In relation to the abnormal frame of hallucinatory fever, Rushdie's protagonist is a participant, and Rushdie's text creates the feverish illusion of itself coming from inside the fever. Conversely, Malouf's Ovid, in relation to the fever, is a spectator (although he is nevertheless the main participant in the child's care and cure).

The very alertness, self-discipline, control, scrupulous attentiveness, and concern for consequences that characterize Ovid's watch over the child—these are also present in the representation of them—the text. Rushdie's and Malouf's prose could not be more dissimilar, and each illuminates the other.

Ovid, then, in relation to the child's fever, is a spectator. What features of his utterances (who, indeed, is he "talking" to?) confirm, consort with, his spectator role? Let's consider a single sentence:

*He looks terrified, and when the convulsions begin I have to hold him, forcing a knife handle between his teeth, while he jerks, stiffens, goes through a whole series of spasms, and then sinks exhausted into a kind of nerveless sleep.*

This is a complex hypotactic sentence, in which the main clauses are starkly simple: "He looks terrified" and "I have to hold him." A paratactic text would hold on to that kind of severe plainness. But Malouf's hypotaxis impels us into a strong and affecting torrent of all that surrounds, resists, and complicates the simple act of holding: the knife between the teeth, the jerking, the stiffening, the series of spasms, and the closure of exhaustion and sleep. It is a very knowing account, and the knowingness can belong only to the spectator; the participant can know little or nothing of it, let alone give an account of it.

Why, then, is Malouf's narrative cast in the *present* tense? Precisely because, for suspense, for pity and terror, it is important for the reader that Ovid (the narrator) should *not* know the outcome of the event. If the child is more in the dark than Ovid, then Ovid must be more in the dark than the reader. Malouf's readers do not know the outcome (unless they have cheated and looked ahead in the book); how much less so can Ovid, as he struggles to save the child. Even as he utters the words, he struggles against the odds. The effect is one of almost unbearable immediacy—as if we were ourselves witnessing the event, directly and not through the mediations of written language.

# THE SHIFT FROM PARATAXIS TO HYPOTAXIS

W hen students have registered and appreciated the dissimilarities of the Rushdie and Malouf texts, they can be invited to try their hand at producing contrastive interacting texts; one riddlingly participant, characterized by a noncontextualized immediacy, a hurly-burly of impressions and effects, and mostly paratactic; the other cooler, more detached, availing itself of the larger view of hindsight, reflecting from a distance, evaluating, considering, and inevitably finding expression in structures that are hypotactic, that represent significant connections and relationships.

Whereas the term "parataxis" derives from the Greek for the act of placing side by side (a spatial metaphor for a temporal sequence), the term "hypotaxis" refers rather to the act of arranging under—what is usually called subordination. One involves the tactic of apposition, the other a vertical ordering, a perspective of relative emphases and of a variety of relationships between the various parts, some of which are dominant and others subsidiary.

When children offer us paratactic utterances, we intuitively translate them, when appropriate, into hypotactic forms. In other words, we transform them in accordance with our sense of the interconnectedness and interdependence of the world. Conversely, when we offer children hypotaxis, what they often have to do is to try to construe our utterances paratactically. For if, as Notopoulos has argued, parataxis is "a state of mind," how much more so is hypotaxis!

The shift from exclusive parataxis toward hypotaxis is a crucial one in the development of any syntax and in the development of every individual. As G. W. Turner has observed:

> *If we had to decide which of the legacies of Ancient Greece has meant most to Europe and mankind, we might well nominate the complex sentence. Along with Greek philosophy, there grew up a language able to express its fine distinctions and carefully ordered thought. Early and popular writing in any country is close to spoken style, with loose paratactic sentences. . . . The loss of intonation in writing leaves paratactic sentences rather bare. G. Vinokur writes of the early popular Russian sentence that it is "decentralized" and lacks "syntactic perspective." The word "perspective" describes well the effect of subordination of clauses in the complex hypotactic sentence which the Greeks first taught Europe to write.*[2]

If, then, despite your possible uncertainty about the relevance or usefulness of these distinctions between what appear to be two polarized options (an uncertainty qualified perhaps by your respect for Auerbach and your interest in stylistics), if, despite these rather shadowy reservations, you have followed this sentence to this point, you have been involved precisely in an experience of hypotaxis.

When we say of someone, "He talks like a book," it may well be that we are paying recognition to the presence of hypotaxis in utterance rather than to an exotic or extravagant lexicon. Of course, hypotaxis can and does feature in utterance, and a text, conversely, can be paratactic; and Turner affirms this. But the basic distinction stands. Writing as a medium enables and facilitates hypotactic structures that, as addressee/reader, we can cope with precisely because we not only build up a body of intuitive expectations about what prose "sounds like," but also because we can read in any way we choose—as recursively as need be in order to effect a synthesis of the various parts of a text and of their relationships, their ways of being interconnected.

# PARATAXIS/HYPOTAXIS AS MANIFESTATIONS OF PARTICIPATION/ SPECTATORSHIP

Our working hypothesis is very simple. (It's a "working" hypothesis in two senses: it is what we work with; and it appears to work for our students, even before they have discovered *explicitly* what it is.) On the whole, participant roles tend to generate paratactic forms;

and spectator roles tend, conversely, to generate hypotactic forms. While we are ready to agree that it is desirable for students to master the more complex reaches of hypotaxis,* we wish to respect the fact that an understanding of each is to be found in their differences. Thus, recognition of the virtues and value of hypotaxis may best be found through recognition of its differences from parataxis, and vice versa. Sometimes we recognize X more clearly when we see it not so much as X but rather as not-Y.

By putting students, or getting them to put themselves, into situations that generate particular states of mind, we bring them to a place inside their heads wherein certain structures become both appropriate and necessary. To put it another way, we compel them to work from the inside out, rather than from the outside in. For all their elegance and apparent ingenuity, most sentence-combining exercises seem to us of very limited value; at worst, they treat language as cosmetic, structure as manipulation. Our way is undeniably more complex and more demanding, at least in its early stages, where we may encounter eddies of confusion and skepticism; but in the longer term it seems to us to involve the students in insight rather than outsight.

Consider again the case of participants generating utterances, inner or outer, unspoken or spoken; within a situation, a happening; they experience it and verbalize it as it is happening; they are stuck in immediacy; their powers of prediction are curtailed. In an image, they see the trees, close up against their faces, but they cannot see the wood as a spectator on the other side of the valley can. Like Dante, they find themselves (or fail to find themselves) in the midst of a dark wood. Inevitably, utterances will come piecemeal, step by step; they cannot represent what is going to happen next because it has not yet happened and they cannot yet know what it will be.

Their utterances, then, will be to a great degree disconnected and snatched. They discover and represent each item, each constituent, each segment as they proceed, inch by inch. Disjointedness and an extreme of discrete particularity—these are criterial features of the situation as experienced and as represented at the time. It is all phenomenal.

The spectator, conversely, enjoys a profoundly different perception of that event. It is neatly framed by distance—either spatial or temporal—and the spectator perceives not only the larger form of the whole but

*The whole question of a *terminus ad quem* is fascinating but problematic. The notion of "the mature sentence" is inherently problematic. Mature talkers and writers play freely across both hypotaxis and parataxis according to the needs of the discourse. Notions and criteria of maturity—as of immaturity—must, to be useful, remain contextualized in terms of the individual student's development and of the responsibilities of the particular type of discourse.

also the ways in which the parts come together to make up the whole. This cohering is inherent in the stance we occupy as spectators and is available to us even before we move to verbalize. Even as we contemplate that distant wood, we can reflect on whether we find it attractive or repellent, inviting or forbidding. We have the freedom, the leisure, the distance.

As spectators, we do not have to make up connections; the connections are inherent in our act of perceiving. We recognize something "as something"; as Walker Percy says, "It is not enough to say that one is conscious *of* something; one is also conscious of something being something."[3]

# FORMS OF SPECTATORSHIP: SIX STUDENT TEXTS

We invite you now to share the spectator counterparts of the six student texts presented in Chapter 7. First is that of Lynn, whose paratactic text appeared on pages 153–154.

> He was always somewhat slow in learning. By now we thought he had made some progress. However, it was those drugs he had purchased on the street which set back all the progress we had made. From the next room I observed him in a conversation with his mother. All that she wanted to know was if he knew where her calculator was. He couldn't give her a clear response. He was hopeless. When she asked him additional questions, his answers, if any, were quite curt. There was no way to reach him. It was as if he was in another world. He strained for the sentences to come out of his mouth. Every sentence was a struggle for him. It was such a sad sight. I wanted to kill those men who had sold him those drugs. They had ruined all the progress we had made through the years.
>
> Lynn Horn (Q)

When we compare Lynn's two texts, what do we find? Why do they strike us as successful, effective writing?

Take the spectator text first. It is presumably intended as a report or comment by a nurse, psychiatric social worker, or drug rehabilitation worker on the person who is speaking in the earlier text. It has the features of mature, adult discourse, both spoken and written: there is the use of fairly subtle modifiers—"somewhat slow," "some progress"— to express degree; there is contextualization, both general (in terms of the patient's history) and specific (the conversation with the mother); and there is a sense of genuine involvement in the well-being of the patient, so that the writer allows herself to express anger and distress, even to the point of hyperbole. Her text is not purely clinical, not totally constrained by institutional conventions; personal attachment breaks in.

Lynn's participant text, on the other hand, is a successful *impersonation* of a disjointed, incoherent speaker. The "voice" that Lynn has invented expresses a strong sense of confusion and disorientation, giving the reader some hard work in the effort to make sense.

In other words, Lynn's participant text is entirely indifferent to any audience: the voice is almost talking to itself; the text, although "spoken," is close to confused, dislocated inner speech. Her spectator text, conversely, is attentive to the needs of its audience.

Here now is Marc's spectator text; its companion piece is to be found on pages 154–155.

Some mornings he woke up broken-hearted, because some nights he dreamed of a better world. That morning he woke up shaking with fear, breathing only with conscious effort. He drew his knees up to his chest, leaned back against the cold metal of the lifeless radiator. He was grateful to see his roommate gone; self-pity struck him as unseemly, grief as an imposition on others, tears as weakness, depression as sickness. Unable to gather his thoughts, he looked at the ice blue sky, the thin cirrus glittering like crystal. Almost perfect, yet marred in a horrible way by the scalding sun, which *rammed right through* the cracks in the shutter, pressing on him, revealing things right and left. When it was dark, he never thought about the dawn, so when dawn came he was more than dismayed.

A book was open in front of him but he did not read, could not comprehend the words. When he looked at them, they spun around and poured together, and very soon his mind was elsewhere. In the future. Light years away, where he was successful and smiling and arrogant, where kindness to others was a gesture of magnanimity, not a half-starved prayer for acceptance. The future is vindication of the past. The present is each day's climb up the wall of a pressure cooker. Some get out, some push back, some implode with failure. He cowered in the corner; what else was he trained to do?

Suddenly an unexpected surge of resolve, rare, not unprecedented. It marches in like an army of liberation; always deserts him without warning. He focuses his eyes and slowly scans the lines, reading out loud in a halting, child's voice. One hour till his test, fifty pages to be understood and tucked away. His pace increases, he experiences a joyful reunion with concentration. He is sailing along now, analyzing, integrating, seeing subtleties as clear as day. Half an hour and his work is done. He closes the book and panic rises up inside him, hissing in his ears, a snake. Who can see where it starts, probably someplace insignificant, obscure as the stream that is the source of the Nile, but becoming just as deep and murky and relentless. He needs to yell out, but people will hear, perhaps they will come running. Has he forgotten everything he just read? He pulls the blanket over his eyes. The sun rams through; he hopes sleep will return, he knows better.

Marc Kieselstein (Q)

Consider the following questions in relation to Marc's two texts:

Which is the more difficult to get into?

Which is more clearly contextualized?

Which is slangier?

Which is more public and which more private?

Which do you find more predictable?

Which is closer to the jumble of inner speech?

You may care to correlate your answers to these various questions. For example, is the more slangy text also the less predictable? Is the less slangy text the one that is also more clearly contextualized?

Here now are Peter's three different spectator texts to correlate with his participant text on page 155.

Former participant, now distant from the event:

I had not been feeling very well that day. I didn't have much for breakfast and felt pangs of hunger throughout the day. I also felt rather lethargic. Perhaps it was due to the hot weather, for the event occurred on a hot day in June. As with all my fainting spells, I lost all recognition of where I was. To my dismay, when I woke up, I did indeed find myself on the floor of the classroom. The entire ordeal led to a somewhat embarrassing situation. I am now glad the event is over with.

A friendly, well-disposed other spectator:

He was sitting there in his seat at his desk, when all of a sudden his head began to drop. He had a long and pale look about his face. He started wobbling in his seat, and, before I knew it, he fell to the ground altogether. At first, I didn't take him seriously. I thought this was all some sort of bizarre joke, for he had been known at times to kid around in class. I watched him lying on the floor. His eyes began to move in a peculiar way. Strange grunting sounds came out of his mouth, almost as though he had been choking on some food. Finally, some of us had to help him back to his seat. That was the only time I had ever seen him do that.

A clinical reporter:

The patient appears to have been suffering a chronic series of faintings. He claims that he is always aware of when he might faint. He was observed at first as trying to prevent himself from fainting by the standard procedure of bending his head down between his legs and pressing his thumbs against his eyes, in order to bring the bloodflow back into his head. He showed no signs of consciousness when he fell on the floor, and, except for a few slight sounds and twitches in the eyes, remained perfectly still. No negative side effects have been found in the patient. His recovery period is very fast.

Peter Mazzola (Q)

The following is Masaru's spectator text, counterpart to the participant text on page 155. It is a *neutral* account of a traveler struggling through deep snow, at night. The observer does not know what is going on inside the traveler's head, so in offering an account of how the traveler feels, his inner state, his state of mind, the observer has to use such verbs as "seems." (In other words, the spectator is inferring.)

In the participant text, the reader *enters the mind of the traveler* as he becomes more and more exhausted and begins to hallucinate. (One of the most peculiar and surprising features of exposure is that it creates a strong sense of euphoria in the victim, who feels good and drifts into a pleasant world of fantasy.)

> As he walks a narrow road with snow accumulating during the night, he seems to be growing weak, and his steps begin to slow down. The snow is falling silently and incessantly. The snow-covered forest stands still on both sides of the road. The whiteness of the snow somehow brightens the night. He holds a shovel in his right hand and drapes a blanket on his head. Whitened by snow, it covers his whole body. He does not show any signs of fear, though the shivering cold air creeps into his body. His tread seems stable but slow. He seems to be breathing regularly but a bit rapidly. The snow is still falling silently. He slouches forward. His legs are sucked into the accumulated snow. It is now more than two feet high. His movement becomes stagnant. His breath is frozen in the icy air. He falls down on the soft virgin snow.
>
> Masaru Matsumoto (Q)

Here now are Don's and Barbara's spectator texts, companions to the participant texts that appeared on pages 156–158.

## A LOOK BACK (TO A DIFFERENT TIME)

I assume it all started when I was 16, a time when most teenagers experiment with different things: I at the time happened to be doing it with drugs. It was at a time when I used to say "Hey, I'll try anything once." It started with marijuana, to give me that so-called "high," that sense of "euphoria." I never did like it, I felt greater highs from just being myself. My opinion of pot, as I remember it, was contradictory to the opinions of my friends—who insisted on feeling so wasted.

From marijuana, the stepping-stone to more severe drugs, I encountered various outrageous drugs: Hash, Mesk, Ludes, Speed are some of the many drugs I encountered. It may be hard to believe, may even be impossible to believe, but I did stick to my "only once" theme—with the exception of alcohol, which will always be present to some degree.

The question was, Where should it all end? When would I stop my experimentations? Was I so overly obsessed with trying everything? Were these experiments a manifestation of a compulsive-obsessive personality: a person who constantly had to struggle to find new experimental drugs? It got to the point where my high wasn't even derived from the drug itself. The thrill came from the feeling of trying something new—waiting in anticipation for its effects to play with my body and mind—that in itself was the high (the rest was merely an addition).

I knew it had to stop somewhere, but as a compulsive person on a conscious level, that somewhere was not visible (in my future). I, like the compulsive shoplifter, "will never get caught, and will never stop," even though it was inevitable. So like the shoplifter, he does stop somewhere— he is caught! The drug abuser also stops, somewhere down the line, due to various reasons (death, overdose). I fortunately was able to assess what was happening to me, from a vantage point not merely my own. I was able to view myself as though I was an outsider giving myself a rational assessment to conquer my problem.

I decided to stop my foolishness of experimenting after I encountered LSD (acid), on a stamp called Snoopy. SNOOPY, what a peculiar name for a drug! My previous amusement at the Charles Schultz character, with all its memories of youth, had suddenly represented something different. This Snoopy was not the same Snoopy I adored and loved in all the cartoons I viewed, but on the contrary, I began to despise it for all the new things it represented. It no longer gave pleasure to its viewers, but more or less began to hurt its users.

Snoopy with its broad, cute smile had actually turned, in my eyes, into a cruel and vicious smile. It had the same smile identical to the ones I've loved, but now in a very different context. Its smile was now equivalent to that of a psychopathic killer. (The psychopathic killer also has a smile, but drastically different from an ordinary smile that we're accustomed to seeing.)

In any case, it was after my experience with LSD that I became aware that I had truly lost control. I felt my only salvation was my ability not to lose a total grip on reality: No matter how minute the grip may be, it must exist—for if it doesn't there is no explanation for our thoughts, and that would surely drive us mad. Seeing battleships, bugs taking over, seeing bodies carried by feet, without interpretations, or any explanations I would have surely gone insane. It is that touch with reality that enables us to have realistic interpretations of our absurd thoughts.

I know now, that to lose touch with reality would, in essence, be to lose a great part of myself. All the images I saw were, surely, signs of a lost mind, but my ability to realize that they were merely images was my salvation. It is through, and only through an outsider's view (point) that one can really see what is happening.

Don Winter (Q)


## REFLECTIONS ON A FEVER

I absolutely despise being ill! The mere thought of lying in bed all day sets my nerves aquiver. Wasting time is not one of my favorite pastimes, and to my mind, any sickness which involves bedrest is a waste of the worst kind. This would explain my disgust when I found myself caught in the grasp of the 72-hour flu a short while ago.

It began suddenly, totally without warning, on Monday, the 7th of May. I came perilously close to passing out over a lump of clay in my sculpture class. My professor noticed that I wasn't faring well and sent me home, promising that I would feel much better next week. Not feeling up to facing a 2-hour odyssey in order to get home, I stayed at my aunt's home overnight.

Tuesday May 8th. The world seemed much brighter this day, so I decided to make a go of school one more time. Silly me! I had completely forgotten that sickness only strikes later in the day—unless you're terribly ill, you don't notice not feeling well at 6 A.M. (In my case, I attribute any ill feelings to the ridiculous hour at which I had to rouse myself from a peaceful slumber and comfortable bed!) Anyway, I made it to school just in time for my 8:00 A.M. Scuba class, jumped in the pool, swam 36 laps, and nearly lost my meager breakfast on the deck. I sat out the rest of the class.

My discomfort worsened steadily. By 12:30—time for English—I was thoroughly blitzed; the fever, though mild, was taking its toll on my feeble mind. Thanks to my *extremely kindhearted* professor, I began the dreaded journey homeward.

My head was throbbing and I was getting very lightheaded. My legs were shaking—I could almost feel the power draining from them. I felt panic begin to well up inside me, but managed to stifle it by singing silly songs and talking to myself. Feeling moderately well, I continued driving home—praying that I'd make it there with the car intact,

I almost made it! Only 8 miles to home-base, when the mild hallucinations started. I felt as though I were in a dreamworld. Things looked a little fuzzy around the edges —almost like looking through a fish-eye lens. I felt as if I was on some sort of amusement park ride—the swaying of the car as it hit imperfections on the surface of the road added to the sensation. Lucky for me I was thinking more in terms of a roller coaster than the bumper cars! That passed, but was soon followed by "The Attack of the Orange Baron(ess)." In my Sopwith Chevelle Wagon (equipped with a toy machine gun which my brother had, in a playful mood, taped to the dashboard) I pursued and "shot down" many an enemy Oldsmobile and Cadillac (the most hideous cars on the road—their drivers are no bargain either). This too passed, though I was kind of sorry to have the feeling go—I was getting used to it. After this, the last leg of my trip was completed without further event.

Home at last! I threw my books into a corner and staggered into the kitchen. There, to my surprise and delight, I discovered about ten containers of tea. I lost no time in finding the one I wanted and putting a kettle of water on the stove to boil. Next mistake. Thinking, which I should never do when ill—it hurts and the results are lousy—that I had time for a short walk around the block with the dog while the water was heating, I stepped out into the fresh air in an attempt to enjoy, for at least a short time, this bright and sunny day. No such luck! I wasn't more than 30 yards from the house when the dizziness hit me and I was forced to return home.

I soon found myself comfortably in bed with a steaming pot of peppermint tea at my bedside. I was sweating so intensely now, from the fever, that I thought for sure that I'd melt. I could picture my father coming home, only to find a small pool of water that my mattress couldn't absorb. I took a sip of tea and snapped back into reality, momentarily. The clouds were drifting lazily across the sky. My eyelids drooped as I watched them. I was trying to write, but my brain wasn't into it, so it fell asleep, taking with it the use of my hands and eyes and leaving me with only the vague memories of billowy clouds and blue skies.

Barbara Schmitt (Q)

# A PUBLIC VERSUS A PRIVATE VOICE

Here now are two texts that set up an amusing contrast between the explicit public event, a theater performance of *Hamlet*, and an implicit private event. In each case, the text offers the reader "high culture" through the overt public voice and a subversive "subculture" through the covert private voice.[4]

CAST:  *King* and *Polonius*, speaking onstage
       *Spectator*, a member of the audience, speaking *sotto voce*

Pol.:  The ambassadors from Norway, my good lord, are joyfully returned.

Spec.:  I don't think I can wait till intermission, I have to go to the bathroom so bad. And I can hardly breathe—my allergy's acting up. Must be I'm allergic to the perfume of this woman next to me.

King:  Thou still has been the father of good news.

Spec.:  I'll tell you what will be good news: the end of this play'll be good news, that's what!

Pol.:  Have I, my lord? Assure you, my liege, I hold my duty as I hold
      my soul,
both to my God and to my gracious King;
And I do think or else this brain of mine
Hunts not the trail of policy so sure
As it hath used to do, that I have found
The very cause of Hamlet's lunacy.

Spec.:  Let me tell you, Hamlet's not the only one that's loony. I'm getting there, too. Boy, I can't sit still much longer: my bladder's about to explode. Now my eyes are beginning to run, with this stupid woman's perfume.

King:  O, speak of that! That do I long to hear.

*Spec.:*  I don't think I can sit here any longer. I'm going to get into one of my sneezing fits soon. Ouch! That hurt, lady! I swear if she elbows me one more time in my side, I'll knock her silly-looking hat off her head. Or, better yet, I'll step on her foot on my way to the bathroom.

*Pol.:*  Give first admittance to the ambassadors.
My news shall be the fruit to that great feast. *(Exit)*

*Spec.:*  Well, if Polonius can leave, I guess I can too. Now's my chance to get even with this lady who made my evening miserable.

Doris Karcic (Q)

In the next text, Doris represents the *public* and *private* voices of the same person: the actor playing Polonius. The contrast between the two voices is well sustained; and the intrusion of the actor's "inner speech" serves to make his prescribed lines sound artificial and strained, reminding us that actors speaking their lines are involved in an impersonation that may have very little to do with their private selves.

CAST:  *King* and *Polonius,* speaking out loud
*Actor* (the actor playing Polonius), speaking *sotto voce*

*Pol.:*  The ambassadors from Norway, my good lord, are joyfully returned.

*Actor:*  I'm so tired! I knew I shouldn't have stayed out so late last night: oh, that party was wild. And that girl was something else! I wonder if she came to see me perform tonight?

*King:*  Thou still hast been the father of good news.

*Actor:*  Oh, my God! I think that's her! The one in the third row, in the end seat! Jesus, I'm getting nervous. I must control myself. If I make a mess of my next speech, I'll die.

*Pol.:*  Have I, my lord? Assure you, my good liege, I hold my duty as I hold my soul, both to my God and to my gracious King;
And I do think or else this brain of mine
Hunts not the trail of policy so sure
As it hath used to do, that I have found
The very cause of Hamlet's lunacy.

*Actor:*  Phew! No mistakes! I hope she's impressed. I wonder if she thinks I look sexy in these tight pants.

*King:*  O, speak of that! That do I long to hear.

*Actor:*  Oh no! I'm starting to sweat. Much earlier than usual. It must be these lights that do it; and the girls. Thank God my exit is coming up.

*Pol.:*  Give first admittance to the ambassadors.
My news shall be the fruit to that great feast. *(Exit)*

Doris Karcic (Q)

# PARATAXIS AND HYPOTAXIS: SOME CLOSING OBSERVATIONS

Finally, we would like to share with you some random thoughts on parataxis and hypotaxis, their characteristics and uses:

1. Cartoon strips are paratactic: A and B and C and D and E. The reader/viewer is left to infer the hypotactic connectives (therefore, because). Generally, these take the form of cause and effect, sometimes used ironically or for surprise (as in Hart's *B.C.*).

2. Popular newspapers use a mostly paratactic prose style — presumably because of the assumptions made about their readers (the targeted reading age of most pop journalism is about 11 years) but also for the effect of immediacy (as in the Pow! Zap! of cartoon strips).

3. Ted Hughes' *Crow* poems are a sustained exercise in parataxis. The effect of this is to reinforce the "absurd" comic-strip tone, in tension with the echo of the parataxis of Genesis.

4. Beckett is the great twentieth-century master of parataxis. Much of the austere power of his prose derives from the fact that it reads as a transcript of the utterances of a participant. Beckett discovered the strength of parataxis (and of the states of mind that it signifies) when he read the *Journals* of Jules Renard, the French novelist. He was so struck by the spare strength of Renard's prose that when he read Renard's entry for April 7, 1910 — the last entry — he felt compelled to repeat it again and again: "Last night I wanted to get up. Dead weight. A leg hangs outside. Then a trickle runs down my leg. I allow

it to reach my heel before I make up my mind. It will dry in the sheets."[5]

5. Perry Meisel, in a comment on an earlier draft of this book, proposed that while comic strips, *Crow,* and Beckett's prose are all ostensibly paratactic, they all depend on an implicit hypotaxis, on being placed within hypotactic frames.

6. When informal conversation moves into *discussion,* it drifts from parataxis to hypotaxis.

7. Writing is always potentially hypotactic. The act of writing (as opposed to utterance) is a condition in which one has the time and often the predisposition to consider, to reflect, to tease out connections. When one chooses or feels the need to explore a question in writing, it is because one needs the resources of hypotaxis—the connections, the subordinations, the patterning.

8. Hypotaxis is a symptom, a sign of the power of the ordering mind; of the coherent possibilities, the recuperations,* of detachment. We can offer no more eloquent case than that of Wordsworth's *Prelude.* In this brief extract, on the solace of reading during adolescence, the perturbation and the reassurance are both present in the syntax. Experience that was earlier confusing is now recollected in tranquillity and coherence —the privileges of the spectator. For emphasis Wordsworth exploits the direct, unconditional force of parataxis, in lines 4, 28–32, and 42.

> *A gracious spirit o'er this earth presides,*
> *And o'er the heart of man: invisibly*
> *It comes, directing those to works of love*
> *Who care not, know not, think not, what they do.*
> *The tales that charm away the wakeful night*      5
> *In Araby—romances, legends penned*
> *For solace by the light of monkish lamps;*
> *Fictions, for ladies of their love, devised*
> *By youthful squires; adventures endless, spun*
> *By the dismantled warrior in old age*      10
> *Out of the bowels of those very thoughts*
> *In which his youth did first extravagate—*

---

*We are grateful to Perry Meisel for this word.

These spread like day, and something in the shape
Of these will live till man shall be no more.
Dumb yearnings, hidden appetites, are ours,                    15
And they must have their food. Our childhood sits,
Our simple childhood, sits upon a throne
That hath more power than all the elements.
I guess not what this tells of being past,
Not what it augurs of the life to come,                        20
But so it is; and in that dubious hour,
That twilight when we first begin to see
This dawning earth, to recognise, expect—
And in the long probation that ensues,
The time of trial ere we learn to live                         25
In reconcilement with our stinted powers,
To endure this state of meagre vassalage,
Unwilling to forego, confess, submit,
Uneasy and unsettled, yoke-fellows
To custom, mettlesome and not yet tamed                        30
And humbled down—oh, then we feel, we feel,
We know, when we have friends. Ye dreamers, then,
Forgers of lawless tales, we bless you then—
Impostors, drivellers, dotards, as the ape
Philosophy will call you—then we feel                          35
With what, and how great might ye are in league,
Who make our wish our power, our thought a deed,
An empire, a possession. Ye whom time
And seasons serve—all faculties—to whom
Earth crouches, th' elements are potter's clay,                40
Space like a heaven filled up with northern lights,
Here, nowhere, there, and everywhere at once.[5]

# NOTES

1. David Malouf, *An Imaginary Life* (London: Picador, 1980), pp. 114–17.
2. G. W. Turner, *Stylistics* (Harmondsworth: Penguin, 1973), p. 71.
3. Walker Percy, "Symbol, Consciousness and Intersubjectivity," *Journal of Philosophy* 55 (1958).
4. Cf. John Barth: "Even the most Stanislavsky-methodist would presumably if questioned closely recollect his offstage identity even onstage in mid-act. . . . It was of course imaginable that much goes on in the mind of King Oedipus in addition to his spoken sentiments; any number of interior dramas might be played out in the actors' or characters' minds. . . ." "Life-Story," in *Lost in the Funhouse* (New York: Bantam Books, 1969), p. 117.
5. Jules Renard, *The Journals of Jules Renard,* ed. and trans. Louise Bogan and Elizabeth Roget (New York: Braziller, 1964), p. 248.
6. William Wordsworth, *The Prelude,* 1799, 1805, 1850, ed. Jonathan Wordsworth, M. H. Abrams, and Stephen Gill (New York: Norton, 1979), p. 178.

# CHAPTER NINE

# GENERATIVE FRAME

## *Role*

*. . . to bring his feelings near to those of the persons whose feelings he describes, nay, for short spaces of time, perhaps, to let himself slip into an entire delusion, and even confound and identify his own feelings with theirs. . . .*
                    *Wordsworth*

# FORMS OF ROLE

When our students produced their "Wodwo" texts, they were writing in role; when Lynn wrote her two pieces—the participant text on pages 153–154 and the spectator text on page 170, she was writing in role.

What, then, *is* role? Why and how is it useful? To what desired ends do we use it?

In her remarkable novel *Memoirs of Hadrian*, Marguerite Yourcenar has her old dying emperor recall his early training:

> As for the rhetorical exercises in which we were successively Xerxes
> and Themistocles, Octavius and Mark Antony, they intoxicated
> me: I felt like Proteus.[1]

And Norman Mailer has observed that "the psychological heft of a role has more existential presence than daily life."[2] It is worth noting that Yourcenar has Hadrian frame his memory not as "We pretended to be" or as "We acted the parts of," but rather as "we were," which is the simplest, most unconditional way of expressing "existential presence"—Yourcenar *is* Hadrian.

If texts, simple or complex, modest or ambitious, are manifestations of forms of life, and if a versatile repertoire of states of mind gives rise to a similarly wide range of textual variety and resourcefulness, then the justification for role-work is simply that it is the most effective way of *realizing* a particular form of life and state of mind, and *verbalizing* its appropriate representation as text. Text is end product. What necessarily precedes it? What is necessarily *prior*? We believe it to be a frame of mind that is generated by effectively taking on, or being taken in by, a clearly defined role.

For our present purposes, we wish to distinguish between three main forms of role:

1. *Daily roles:* In daily life, we take on a variety of social functions that we *must* perform. For example, young adults "become" parents and slowly acquire the skills, habits, and mannerisms whereby we identify them as parents. On Saturday afternoons they snatch a break—a grandmother takes on the role of baby-sitter—and they rush off into the role of football fans. Within each day, they switch from one role to another, without even noticing—the shifts have become habituated. The wife is one moment a dentist, the next a vegetable

gardener or an interior decorator; the husband, paid for being an accountant, changes his clothes to become an amateur auto mechanic.[3] But we can object to such categories on the grounds that they are merely various activities, involving no significant social change. At a deeper level, changes of relationship involve much more, the major switch being from private to public function, or vice versa. For students, the shift that concerns us is that into membership of an academic community: the switch into any one or more of a variety of roles that constitute being a student: research roles, academic roles, student roles.

2. *The self idealized in daydreams and fantasies.* Jerome Singer, who has devoted many years of his working life to the study of fantasizing, is inclined to believe that there is almost a conspiracy of silence about fantasy. We can assume, nevertheless, that we all fantasize, transforming ourselves into enlarged, idealized, enhanced selves—more eloquent, more attractive, and so on, even omniscient and omnipotent. Through such fantasy, we reconstruct our past selves retroactively and prepare ourselves for tomorrow. Ah, yes, tomorrow we will do better!

3. *The self as other.* In this form of imagining, it is as if we *become* another. Through a virtual or vicarious entry into another identity, we enjoy the illusion of living other lives. For the readers of this book, the most common form of this kind of role-play is probably in the experience of fiction; for those who don't or can't read, we presume that the repertoire of possibilities is conveniently offered by movies and TV soap operas.

It is clear that fantasy fulfills a crucial function in the evolution of personality in childhood, as the work of D. W. Winnicott so vividly demonstrates.[4] What legitimate place can fantasy find in the lives of our students? Is it not enough that they should be themselves?

What, then, is the actual role of our students *qua students*? As they sit in our classrooms, they are persons under constraint; they are inexperienced writers; they are rusty or underdeveloped readers; they are makers of mistakes, producers of error. That is, to borrow Mailer's term, the nature of their "daily life." One of our first priorities must be to remove them from this disabling and dispiriting role, and nudge them into a variety of vicarious roles that will allow them, force them, to find a strong voice—a voice other than their own "private voice."

# WHAT ROLE DISCOVERS

Consider the following scenario: A class of elementary school children in Northeast England are studying the Roman invasion and its effects on the lives of the native Celts. Half of the class are Romans, and they gather outside the classroom to plan their attack; the others are Celts, who apportion their classroom space: here is our village, here are our livestock, and *here* is the clearing in the trees that is our place of worship, our temple. In due course the Romans burst in with all their material power. The villagers are mostly overwhelmed, but as one Roman goes thundering arrogantly across the place of worship, a Celtic girl springs out at him, bars his path, and raises her hand imperiously. "Stop!" she declaims (it is more than mere saying). "You are treading on holy ground!"

The work of these children was being guided by Dorothy Heathcote, who of all the teachers we know uses role-play to greatest effect. She later observed that the utterance the small girl had produced fell into a category that she chooses to call "epic speech." In the event, it possessed remarkable "psychological heft," and it clearly offered the student and her adversary a sense of intense "existential presence" such as they would rarely enjoy in "real life."

The points that we wish to draw from this exemplary tale are these: first, that the student was *not* acting; second, that the student's utterance was a truth—not in actuality, not in real life, but a truth discovered in or through role, imbued with remarkable moral force, and expressed with a power that was more than merely personal. To raise, in such matters, the question of sincerity is merely to invoke a red herring. What counts is that the words were *meant*. They made marvellous, urgent, intent sense. They had effect. Through role, the small girl joined the community of those who respect holy places, those who resist sacrilege, those who dare to question the claims of Caesar.

Such a case offers us a useful analogy for effective role-play in the making of texts: Strong texts get made through a commitment to role. A well-focused, clearly delineated sense of role, operating within given constraints, sharpens the writer's sense of function; it imparts a bracing, athletic tone; it obliterates all the fuzziness, indeterminacy, and unknowableness of the "real self"; it generates energy, dynamism, a clear sense of audience, and a coherent grasp of all the felt intangibles that make up the context of writing. The key virtue in all this is a kind of inclusive *clarity*. The text that gets made may well be "difficult"—as exemplified in Sakura's text on page 86—but that is not the issue; the mental functions, the acts of mind, the realms of being that were committed to the shaping of that text—these were all *clear*. And it is on their own experience of that sheer clarity that our students can build belief and further commitment. Writers in role create strong texts—that is our case in a nutshell. And given a variety of roles, within a variety of contexts, they can produce a corresponding variety of texts.

As Marguerite Yourcenar's Hadrian observed, the possibilities are protean. Yourcenar's feat of impersonation in her *Memoirs of Hadrian* is, indeed, a supreme example of sustained, coherent role-play. As she remarks, she had to "forget" what he, almost two thousand years before, would have forgotten; and she had to remember in the ways in which he would have remembered.

# TEXTS IN AND OUT OF ROLE: GOING BEYOND THE INFORMATION GIVEN

B ut let us come down from such dizzy heights of role and look at the texts written by two teen-agers in their school history classes:

### *JOSIAH WEDGWOOD 1730–95* *

*Josiah Wedgwood was born in north Staffordshire. He was the 13th son of a master potter. He began work in the family pottery business at the age of 9 years old and was self educated. When he was twelve he contracted small pox, which as a result caused him to have a leg amputated in later life.*

*The pottery industry was already well-established in Staffordshire where there was plenty of clay and coal. However, the pottery produced there was of poor design and texture. Josiah Wedgwood saw possibilities for expansion. Roads and canals allowed easier transport of heavy commodities such as coal and clay since they had been improved, and also allowed safer transit of fragile pottery.*

*The 18th century saw a rise in population and an increase in the standard of living. Tea, chocolate and coffee drinking, already popular with the rich, was becoming the poorer people's habit. The rich wanted high quality ware, while the rest of the population sought less expensive sets of pottery. Plate was expensive, pewter was scarce, porcelain too fragile.*

---

*Written by Clare, aged 15–16.

*Wedgwood's pottery was to supply the needs of all tastes. His success was due to the quality of his produce, his original designs, the specialisation of labour, and his sales organisation. Wedgwood established a new factory at Etruria, near Burslem, in 1769. There using the new discoveries of green glaze, cream-ware and jasper-ware he produced quality goods for the rich. He soon won world fame. The most famous were the elegant vases with a white decoration on the "wedgwood blue" backgrounds. As Italian or classical motifs were in vogue, he employed the great designer, Flatman. Wedgwood used the heads of Popes for goods sold in Spain, Italy and South America. He had a display room at Etruria and in 1765 opened a showroom in London.*

*Wedgwood was a perfectionist. He used to walk around the factory smashing with his stick any piece which was substandard and chalked onto the bench, "This won't do for Josiah Wedgwood." His workers responded well. He increased production by a division of labour. Instead of one man performing every process, Wedgwood employed specialists—some mixed clay, others worked on the potter's wheel, some did the firing and some the glazing.*

*Sales were increased. In order to cater for the popular taste the "willow pattern" was produced. Advertisements appeared in newspapers, discounts were given and catalogues appeared translated in Europe. In his time Wedgwood was called "Vase Maker General to the Universe." Josiah Wedgwood died in 1795 worth £500,000.*[5]

## MY FIRST DAY IN THE WORKHOUSE*

*I woke up on a hard bed with a sheet hardly the size of myself strewn across my body. The bell rang through my head, it rang and rang "Get up you lazy rat no sympathy for new 'uns" was bellowed at me. A push from behind and I was on the hard stone floor. It was cold and burned my skin. I got up and walked towards the crowd gathering at the door. We all had brown smock-like dresses on but the older people had thinner holey ones where they had obviously worked harder.*

*We were all told to go to a room the name of which I didn't catch. Everyone hurried along to the dark damp room where more people, mostly females crouched over wooden tables and ate a sloppy broth that was obviously nasty. We all spread around the wooden tables and in turn collected a bowl from one table and a ladle full of the lumpy food. I sat on the long wooden bench between a young girl*

---

*Written by Jackie, aged 15–16.

who, like the others looked very sad but she had tears in her eyes. On the other side of me sat an older lady about 50 years of age who smelt stale and occasionally broke from slurping her broth to comb her greying hair with her thin dirty hands. The broth was sour and only just warm I forced it down my throat knowing it was probably the first meal for some hours.

I turned my attention towards the girl. She was thin and tears were streaming down her high cheekbones. "What's up" I said hoping to make friends with someone as soon as possible.

She stared at me as though it was my fault and then looked away again.

"Er brothers in the punishment room, 'e was caught drinkin, poor soul, treat ya bad 'ere ya know, ever bin in a workhouse before then" it was the woman from the other side of me who had nudged me from behind.

"No," I answered "never"

"Well you'll have to learn not to speak to your family or they'll punish ya too see" she said scraping her bowl with her hands.

We were all filed out in two different groups, some were to "do the ropes" the others were to "do breaking." I was to do the ropes. Some people were to clear up after the meal and were picked at random. It shocked me that everyone's faces were showing no emotion at all.

I wondered as I walked into a small stone room what the rest of the family were doing. My brother was in a different part of the building and my mother wasn't around at breakfast—we'd been split up.

Doing the ropes was splitting up old ropes to the smallest possible amount. It was a tedious job, my nails broke and my fingers were red. If anyone communicated they were either beaten or dragged out if it was often. After what seemed twelve hours work we had a break. We were all sent into a yard where the older people slouched against the wall. I talked to the lady who had spoken to me at breakfast and learned that we got up at 6, worked until one (this was one), and worked right through until 6 again. Then we went back to the room where we ate another meal which was usually a broth again and a chunk of cheese.

I saw my mother while wandering around the grey dark yard but when I approached her we were split up and she was beaten. It was so cruel. I looked around as I sat picking at the ropes, wondering how much I was going to see of this room and how much I would end up hating it. Was my life really going to carry on in this gloomy, cold grey building with monotonous work and hard beds. No friends, nothing to enjoy and no personal life, now I could see the reason for all the unemotional faces.[6]

191

Jerome Bruner has suggested that one of the signs of intelligence is the act of "going beyond the information given." If part of our task as instructors is to promote and encourage intelligence, it follows that we must design writing assignments in such a way as to invite precisely that—the need/willingness to go beyond . . .

This is surely one of the distinctive differences between the Wedgwood text and the workhouse text. Whereas the Wedgwood text, with all its competence, exemplifies merely conformist and convergent virtues, the workhouse text, by entering and sustaining role, goes beyond the information given; it *uses* that information to create a plausible scenario.

The relationship between Jackie and the historical facts has become remarkably interesting. It is, in the first place, an *active* relationship: she is *using* her knowledge to produce a believable narrative—a narrative that offers a great deal of information but is never crudely didactic. Using the naive, surprised, confused responses of a new arrival, she appropriately registers a sense of sharp incongruity: the situation is awful, but the inmates don't seem to care.

Since she is writing retrospectively, she can claim to have been involved in exactly what Yourcenar speaks of: "participation, as intensely aware as possible, in *that which has been.*"[7]

# THE REACTIVE TEXT AS A REALIZATION OF ROLE

Just as Goffman in *Frame Analysis* discovered frames within frames within frames within . . . in the ways we construct our "reality," so can we discover roles within roles. Let us offer some examples.

In the following texts, the students are in the constraining role of student writer constructing a text that reacts, by imitation or otherness, to the structures offered by the passage from Beckett's *Watt* (see p. 148). But within or behind that role, they have another, existential role: Watt was in role, fictively, as one who curses, one who offers complaints; here three students take on the contrary role of one who celebrates. The first text closely echoes Beckett's in structure, while inverting, contradicting, denying, Beckett's meaning. The second and third are more freely reactive in nature.

> Personally of course I celebrate everything. Not a word, not a deed, not a thought, not a need, not a grief, not a joy,

not a girl, not a boy, not a doubt, nor a trust, not a scorn, not a lust, not a hope, not a fear, not a smile, not a tear, not a name, not face, no time, no place, that I do not celebrate, exceedingly, A pureness, from beginning to end. And yet, when I sat for Fellowship the boil on my bottom burst . . . The rest, a pureness. The Tuesday smiles, the Wednesday laughter, the Thursday blessings, the Friday songs, the Saturday sleeps, the Sunday alertness, the Monday grins, the Monday grins, The loves, the melodies, the reachings, the lullabies, the squeezes, the chants, the hugs, the caroling, the sympathies, the prayers, the embraces, the laughter, the fondlings, and the crooning. And the rich new lovely new earth, my earth and my father's and my mother's and my father's mother's and my mother's father's and my father's mother's father's and my mother's father's mother's and my father's mother's mother's and my mother's father's father's and my father's father's mother's and my mother's mother's father's and my father's father's father's and my mother's mother's mother's and other people's fathers' and mothers' and fathers' fathers' and mothers' mothers' and fathers' mothers' and mothers' fathers' and fathers' mothers' fathers' and mothers' fathers' mothers' and fathers' mothers' mothers' and mothers' fathers' fathers' and fathers' fathers' mothers' and mothers' mothers' fathers' and fathers' fathers' fathers' and mothers' mothers' mothers'. A pureness. The crocuses and the larch turning green every year a week before the others and the pastures white with new born lambs and the long summer days and the newmown hay and the wood-pigeon in the morning and the cuckoo in the afternoon and the corncrake in the evening and the wasps in the jam and the smell of the gorse and the look of the gorse and the apples falling and the children walking in the dead leaves and the larch turning brown a week before the others and the chestnuts falling and the howling winds and the sea breaking over the pier and the first fires and the hooves on the road and the consumptive postman whistling "The Roses Are Blooming in Picardy" and the standard oil-lamp and of course the snow and to be sure the sleet and bless your heart the slush and every fourth year the February leap year and the endless April showers and the crocuses and then the whole wonderful business starting all over again. A spirituality. And if I could begin it all over again, knowing what I know now, the result would be the same. And if I could begin again a third time, knowing what I would know then, the result would be the same. And if I could begin it all over again a hundred times, knowing each time a little more than the time before, the result would always be the same, and the hundredth life as the first, and the hundred lives as one. A cat's purr. But at this rate we shall be here all day.

Lyle Wakefield (U)

Jenny, Rachel, Anna, Ben, hiking Waterfall Canyon, rocks, mud, birds, trees, muddy untied canvas sneakers soaking wet, gritted with mud from walking up the creek, cold, clear, wet, frothy, former winter snow now springtime hiking's refreshment from sun, dust, heat, rocks, a Great Basin sunning itself on sandstone near Ben's path, rattle, strike, cry, fear, panic is rocks in untied shoes, numb arms from carrying, the car that won't start, red semaphores that won't change, left turns, traffic jam, fender bender, curses, the brutal halting of time, the swelling of Ben's hand, the brisk, cold professionalism of the emergency room, nerves, sweat, disinfectant, white, reading meaningless magazines, Time, Newsweek, Sports Illustrated, Reader's Digest, words forced into one eye vomited out the other, my mind is in the other room—Ben's room, recovery, room, me, recover, recovered, recovering, he, Ben, recover, will, they, me, will, recover— the dining room where now I'm eaten, a jaundiced-skinned, hollow-boned, ninety-five pound, Thanksgiving turkey, devoured by cancer, doctors, knives, and drugs, but it doesn't matter, it doesn't matter, Ben got better.

Craig Shertloff (U)

## Reflections

This is, in a way, the most fictitious piece of writing I did the entire week, and yet it is also the most honest. Fictitious in that I have never had such an experience with my children, nor have I heard any particular accounts of snakebite that parallel closely this one. It is honest in that it reveals my own concern for my children, particularly, in this case, for my son. I chose, as my persona for this text, to be a 25-year-old woman with terminal cancer. It was an arbitrary selection, but as the writing progressed, I could see why I had selected that particular mask to write from. My mother died some twenty years ago of cancer. She was fifty, not twenty-five. I remembered taking her to breakfast, shortly before she returned to the hospital to die. Her skin was yellowish, from jaundice; she died in November, shortly before Thanksgiving. At the time I wrote this piece, however, I did not consciously think of one of those details. I wrote the names, events, magazine titles, and so on, as they came, without stopping to edit or analyze why I had placed them there. It is an astonishingly personal account of my different familial relationships with my wife, my son, my mother and her death. It represents, to me at least, some kind of reconciliation with death (which to me is represented by my mother's death) and with life after the death of a loved one. This text says something about the way a fourteen-year-old views death, doctors, and the impersonality of professionalism, which many feel encourages confidence in patients. The frustrations, fear, anxiety, and tension of the snakebite scene, somehow suggested to me similar tensions about sickness and death, which I believe everyone shares.

Craig Shertloff (U)

Looking in the rear-view mirror of my small truck, I see my blood and flesh deeply planted in the soil, and I celebrate the sacrifice of life for life: The seed, the rain, the blisters, the pain, the sun, the grain, the loss, the gain, the beet, the bean, the prayers, the unseen, the hoe, the soil, the sweat, the toil, the greens, the golds, the droughts, the colds; and yet, I have no regrets for good or bad; they are one in purpose; one cannot exist without the other's embrace. These are sweet.

Sand and soil do not create the subtotal of my satisfaction, for the hub of my life lies in the heart of my heart, in the home I have built. My eldest daughter, my dancing perfectionist; my second, my son, my left and right hand; a third, a daughter, giving and caring, and most of all laughing; the fourth, a son, the one who must dare; and my youngest, a son, the me blonde again. But beyond all my young, beyond all my pride, the woman, the spine, the strength, the line, my wife is my partner in building my land; and with her I share the plans I dare and with her I climb beyond boundaries of time. And through her I see things I've never seen before, and this I celebrate. But this is enough poetics for one afternoon. Life is good; and I fasten my eyes to the road, and drive ahead.

Elaine Turner (U)

# ROLE AND IN-PERSONATION

Let us now offer a distinction: Lyle writing as "one who cele-brates" can be said to be writing as himself in the role of cele-brant. Conversely, Elaine, like Jackie, is writing in the role of someone else—Elaine's father in the present or in the recent past—yet she must retain, however covertly, elements of her own self. In general, our policy is to involve students in role-work of both kinds: in role as a "special" self and in role as another, expressing a particular frame of mind or a specific sensibility.

But if students are asked to write in role—not only as a particular self but also as others—where exactly do they find a plausible language, a "voice," for each of those other selves? The answer is that within our memories, we carry a rich funding of aural/oral images. Here is William Stafford acknowledging one of his. He is talking about the needs of a writer:

> *No special sensitivity or intelligence is required—though for other activities, sensitivity and intelligence would be good to have. The crucial thing is just willing involvement with the nuances and suggestions that thrive in language and thought. Influences that make the most difference are close and sustained. For myself, I have not been able to dredge up a literary voice that influenced me so much as my mother's voice did. I must witness for the influences of immediate, ordinary interaction. We talk and write the days of our lives, and it is willingness to start from where we are that enables us to have a good life locally and make "original" things—art.*[8]

The voice of Stafford's mother we would tentatively describe as "a dominant voice." We all have them—they are often maternal, and seem to have been imprinted on "our inner ear" before we developed the defenses of critical distance. And they will surface, both in our expressive writings and also at moments when we require of our texts that they take on a particular force or tone. But alongside such dominant voices—definitive voices—lie hundreds of others—less potent, very various, and quite serviceable.

When students prove to us that they can produce a great variety of "voices" in their texts, we ask where they get them. Neil's answer was perfectly simple and absolutely confident: "I have hundreds, perhaps thousands. You just pick them up."

"Where?" we asked.

"Oh, from conversations, and listening in, and television, the movies, and books."

"So, do you think you could convincingly create a text that would simulate any kind of voice?"

"Oh, sure," he smiled. Then he proceeded to write a gushing letter, in role as a spoiled, plutocratic Manhattan widow writing to a close friend. It's a text that has slipped from our grasp and our filing system, but it was indeed plausible, an authentic forgery.

Impersonation, then, we prefer to construe as "in-personation": as a retrieval of, an entry into, the psyche and the voice of an other, or as that other's entering into one's own voice—the process invariably strikes us as inseparably two-way, reciprocal.[9] Making a plausible impersonation requires a salutary level of attentiveness. One has to be on the qui vive for unintended lapses or changes of tone, of idiom, of idiolect, of those nuances in text that constitute an important part of its identity. But once its distinctive fascination has been experienced, impersonation lends itself to a remarkable variety of uses, both academic and vocational. In exploring the reach of impersonation, one discovers an extension of one's options. One is freed from the preemptive jaws of "sincerity," and from pursuing the illusory and deluding grail of "one's own voice." If indeed there can be said to be such a thing as one's own voice—an elusive phenomenon dear to many teachers of creative writing—then its pursuit, like that of happiness, is a waste of time and effort. For like happiness, it will come not out of a willed effort but as a mostly retroactive discovery and as a donnée. And if it comes at all, others will be more likely than oneself to recognize its arrival: "Ah," they will exclaim, "you have finally found your own voice!"

Is impersonation anything more, some people ask, than pretending? We consider the question tendentious. Implicit within it is a devaluation of the act of pretending—an unspoken assumption that it is, perhaps, something childish and therefore to be outgrown, possibly dishonest, probably trivial. We contend that such views derive from a narrow, philistine, and positivist view of the mind and its acts, and that the work to be done in creating a convincing and sustained impersonation is indeed valuable. Linguistically, it involves a move toward repertoire expansion; and in philosophical and ethical matters, it is what we *have* to do in order to understand as fully as may be not only another person's position but also the grounds for that position. Implicit in any well-managed assignment is some degree of impersonation of those who would be adversaries. At best, we recognize such impersonation as identification—as exemplified by Keats *in* the society of the Grecian urn's frieze.

Impersonation has had a bad press. It conjures up images of people posing as others in order to steal, defraud, gain entry, or otherwise win the battle of life by devious means. On occasion, when done with style, it has admittedly tickled the funny bone. One recalls the virtuoso act of impersonation in which Virginia Woolf was involved, the Dreadnought Hoax.[10]

If, then, role-play involves some form of impersonation, how do we seriously justify it? The answer is a simple connotative one: the impersonation we wish to promote is primarily a matter of reconstruing, and representing, some part of our previous fundings. Let's put it another way: It is a process of "hearing voices," and of choosing the most appropriate ones. Hearing voices is, admittedly, what some people in some mental hospitals do; but it should be clear by now that we have something rather different in mind. It is what Yourcenar expressed in two words: "We were."

For much of our lives, we are involved in a process of "becoming." In our personal lives, we take on, explore, rehearse, new ways of being: A middle-aged woman has probably done much really strenuous learning in the process of becoming a mother to her children; but she may well be just beginning to learn the skills of being a "mother" to her aging parents. As her children move out of adolescence, she will be learning new, more symmetrical ways of being a friend to them; and they will be busy learning how to be young adults.

We ourselves can recognize the shift from one role to another, the switch from one "voice" to another, as we switch, for example, from a voice speaking to teen-agers to a voice that answers the telephone. One minute our voice is raised in annoyance, frustration; the next it answers the phone in cordiality and equilibrium: "Hello," we say, amicably. Our students know these switches well. The "voices" in the classroom differ from the "voices" in the home and both differ from the "voices" in the street.

The other major form of role-play is found on the job—in people's professional lives. As a lawyer takes up her work from her desk, she enters into her role as a lawyer. Over coffee she enters a shifting twilight zone, in which she is both individual (personal) and lawyer (professional). The conversation over coffee, similarly, will display twilight characteristics—partly informal chat and partly legal talk.

(We often feel more *effective* in clearly defined roles than in those parts of our lives where roles are blurred: good teachers/counselors are often unsatisfactory parents!)

# THE BENEFITS OF
# ROLE-WORK

Within the constraints, guidelines, and frames of role, our purposes and our means are clarified. We can do things well that we might fudge *in propria persona*. It is a matter of "existential presence" and of the clear focus that is offered, made available, by such presence. Role-play creates a strong, clear sense of environmental determinants: all those factors of context or situation that, when recognized, make an appropriate/effective utterance what it is and not otherwise.

As early as primary school, we learn to internalize and habituate such social-conventional factors. We learn, for example, to modify our language in directions that we can recognize, even though we cannot yet name them. Our sociolinguistic abilities are preconceptual but none the less effective for that. We *perform* the conventions.

The virtue of writing in role is that the crucial features of context and especially of audience are clearly focused, often explicitly so. In *actual* life, daily life, many of our uncertainties in the production of language stem from uncertainties about context and audience, uncertainties about the roles of daily life. There is no such uncertainty in the tasks we perform *in role*—vicarious, virtual role. In role, our *functions* are often crystal clear. For example, the lawyer knows precisely: "I have to disentangle this mess in order to prepare a brief for the defense." Here—as in many of the clear-cut roles of actual life—the lawyer must be a cool-headed spectator of the confusion of other people's lives.

Filling a role involves taking on, or entering, a *language*, a "cultural syntax." The term is that of James Boyd White, a professor of law at the University of Chicago. Before we examine it, however, let's consider G. W. Turner's observations on initiation:

> There is something of the initiation ceremony in the training of *apprentices and scientists. The magic of secret names is powerful. The student of geometry is never to* draw *anything; he may describe* circles, *construct a* triangle, *produce its sides and drop a perpendicular, so that geometry is in part the learning of new collocations of words special to the subject. The student goes on to chemistry and learns to discuss milky limewater in terms of a* white precipitate *or interesting cracklings as* decrepitation. *It is all linked with training in precision of thought and care about language, and I know I am grateful for such stylistic training as I had in school labs and, even more strikingly later, in university lectures on palaeontology, a rigorous training in*

*describing spiral staircases without waving your hands, since it
includes a description in words of all the possible shapes of fossil shells.*[11]

Here now is White:

> *To sum up my point in a phrase, what characterizes legal discourse is that it is in a double sense (both substantively and procedurally) constitutive in nature: it creates a set of questions that define a world of thought and action, a set of roles and voices by which experience will be ordered and meanings established and shared; a set of occasions and methods for public speech that constitute us as a community and as a polity. In all of this it has its own ways of working, which are to be found not in the rules that are at the center of the structure, but in the culture which determines how these rules are to be read and talked about.*
>
> *I have identified some of the special ways of thinking and talking that characterize legal discourse. Far more than any technical vocabulary, it is these conventions that are responsible for the foreignness of legal speech. To put it slightly differently, there is a sense in which one creates technical vocabulary whenever one creates a rule of the legal kind, for the operation of the rule in a procedural system itself necessarily involves an artificial way of giving meaning both to words and to events. These characteristics of legal discourse mean that the success of any movement to translate legal speech into Plain English will be severely limited. For if one replaces a Legal Word with an Ordinary English Word, the sense of increased normalcy will be momentary at best: the legal culture will go immediately to work, and the Ordinary Word will begin to lose its shape, its resiliency, and its familiarity, and become, despite the efforts of the draftsman, a Legal Word after all. The reason for this is that the word will work as part of the legal language, and it is the way this language works that determines the meaning of its terms. This is what I meant when I said that it is not the vocabulary of the legal language that is responsible for its obscurity and mysteriousness, but its "cultural syntax," the invisible expectations governing the way the words are to be used.*[12]

Within the time constraints of our work, we can't hope to bring our students to any degree of mastery of a range of "cultural syntaxes"; but we do nevertheless believe that after having worked in role and produced a variety of forms of discourse from within a variety of roles, they are in a better position to understand what factors are involved, what conditions are necessary and sufficient for a syntax to be seen as operating plausibly, appropriately, effectively. They achieve that modest level of insight by having come to know how to do it by doing it, and by having acquired a reasonably coherent sense of what is involved: the issues and the options.

# BEING IN ROLE
# VERSUS ACTING

An elementary confusion sometimes arises between role-play and acting. Elaine Maimon provides a classic example:

> *In your science courses you will learn how to formulate and test hypotheses. You will learn systematic and objective approaches to explanations of cause and effect. In science courses, your role demands that you perform rituals that establish distance between you and the material you are studying. In that sense, the methods that you will learn for performing and recording experiments are theatrical techniques to help you maintain your objective stance. Effective writing in the sciences is impersonal without being frigid. The best scientific writers are the best actors; they understand the complexities of the scientific role.* [13]

The influential book in which this passage appears is, alas, marred by epistemological confusion, and its failure to recognize the *dynamic* nature of our engagements in role renders its discussion of these matters very misleading, not to say obfuscating. The conceptual muddle here seems to arise from a failure to discriminate clearly between the environmental determinants and acts of mind that characterize role, and those that are required in acting. The implication seems to be that even experienced scientists persist in "acting" as scientists. The notion of theatricality, of a contrived *illusion*, is reinforced by the curious view that laboratory disciplines and procedures are "theatrical techniques." This is deeply misleading. It is as if a responsible, mature scientist could properly confess, "I'm not *really* a scientist, I just act the part." But the internalizing of a role is quite another matter. And if the distinction is not grasped, then illusion is twice compounded. Imagine a laboratory on a theater stage: the actors enter and pretend to be scientists; they are clearly doing something very different from what real scientists do in actual laboratories. To speak of scientists as actors fails to distinguish between the effective illusion of the theater and the inherent actuality of the laboratory, between "acting" and "role."

The peculiar virtue of role is that it is a way of entering/taking on the conventions, the determining environmental constraints, of a particular task/function or discipline/tradition and genuinely performing—*not pretending*. The impersonations of role move away from illusion, even though they may start there; the impersonations of acting move toward a more finely tuned, a more complete illusion, even though they may start in some perceived "reality."

Fortunately, students seem to possess a strong intuitive grasp of these distinctions. Or perhaps we have been lucky. Certainly, we have not yet encountered any student who failed to grasp and use the conventions of writing in role.

This is not to deny that every discipline has its distinctive rituals. But such rituals have a great deal to do with promoting and sustaining effective control of role, and little or nothing to do with theatricality. When we see a video or film of a real operating room, that the scene may strike us as theatrical is not in question. We are simply imposing a mostly inappropriate frame on an unfamiliar event in order to make sense of it. But at no point do we murmur, "Ah, the surgeon is pretending to open the rib cage, and the fake blood is beginning to pour with powerful illusory effect out of the patient's body."

Phenomenologically, role-play is very subtle, and we need to tread very carefully through its conceptual minefield. To confuse role with acting is to demolish the possibility of crucial discriminations at one stroke. It may, however, help to remember that actors always speak someone else's lines, the lines are "out there"; in role we speak lines that come out of ourselves, lines that we have already made our own or are in the process of making our own. Acting is a process of replication, role is an act of retrieval. In acting, we represent or mediate another's text; in role, we shape our own utterances.

Let us borrow a metaphor from Marianne Moore: if acting is the presentation of imaginary toads in imaginary gardens, then role begins as the presentation of real toads in imaginary gardens and moves toward the presentation of real toads in real gardens. "Reality" is not a given; it is what we learn to construct. We continuously imagine that which is to become "real"; and our imagining comprises expectation, preparation, anticipation, rehearsal. (Cf. Keats's metaphor of Adam's dream.[14]) Role depends, above all, on the social endorsements and validations offered by those who constitute our little world. If our roles don't work for/on others, we generally know when and how to drop them. We know our envisaging was faulty: the envisioned failed to enter the realm of what those around us who matter accept and respond to as "real." Erving Goffman puts it this way: "I hold society to be first in every way."[15]

Here is another example of misapprehension of role. In a rather solemn essay, Dan Fader quotes from a letter to a newspaper: "As both a woman who has been in the role of client and therapist, I strongly disagree." Fader notes the misplaced "both" and then remarks: "I want first to ask her why she is 'in the role of' client and therapist instead of simply being what she claims she has been—both a client and a therapist?"[16] (We note the misplaced question mark.) He mistakenly argues that she "invokes a metaphor of the stage to communicate her feeling," and he goes on: "The actress who plays a role may be profoundly convincing in that role, but she is nevertheless not the thing itself. She is substitute and surrogate, a woman representing reality rather than being reality."

Fader's observations are identical, in one crucial respect, to Maimon's: he assumes that "being in role" is synonymous with "acting." It is odd, to say the least, to find such writers and readers at this late hour leaping to assume that "role" refers only to acting on a stage. The woman was, of course, right: when she visited a therapist she *was* in role as a client—that is, she entered the therapist's office as a client (not as any of her other selves). The frame was entirely appropriate and necessary. The "constraint" (role of client) was enabling—that is, she could say things as a client that in other contexts she would not have said. Conversely, when she worked as a therapist, she had to *be* in role as a therapist—that is what her clients paid her for!

Fader goes on to give a long account of a segment of his teaching— an account that reflects great credit on him as a teacher—that is, in role as a teacher; just as, when he wrote his essay, he was in role as a teacher writing about teaching; just as, when he lectures, he goes into role as a lecturer and does some of the role-typical things that a certain kind of lecturer does—such as taking off his coat and rolling up his sleeves, to signify, in role, an increase in intensity, in his wish to arouse his audience—saying, in effect, "I mean business; pay serious attention to my words."

# STUDENTS IN ROLE AND THEIR AUDIENCE

If we claim that having students write in role, as opposed to *in propria persona*, is advantageous, productive, and enabling, then this has to be true also of the fundamental elements of the writer's conception/envisioning of reader.

As Walter Ong has amply and wittily demonstrated,[17] the act of creating a reader for text is one of the student writer's most difficult tasks: indeed, Ong argues that judging the degree to which one's reader may be legitimately, properly ignorant of the matter in hand is a skill that separates the undergraduate, however brilliant, from the mature scholar. "It takes time to get a feel for the roles that readers can be expected comfortably to play in the modern academic world."[18]

Our case is that one of the most valuable *products* of writing in role is, precisely, that the writer-reader relationship is more clearly defined, delimited, contextualized, constrained than it is when a student *in propria persona* writes for an instructor who is more or less a stranger, indeterminate and threatening—threatening because indeterminate.

Have the student take on a role in an established scenario—established in the sense of offering a social context, a pattern of comprehensible relationships, its salient conditions explicitly known—and whatever text he or she may then produce will enjoy the benefits that accrue from having, also, a reader-in-role. The reader is no longer an indeterminate instructor or a hardly known peer but, rather, a recipient whose relationship with the role-writer can be appreciated. Such reciprocity clears up, or wipes out, many of the uncertainties about "readership" that retroactively make for uncertainties in the writer.

The desires of the *persona* who writes the text are understood, and so are the needs of the *persona* to whom the text is addressed. As we hope to demonstrate in the next chapter by looking quite closely at two scenarios, there is, at one swoop, a significant gain in clarity, purposiveness, and effectiveness.

# NOTES

1. Marguerite Yourcenar, *Memoirs of Hadrian*, trans. Grace Frick and the author (New York: Farrar, Straus & Giroux, 1981), p. 34.

2. Norman Mailer, *Marilyn* (New York: Grosset & Dunlap, 1973), p. 18. A vivid example can be found in John Barth, *Lost in the Funhouse* (New York: Bantam Books, 1969), last three pages.

3. Cf. Erving Goffman: ". . . In taking on a role, the individual does not take on a personal, biographical identity—a past or a character—but merely a bit of social categorization, that is, social identity. . ." in *Frame Analysis: An Essay on the Organization of Experience* (New York: Harper & Row, 1974), p. 286.

4. D. W. Winnicott, *Playing and Reality* (London: Tavistock Publications, 1971).

5. Nancy Martin et al., *Writing and Learning Across the Curriculum 11-16* (London: Ward Lock, 1976), pp. 64–65.

6. Ibid., pp. 87–88.

7. Yourcenar, *Memoirs of Hadrian*, p. 328.

8. William Stafford, personal communication.

9. Cf. Seamus Heaney on Wordsworth's impersonation of such persons as Peter Bell: "I suspect that there was nothing fundamentally dramatic about Wordsworth's surrender to the speech of the character. It was not a question of the poet's voice performing a part but of the poet's voice being possessed; it was not a question of technical cool, of finding a dramatic pitch, rather a matter of sympathetic warmth, of sinking into a mood of evocation." *The Makings of a Music: Reflections on the Poetry of Wordsworth and Yeats,* the Kenneth Allott Lecture, 1978 (Liverpool: Liverpool University Press, 1978); reprinted in *Preoccupations: Selected Prose 1968-1978* (London: Faber & Faber, 1980).

10. Quentin Bell, *Virginia Woolf: A Biography* (New York: Harcourt, Brace Jovanovich, 1972), vol. 1, pp. 157–60.

11. G. W. Turner, *Stylistics* (Harmondsworth: Penguin, 1973), pp. 172–73.

12. James Boyd White, "The Invisible Discourse of the Law: Reflections on Legal, Literary, and General Education," in *Fforum,* ed. P. L. Stock (Montclair, N.J.: Boynton/Cook, 1983), pp. 55–56.

13. Elaine Maimon et al., *Writing in the Arts and Sciences* (Cambridge, Mass.: Winthrop, 1981), p. 5.

14. "The Imagination may be compared to Adam's dream—he woke and found it truth." (Letter to Bailey, 22 November 1817.)

15. Erving Goffman, *Frame Analysis: An Essay on the Organization of Experience* (New York: Harper & Row, 1974), p. 13.

16. Dan Fader, "Narrowing the Space Between Writer and Text," in *Fforum,* ed. P. L. Stock (Montclair, N.J.: Boynton/Cook, 1983), pp. 108–09.

17. Walter J. Ong, *Interfaces of the Word* (Ithaca, N.Y.: Cornell University Press, 1977), Chapter 2.

18. Ibid., p. 77.

# CHAPTER TEN

# APPLICATIONS
## Student Writers in Role

*I can contain thousands.*
*Whitman*

In this chapter we offer two examples of students' role-work. They are extremely different, one from another, and the contrast may itself exemplify something of the potential range of role-work. We debated for some time about the sequence: the prison texts are extremely serious, even grim, whereas the filler texts are often lighthearted, even—some may feel—frivolous. Which, then, should come first? We decided to offer the filler section as light relief after the prison section, but the switch from one to the other may still be felt to be disconcerting.

# Part I
## Solitary Confinement:
## A Role Sequence

# ACTUAL PRISONERS

*I t was in May of 1975 that Kim Chi Ha—thirty-four, the father of a baby boy (he had been pardoned and freed for a while after his earlier imprisonment, only to be re-arrested in 1974 and given a life sentence), and ill with a recurrence of tuberculosis—wrote in a postscript to his* Declaration of Conscience,

> *I am not allowed to receive visitors or mail, or even read the Bible. I have been forbidden to write anything. I cannot move around much. This underground cramped cell is scarcely seven by seven.*
>
> *I sit here in the dark thinking about the uncertain future. But prison has not dimmed my spirits. These miserable conditions and the endless waiting have made me more determined than ever.*
>
> *I feel a quiet composure, almost serenity. But I am very anxious about what might happen to the individuals involved in making this statement public. My friends, please help these good people.*
>
> *Do not grieve for me. We will surely see each other soon.*[1]

Anatoly Shcharansky was imprisoned by the Soviet authorities in 1977. He had married in 1974, and his wife Avital had emigrated to Israel, confident that he would soon follow.

In a newspaper interview, Avital indicated that:

*Mr. Shcharansky's recent letters have been full of the romantic, witty philosophizing that his wife knew when they were together in Moscow. It buoys her own spirits. "When I see his letters, they make me really excited," she said. "It makes me see how the spirit of a human being can win everything.*

*"The K.G.B. try to kill him emotionally," she continued. "They try to break his soul and make him one of them. They came and said if Anatoly writes to the Supreme Soviet and says he's sick and asks for a pardon, they would release him after half his sentence. But he wouldn't do it. In an appeal for a pardon, you somehow say that you're guilty, and you play the game."*

*Mr. Shcharansky, who was pressed by the authorities to brand the Jewish emigration movement as having links with American intelligence, alluded to this in a letter a year ago, when he wrote:*

*"In addition to Newton's law on the universal gravity of objects, there is also a law of the universal gravity of souls, of the bond between them, and the influence of one soul on the other. And it operates in this manner, such that with each word that we speak, and with each step that we take, we touch other souls and have an impact upon them. So why should I put this sin on my soul? If I already succeeded once in tearing the spider web spun by the uncontrollable forces of life . . . how is it now possible to take even one step backwards toward the previous status?"*

*Last month, writing about his mental efforts to survive interrogation, he said he was compelled to summon up "pictures from my past, and thoughts concerning history and tradition; the Hebrew language and the books that I read; all that remained in my memory from my preoccupation with mathematics and chess; even visits to the theater, and of course, the ability to laugh—not at jokes or clever plays on words, but as if I were a spectator viewing the world from the sidelines, without undue melodramatics, discovering many interesting things, both comical and absurd."[2]*

# VIRTUAL PRISONERS

## The Student Writer/Prisoner

Consider, if you will, the similarities between a student writing in a composition class and a prisoner in solitary confinement.

Each is subject to the instructions/orders of a higher authority. Each has lost the privileges and pleasures of conversation. Paradoxically, each may, because of the loss of social intercourse—talk, gossip, story-telling—discover the distinctive satisfactions afforded by writing. It was on the basis of these suggestive correspondences that we decided to involve our students in writing in role as prisoners of conscience. We provided short-term funding in the form of a brief account of two remarkable prisoners of conscience: Edith Bone, who in her sixties was in solitary confinement for seven years, a prisoner of the Hungarian Stalinist regime;[3] and Jacobo Timerman, who was a victim of the fascist military dictatorship in Argentina.[4] We concentrated especially on Edith Bone: on her extraordinary resourcefulness (for example, her success in fashioning an almost childishly simple but effective "printing press"—duly concealed in her mattress—by means of which she printed her prison writings); on her rich funding of people, places, and books, which she drew on for sustenance; on her battle of wits with her guards, whom she despised.

We then asked our students to put themselves into the situation of a prisoner. To put it another way, we asked them to allow the sense of being confined and isolated to enter them. It's a two-way movement—the outer coming in and the inner reaching out.

## *Writing a Last Letter*

The prisoner role was a sequence lasting several classes. The first assignment in the sequence was this: as a special privilege, students would be allowed paper and pencil to write a letter to their nearest and dearest. We suggested that it might well be a message of prudent warning (don't expect too much) and of reassurance (they can't destroy my spirit). We also urged them to think of it as the last letter they might ever write.

The first comment we wish to offer on student reactions to the prisoner sequence is that no student seemed to experience any difficulty in taking the task seriously, in entering into the role of self as solitary prisoner, and producing a reasonably convincing text—an "authentic forgery." In role, they transcended or side-stepped the actual role, the daily reality, of student writer in a required course. Affectively, they discovered a sense of urgency, a sense of having something important to say, and an intensified sense of a bond between themselves and those who were to receive their letters. The framework of the role allowed them to write with passion, tenderness, and commitment; but the same framework allowed them the freedoms of a fantasy or a fiction—not so much a disclaimer ("I didn't really mean it") as a range, a reach, an intensity that they could not normally avail themselves of in daily life—and the detachment of the artist ("That's not really me, not myself, personally"). The vicariousness, the virtualness, of the role is perhaps its greatest virtue: no personal confession is involved. But the very detachment of the fiction promotes, paradoxically, a greater intensity and concentration of "existential presence," of personal truth.

"This, my text," the student can say, "represents someone other than me." But, paradoxically, it will be "informed" by the resources of the self, the hidden self. Thus students can represent and present their truths—delicate, difficult, sensitive truths, perchance—and offer them confidently as belonging to another, the other of the role. What strikes us about such texts, among other features, is the immediacy, the intensity of their realization of the sheer solitariness of "solitary confinement"—something they have never *actually* experienced. The clue is offered when students later write explanatory commentaries on their texts. And the consensus is: we all know loneliness, what it feels like, how we cope with it. *Retrieved actualities* are thus used in the task of realizing a vicarious, virtual experience.

## Stacey Silverman's Last Letter

Here is the letter written by Stacey Silverman (Q):

February 4, 1984

Dearest Mother and Father,

Why was I given a voice, so only I could hear the screams of my torment? And why when I am silent does the serenity pierce my eardrums like gunfire? I long to hear the voice of another animal. I have taken to shouting kind words to the far end of the room, so the echo brought back to me is the voice of another being who shares this bleakness with me. I pray to God every time I close my eyes, that when I open them, I will be in a crowded room, but it never happens.

There is a wooden chair standing by the huge bolted door towards the corner of the room. It is covered with layers of dust. I think it must have occupied that same spot for years. I fear what has happened to that chair will happen to me.

When the jailer led me to this room, he looked annoyed at having to walk the extra flights down to this hell that I must now call home. Just before he shut me into my aloneness, he maliciously grunted, "I guess I won't be seeing you around anymore." With that he slammed me in. I quickly rushed to put my ear to the door, and strained to hear his footsteps, which grew fainter and fainter and fainter. Then there was silence.

I fear the worst for myself now. I will undoubtedly go insane. No one could possibly save their mind in this position. The constant pressure of solitude is unbearable. I will, however, make it to tomorrow. It takes more than just one day to die of loneliness.

With love,
Your daughter

## Commentary

Stacey is capable of eloquence, and derives pleasure and satisfaction from achieving it. She rehearses much of her text, as inner speech, before writing (see p. 222 for a fuller discussion of this) and shapes to good effect. Hence the "textuality" of her opening two sentences, with the careful placement of "only"; the paradox of her opening question (surely we would expect her to be pleased to have been given a voice); and the element of self-dramatization in "the screams of my torment." Note also that she focuses *immediately* on the loss of utterance, of conversation.

She has clearly internalized / realized the plight of the prisoner: the chair is a vivid bit of apprehending and offers a plausible analogy; and the little dramatic cameo in the third paragraph effectively presents her first moment of realizing the extent of her calamity, the enormity of such imprisonment.

As for the last paragraph, it seems, in its precarious equilibrium, finely judged: it is both a stark warning ("I will undoubtedly go insane") and also a provisional (but convincing) reassurance ("I will, however, make it to tomorrow"), which is effectively reaffirmed or reinforced by her last sentence. What we find, here, is akin to what John Stuart Mill valued in the poetry that pulled him out of the mire of utilitarianism—"the true voice of feeling."

## *Writing the Psychiatrist's Report*

Barbara Herrnstein Smith has observed that "We perform verbal acts as well as other acts . . . in order to extend our control over a world that is not naturally disposed to serve our interests."[5] The next stage of our sequence was designed to make this unobliging world felt rather severely. The letters are intercepted by the prison authorities, and placed in the hands of the resident psychiatrist. This is the scenario. Prisoners of conscience constitute an awkward category for the prison governor: international pressures of various kinds are exerted on their behalf; it is important that they survive; suicide would cause intense embarrassment for the commissars. The prisoner's letter is to be used, then, as a diagnostic tool. What evidence does it offer about the state of the prisoner's mind? Is he or she likely to crack up or break down? Might he or she "do something foolish"?

Each student then goes into role as a psychiatrist and is given the prisoner letter of another student. It is to be read carefully—both for what it says and for what it does not say—and used for diagnosis, prognosis, and recommendations. This reading is of a specifically pragmatic, transactional kind; it is work to be done, a task to be performed. It comes both as a *real* shock, an actual bit of disconcertingness, and as a vicarious slap in the face, this interception. Yet in no time at all, each student has become a psychiatrist, "on the other side." The report, with its diagnosis, prognosis, and recommendations, takes the form of a memorandum to the governor, and the writer must keep in mind that he is a busy man and not deeply versed in the language of psychiatry. These constraints are, again, pragmatic. This is how real life is. Questions of efficient communication, mediation, classification, and economy inevitably arise.

Once the memoranda are complete, they in turn are circulated so that each student, now in role as governor, can judge the efficacy or otherwise of the psychiatric work and its record.

The students' production of "authentic forgeries," in role as psychiatrists, convinced us of the truth and usefulness of Erving Goffman's remarks about soap operas and the like:

> *Consider now dramatic scriptings. Include all strips of depicted personal experience made available for vicarious participation to an audience or readership, especially the standard productions offered commercially to the public through the medium of television, radio, newspapers, magazines, books, and the legitimate (live) stage. This corpus of transcriptions is of special interest, not merely because of its social importance in our recreational life, or, as already suggested, because of the availability of so much explicit analysis of these materials, or because the materials themselves are easily accessible for purposes of close study; their deepest significance is that they provide a mock-up of everyday life, a put-together script of unscripted social doings, and thus are a source of broad hints concerning the structure of this domain.[6]*

As with such various forms of drama, so with sports and the rituals of organized games: for spectators, they offer engrossment, an entry into and participation in other worlds, alternative realities. Such absorption brings in its train the blessedness of self-forgetfulness. The vicarious world of the soap opera or the game generates its own forms of life, its own "realm of being."

> *The value of these materials for us is apparent. Above all else, dramas and contests provide engrossables—engrossing materials which observers can get carried away with, materials which generate a realm of being.*[7]

When we questioned students about the plausibility of their impersonations, several interesting points emerged. First of all, our students confirmed Goffman's view that, for example, television mock-ups—of doctors, nurses, psychiatrists, and so on—provide young viewers with fairly reliable stereotypes, not so much of characters as of idiolect. They know "how a surgeon talks," they know "how a psychiatrist would write about a patient." They established that their long-term funding had fed into them a remarkable repertoire of "voices." The resources are indeed there, waiting to be tapped and put to constructive, controlled, purposeful use. One student, Ulric Ortiz, produced a psychiatric report of such distinctive expertise, that we had to conclude that the governor would understand hardly a word. "How did you do it?" we asked. "Oh, simple," he replied. "I work part-time in a mental hospital." Ulric's paraprofessional work had provided him with an esoteric "overkill" language with which he could not resist cutting a dash.

## Designing Rules for Survival

The prison, then, has its rules. But so may the prisoners have theirs. How do you hold on to your sanity? The next task for each prisoner was to design rules for staying sane. These had to be economical, brief enough so that they could be written on a small piece of paper that could be concealed inside a straw mattress. The rules had to be pared down to essentials, to high priorities.

Our case is that such a text qualifies as the truly important form of "basic writing"—that is, writing that serves basic, fundamental human needs. By comparison, the kind of nit-picking grammar grinding that passes in many quarters for basic writing is no more than a trivializing, unproductive waste of lives. Given effectively realized vicarious participation in the life of a prisoner, such tasks as the making of rules for staying sane are indeed experienced as if freely chosen. The paradox will be familiar to anyone who knows Marianne Moore's poem "Poetry," where she writes of "real toads in imaginary gardens": the prison-cell (or any other appropriate fiction) constitutes the "imaginary garden," and into it students introduce their "real toads"—their passions, needs, commitments, desires, fears, and so on.

Here now are some of our students' rules for staying sane:

1. Keep hope alive.
2. Think positively.
3. Try to remain happy.
4. Hate those who have imprisoned you and think of the different ways of revenge, once you get out and are free.
5. Their main object is to see you suffer. So always smile.
6. If you feel helpless, cry when nobody is around.
7. Exercise mornings and evenings.
8. Write: About all the fun moments of your life. And about your experiences in solitary confinement.
9. Write to all of your friends and family members. You won't be able to mail the letters but even then you will feel some satisfaction.
10. Sex no doubt is as necessary as food. But as you can resist food by not thinking about it so can you resist sex by not thinking about it. Do not think erotic thoughts.
11. Remember you are right. You are on the right side so you will win in the end.
12. Keep on thinking about the different ways of escaping.
13. Remember these rules. Repeat them whenever you get a chance.

Farukh Kamal Khawaja (Q)*

1. Don't try to remember any of the good experiences you had with friends and family. When you come back to the present you will only hurt more because there is still no change in your situation.
2. Never ask the question Why me? because you will never get an answer.
3. Occupy as much time as possible doing little things such as:

---

*Farukh, a Pakistani, had been a political prisoner when a student in Pakistan.

a. Keep everything as clean as possible.
b. Try to repair and clean clothes.
c. Exercise.
4. Meditation: It helps; the inner soul become one with "you." It helps to develop "ki."
5. God: people need to believe in something.
6. Mark down the days you spend in the cell, possibly by meals.
7. Whenever somebody comes to look in on you, show that person you haven't lost your fighting spirit.
8. Show yourself that you haven't lost your fighting spirit.
9. Masturbation. It's not one of my favorite topics but it has to be mentioned. Keep clean!
10. Accept your situation as it is.

Ulric Ortiz (Q)

1. Make cot; shake mattress.
2. Scratch a line on the wall every day. Every seventh day spend the day singing hymns, talking to God.
3. Comb hair with fingers.
4. Exercise: crunchies, pushups, windmills, wall presses.
5. Sing: everything/anything.
6. Mentally clean house: make beds, pick up bathroom, do breakfast dishes, tidy living room.
7. Mentally play piano, organ, guitar.
8. Eat all meals as if dining at Waldorf Astoria.
9. Mentally write: think through a short story and then a novel. Describe in detail the scenery, people, settings— pay attention to detail!
10. Mentally write letters to: children, parents, friends.

Pat Campbell (U)

## *Returning to the World*

At an appropriate moment and, as in Edith Bone's case, without warning, we tell our students that they are free to go. They may reenter "the world which is the world of all of us" and set about reestablishing their relationship with all that has become defamiliarized. Questions of reentry arise: how to rebuild friendships, how to accept the fact that people have changed, how to learn to take freedoms for granted.

## Peter Mazzola's Reentry Text

Here is how Peter Mazzola (Q) described his reentry:

Dear Anthony,

It has been 20 years since I have seen the light of day. I have spent the better part of my life in solitary confinement. I cannot believe that I was freed from my prison cell just last week. Like a child, I must now relearn how to communicate with others. You are the first.

Being in solitary confinement did irreparable damage to my psyche. All that I have witnessed or learned in the past is, in effect, wasted. When I first entered prison, I entered an unwilling subject, railing at the guards who slid my meals under the door. I was determined to find a way out of that madhouse at all costs. After countless efforts, and many beatings as a consequence, my morale became somewhat "bent." Although I realized that I was not going to escape immediately, I always had the notion in the back of my mind that my time to escape would eventually come. It was just a matter of buying time, waiting for the right opportunity to come.

I think it was 10 years before I totally gave up all hope of resuming a normal life. I had become like an animal, driven by hunger. I no longer thought about the guards and what they were doing outside my cell. I did not think along the lines of my past or future. I simply existed. My words were reduced to simple utterances, and while I often talked to myself about many things regarding the prison, I found myself forgetting the significance of what I was saying. I do not recall what exactly, on a day-to-day basis, I did. I just remember the times that I had been hurt badly, and the duration of my suffering.

I never did have a chance to develop many friendships in the past, present company excluded. Certainly, my prison sentence destroyed the future of any "social life" that I might have had. As I have mentioned earlier, I do not think that I will ever lead a normal life in the future, although I will try my best to live constructively. Maybe I'll get a job stationed at an ocean oil rig. I hear the pay is good, or at least it had been prior to my confinement. Besides, I won't have to come in contact with too many people outside of my co-workers.

(I fear people now.) I will try to catch up on my reading, in the meantime, on how the world has been for the past 20 years.

Many things have changed since I left the "civilized" world. For one thing, I hear that man is now able to fly to the moon in spaceships! Imagine that! What will they think of next? The cities seem a lot more crowded. My stay in New York this past week has been quite an experience. I can't remember the last time that I had to pay so much to do so little. I almost didn't want to ask about a room. I spent an hour rehearsing my lines. I looked in a history book the other day and read that we are in a Cold War with Russia. When was Kennedy shot? It must have occurred a month after I left. Anyway, Johnson seemed to have carried a good administration afterwards.

But enough talk. I have long forgotten the beauty in idle nature. The grass, the trees, the birds in the sky. I forgot what the color blue looked like! I am free to walk the streets, buy food, even watch a movie or two. I am not kept under surveillance, and I can take a bath as often as I like, any time I want to.

Fashions have changed too! Why, just the other day I saw a girl walking down the street with PURPLE HAIR! I have resumed my long-lost hobby of coin collecting. Do you know that they stopped minting silver coins the year after I left? I didn't know that silver had become so valuable.

At any rate, I will try my best to keep up-to-date on the situation of the nation, although I will always remain a silent person in the crowd, somewhat hesitant in receiving hospitality and friendship. I forgot most of the manners I had been so accustomed to using. Just the other day I was leaving my apartment, and I slammed the door in the landlady's face. Without even looking back to apologize, I continued walking just as if nothing had happened. Things will never be the same, and yet I still have "blind hope" in possession. Every day now since I left prison, I have kept praying and praying. . . .

Peter

## Commentary

This letter is not exactly *de profundis*, but it's pretty close. Yet it holds within it a quiet, modest determination. Peter seems to us to have effectively internalized/realized the likely consequences for him of social deprivation. Even though he accepts himself (i.e., this persona) as a not specially social animal, he has developed a fairly acute sense of the keenness of social needs and of the importance of satisfying them.

The sheer recognition of the difficulties of reentering society is a distinctive strength of his letter, and at two moments he offers us a vivid sense of this. The first is: "I almost didn't want to ask about a room. I spent an hour rehearsing my lines," which is quietly embedded in his account of his week in New York ("quite an experience"). The second is his admission that he has forgotten his social competencies, illustrated by the vivid little cameo of slamming the door in the landlady's face and his rueful confession that he went on walking "as if nothing had happened."

One peculiar feature of offering Peter's text to you, our reader, is this: we have had to decontextualize it to a considerable degree. It was produced, and responded to, as a stage in Peter's writerly journey through our semester together. That it was an important step, carrying with it a significant sense of accomplishment—of this we have no doubt. But it is also disembedded, alas, from any sense, any immediate sense, of Peter as a person. Yet (for reasons that we shall not pursue) we are convinced that here, through his prisoner persona, Peter is realizing one way of exploring questions of "presentation of self in everyday life" that are, in fact, of personal importance to him. That claim you will simply have to take on trust!

## Stacey Silverman's Reentry Text

Here now is Stacey Silverman's reentry text:

> I assumed it was daylight outside, because the prison officials entered my cell wearing sunglasses. I knew something was different because the guard at the end didn't bolt the door shut as soon as everyone had entered. Instead the door stayed ajar at least two feet. The largest of the men told me to grab my things and come along. I slowly got up, grabbed nothing for I had nothing, and followed the men out of what had been my dark existence. Within twenty minutes I was free. After five years in solitary confinement I was free.
>
> I arrived at Kennedy Airport two weeks later. This would be the first day of the rest of my life. I was met by family, friends, and people I had never seen before. Everyone was

hugging and kissing, yet I felt estranged. I had not been shown affection for five years.

For the next months I lived with my parents. I ate every meal as if it were my last. This was an unfortunate habit I picked up during my years in solitary. Those bologna sandwiches I had taken for granted as a child, I now savored with every bite.

It was two months before I came out of my dazed existence and really started noticing the people around me. My parents looked older. My father's once dark brown hair looked faded with strands of silver. My mother's eyes looked so tired. Even more tired than the time I had the fever and she stayed up three nights with me. My little niece, who was a toddler when I entered solitary, was now quoting the multiplication tables. I felt robbed of all the years I had missed. Most of my friends were married, a few were pregnant, and some even had small children. I cried when I learned my best friend from high school had named her daughter after me. I suppose a lot can happen in five years, although for me, it was half a decade of nothing.

I have high expectations for my future. I realize that I have a lot of trauma to overcome, but at least I am aware of the problems that lie ahead. Luckily, I have the support of my family and friends, who never stopped believing in me. I love them all.

"I have high expectations for my future"—a good note to end on!

# THE CLASSROOM DYNAMIC

W hen we prepare our students to write, we tend to operate very economically, with the minimum of guidance and instructions. We believe that if the short-term funding that we offer has done its work, then students will experience a sense of arousal, a reactive energy, even a sense of provocation.

After they have written, however, our contribution becomes more important. In the first place, we help students to find a readership, a community of readers. The first reader, we stress, is the writer himself or herself. Then come others—students in small groups—who respond reciprocally to each other's texts. The only rule here is that commentary shall be nonjudgmental. From that stage, student papers are selected for appreciation by the whole class. How are they chosen? The mode of selection is this: The small-group readings are guided by a set of nonjudgmental descriptive epithets, from which the group may choose one. Examples are:

amazing   complex   intriguing   surprising   disconcerting
passionate   cool   formal, etc.

The group chooses one of these and adds the word "most," making the superlative. Members of the group then read four or five of the class's texts and from them they choose the "most x" text. The task is to work for a consensus or a majority decision. Having highlighted a distinctive characteristic of the chosen text—for example, it is the most *surprising* of the group—they can then explain which features of the text made it so.

*Our* task is to help them to fine-tune these observations; to press for a sharper, more clearly focused characterization of particular features of a text; to note particular moments in the text and observe how they "work"—that is, what kinds of *effects* they have on the reader.

In our annotations of student texts, we ourselves can operate less publicly. For example, shoddy, perfunctory work can be designated as such. But again, the main tendency is positive—to point to the nature of particular achievements in the text. This is complementary to what students themselves do when they write retroactive commentaries (reflections) on their own texts, looking as spectators on texts in which they had participated.

# WRITING FROM INNER SPEECH

*Inner colloquy as a means of communication with others. . . .*
**Denise Levertov**

H ere is Stacey Silverman (Q) talking about writing:*

---

*The text that follows was drawn from a conversation over coffee. In editing, we have omitted our little nudgings and some redundancies; in other words, we have translated a string of Stacey's conversational utterances into an unbroken text.

When I think about doing an assignment, I begin to hear sentences inside my head, in my own voice. But I also listen to how it "sounds" as I "say" it.

There seems to be a shift when I move "writing" inside my head to writing on paper, a shift in the position of my audience. It's less close when I actually write.

When I put pen to paper, the parts that go well are those that I've already composed inside my head, or at least prepared or rehearsed. When it's written down, I read it *out loud*, so that I can hear how other people will "hear" it when they read it. A good text always *sounds* good!

What did I enjoy most this semester? The solitary confinement assignments. I had a strong hold on the emotions involved. I envisioned myself in solitary confinement, it was a dramatic experience. I enjoyed it because I'm *not* in solitary. It wasn't painful. I could feel the pain that I would have felt if it had actually happened, but it wasn't *happening*. I felt the pain of the prisoner in my head. That prisoner was *me*, but it wasn't the person who was sitting at home writing. There were two selves—one doing the experiencing and the other doing the writing.

How did I get into it, "psych myself up"? I thought about it—I actually closed my eyes while I was doing the real thinking about it—not just the sentences that popped into my head, but the stuff that I had to think about—to be *in*. I had to invent a cell, the whole scene. This wasn't all that difficult: I'd seen prison cells on TV and in movies.

We want, now, to isolate one element of Stacey's representation of how she envisions/writes: her account of her use of inner speech in writing. And we want to relate this to a rather more formal account of the same experience offered by Barbara Herrnstein Smith, whose term is "interior speech." Smith observes that "we are almost continuously 'saying' things to that most intimate, congenial and attentive listener whom we carry within our own skins."[8] She concurs with Vygotsky's view that the ability to produce inner speech is "appropriated" or "derived"—a "capacity that could not arise prior to, or independent of, one's participation, as both speaker and listener, in a linguistic community."[9] The implications of this for composition teachers are clear and important. The ability of students to engage in usefully productive, reflective inner speech about their work with us—to think about it, to consider it—will depend in part on what we as instructors offer in the way of talk to be internalized. In other words—and it's worth stating the obvious—if in our office hours and classes we find time for conversation or discussion about our work as writers, students' inner speech is likely to be enriched, to be equipped to think usefully about what they are doing. In a word, an important element of the short-term funding that our course work aims to provide for students is a variety of ways of reflecting on, of talking to themselves about, writing. When we ask students to write informal but considered commentaries on their texts, we are asking them to make public and visible that which can profitably be shared, that which, if allowed to remain private and invisible, will never be shared and will thereby be less useful. Our aim is to promote an enlightening consciousness rather than an inhibiting self-consciousness. The occasion for having students reflect on their texts arises not while the texts are getting made but when they are in some degree felt as completed, at least for the time being.

# Part II
## Fillers: An Endless Fund of Vicarious Roles

# THE NATURE OF FILLERS

E rving Goffman has much to say about stories that are so much a part of our daily lives that we hardly notice them—or, if we do, rarely take them seriously:*

> *There could hardly be data with less face value. Obviously, passing events that are typical or representative don't make news just*

---

*But cf. Edwin Morgan: "I like a poetry that comes not out of 'poetry' but out of a story in today's newspaper, or a chance personal encounter in a city street, or the death of a famous person: I am very strongly moved by the absolute force of what actually happens, because after all, that is it, there is really nothing else that has its poignance, its razor edge. It is not an easy poetry to write, and I think it requires a peculiar kind of imagination that is willing to bend itself to meet a world which is lying there in the rain like an old shoe." (*Worlds*, ed. Geoffrey Summerfield [Harmondsworth: Penguin, 1974], p. 229.)

*for that reason: only extraordinary ones do, and even these are subject to the editorial violence routinely employed by gentle writers. Our understanding of the world precedes these stories, determining which ones reporters will select and how the ones that are selected will be told. Human interest stories are a caricature of evidence in the very degree of their interest, providing a unity, coherence, pointedness, self-completeness, and drama only crudely sustained, if at all, by everyday living. Each is a cross between an* experimentum crucim *and a sideshow. That is their point. The design of these reported events is fully responsive to our demands —which are not for facts but for typifications. Their telling demonstrates the power of our conventional understandings to cope with the bizarre potentials of social life, the furthest reaches of experience. What appears, then, to be a threat to our way of making sense of the world turns out to be an ingeniously selected defense of it. We press these stories to the wind; they keep the world from unsettling us. By and large, I do not present these anecdotes, therefore, as evidence or proof, but as clarifying depictions, as frame fantasies which manage, through the hundred liberties taken by their tellers, to celebrate our beliefs about the workings of the world. What was put into these tales is thus what I would like to get out of them.*[10]

These "data," these "tales," these "frame fantasies"—each a "cross between an *experimentum crucim* and a sideshow"—are stories that we and our students encounter daily. They are what newspaper people call *fillers*—those compelling human interest stories that newspapers print to fill up space. They encapsulate our interests, our dreams, our terrors, our fantasies, our nightmares. And they are "open" texts, precisely because they begin *in medias res*, because they are what Goffman calls a "strip"—a slice that has been cut from a "stream of ongoing activity." They represent *a* point of view, *an* angle of vision: the news reporter or editor has selected the bare bones out of what we can readily imagine to be a richer, more resonant, more extended version of "the" story.

Fillers are the *extraordinary*, the moment that John Doe hits the news. They are a carving out of his daily life, a moment, a once, that makes us laugh or cry or stop to think. Often, these bits and pieces of daily life leave us wondering, speculating, reflecting on the world as it is reported to be; and we stand here, as spectators, thankful that we were not there or envious that we were not there. Fillers leave us spaces to fill up in our minds. We invite our students to *enter* the stories—as spectators and as participants.

# THE CHARLES SEQUENCE

## Primary Text: A Six-Year-Old Driver

Here is one of our favorite fillers:

### 6-YEAR-OLD BOY QUITE A DRIVER

*Six-year-old Charles Boyd wanted to visit his father at work Monday morning in Kings Mountain, N.C., so he hopped into his mother's car and started driving.*

*One-half hour and five miles later, just as he was getting ready to turn onto Interstate 85, the car rolled off a road and bumped to a stop.*

*Charles opened the door and climbed out, startling the man who had been driving behind him.*

*"He thought he was following a drunk, but he never saw the driver," Kings Mountain police dispatcher Roy Dyer said.*

*A little lost, Charles rode with the man to Garlock Industries in Gastonia, where his father works. That's about 20 miles from his home.*

*Dyer said an officer asked Charles how he worked the brakes and the accelerator, "and he said he looked through the windshield until it was clear, and then he'd get down and push the gas. Then he'd jump back up and steer until the car slowed down."*

Daily Times (Gannett Westchester), May 10, 1983

## Reactive Texts: Participants

The first assignment in the Charles sequence is for the students to write as participants, as one of those involved in the event *as it is happening*. They select a role: Charles or Mr. X (the driver behind) or Roy Dyer (the police officer) or Charles's father or Charles's mother. In one class we debated whether or not to include Charles's mother in our list of participants; she, after all, is not explicitly named as a participant in the newspaper version. Lisa Portnoy's portrayal of Charles's mother, however, convinces us that she was indeed a participant.

### Lisa Portnoy's Participant Text

"Charlie, Charlie, where are you?"
*Damn kid, I hate playing hide and seek.*

"Charlie, you get in here right now or you're gonna get it."

*He wants another one. The hell with that. I can't even handle this one. No more babies for me.*

"Charlie, Charlie!"

*I'll bet he's hiding outside. Damn kid.*

"Charlie! Charlie!"

*Oh my god, where is my car?*

"CHARLIE!"

"Oh no, oh no, oh no. Help, my baby's been stolen, my car's been kidnapped. Help."

*Calm. Be calm. Breathe. O.K. Breathe some more. Go back inside. Call police. Be calm. Breathe. Pick up phone. Dial. Very good. Calm. Take deep breath. Oh, why the hell aren't they answering?*

"Oh, help, someone has stolen my baby and my car. Yes, he's six. Blonde hair, blue eyes. Yes, about 40 lbs. Omigod. Have you found him? Is he dead? Is my baby O.K.? Where is my baby? What, no. No. He . . . what? No. My husband is driving him home? Could you explain this to me again? Yeah. O.K. Thank you."

*I'm gonna kill him.*

Lisa Portnoy (Q)

Lisa's text typifies the participant texts of more than fifty students in two freshman composition classes. The students represent the event as if it is happening by filling in the "once," by seeing it for what it is— an event that is happening as it does and will never occur again in the same way. Lisa breathes the life of *particularity* into the event by allowing Charles's mother to speak; she takes on flesh, comes to life. We feel her "states of mind": irritated, annoyed, puzzled, persistent, bewildered, exasperated, breathless, anxious, incredulous, resolute ("I'm gonna kill him"). The text, its verbs cast in the present, captures the immediacy of the moment. The voice is both monologic (talking to herself) and dialogic (calling to the absent Charles, speaking to the nameless police officer). Her text represents utterance, is paratactic. The participant, uncertain, inconclusive, speculative, is so deeply involved in the event that she cannot see the forest for the trees; she sees the parts but not the whole; she does not evaluate. Interestingly, once Lisa's "mother" knows that Charles has not been kidnapped or harmed, she's "gonna kill him." The first sign of relief to the participant, who now, instantaneously, has become spectator, is to prepare for the future. The present gives way to the past as she anticipates the future.

### Roberta Meacham's Participant Text

Here is another of our favorite participant texts in the Charles sequence; Roberta Meacham takes on the role of the driver behind, who weaves, oscillates between participating (driving his car, talking to his wife) and spectating (trying to figure out what's going on). He is a participant-spectator:

> "Put that book down and look. I tell you what Mildred, that's the damnedest thing I ever seen in my life."
>
> "What's that, Billy Jack?"
>
> "Well, that car up yonder. D'you ever in your life see anything weave so bad? Hell, he's got more moves than a box of Exlax. I just don't dare git close enough to see who or *what* is drivin'."
>
> "They're probably just drunk, Billy Jack. When we get over to Ersel's station, we maybe oughta call the police. They can check them out before they hurt somebody."
>
> "Shoot. If we even make it that far. Geez, Mildred, now just take a look at that sign on the back of that thing. 'DRINKIN' AND DRIVIN' DON'T MIX'. . . now ain't that something. You reckon that's one of them midgets from over to Rahleigh?"
>
> "Lordy, I wouldn't know. But that intersection's comin' up and they'll never make that turn. Now you just mark my words."
>
> "Jesus Christ! Look at that, Mildred. They've drove clean off the damn road."
>
> "Now what did I tell you. You reckon we ought to stop to see if anybody's hurt or anything?"
>
> "Yeah, we'd better check it out. But Mildred honey, you know what they always say . . . The Lord looks after drunks and kids."
>
> Roberta Meacham (U)

## *Reactive Texts: Participant Becomes Spectator*

When students represent the same event as *erstwhile participants*—participants who have now become spectators—they remove themselves in time from the event as it is happening and look back on the event as it happened. They are no longer in but out, no longer there but here. And the forms of discourse reflect the difference. The move parallels what we do in our daily lives when we tell of something that

has happened to us: we remove ourselves in the telling; we become —
even if we are still emotionally involved in the event — spectators of our
own lives. And often we tell, precisely *because* we are trying for distance. We look back, remember, reflect on — and evaluate.

Take Mr. X, for example. As participant, numerous questions arise in
his mind as he tries to make sense of the "driverless" car in front of
him. Here is a sampling:

> I can't believe it — am I seeing things?
> Is the guy crazy, drunk, asleep, short?
> Is it a remote-controlled car?
> Is it a drunk midget?
> *Is* there a driver?
> Am I having a nervous breakdown?
> Is it some old lady who can't see over the wheel?

Later, looking back as spectator, Mr. X puts many of the pieces together
to construct a representation of the event; he orders it anew and orders
it within the particular evaluative frame he has "chosen." We might say
that the choosing chooses him, unwilled, for it emerges out of his own
conceptual, evaluative frame — what psychologist George Kelly would
call a "templet," a "transparent pattern," through which he sees the
world;[11] so that, depending on what the spectator foregrounds and
backgrounds (hypotaxis), the reader sees how *he* sees the world, how
he informs the event through his own values.

Here now is a sampling of Mr. X's later evaluation of the event:

> What an amazing little boy.
> I'm sure I wasn't that smart at that age.
> I really felt sorry for that little kid. He must have been
> desperate to see his father.
> If he were my kid, I'd give him the beating of his life.
> Thank God, no one got hurt.
> Somebody could have been killed.
> Now, at least I know I'm not crazy.

## Reactive Texts: The Noninvolved Spectator

We push further, asking our students to write as spectators who were
not involved in any way in the event. They can be a teacher, some other
child's parent, a child psychologist, a journalist — they can assume
whatever spectator role they choose.

### Neil Frederickson's Noninvolved Spectator

Here is Neil Frederickson (Q) in role as an editorialist taking a strong stand on the issues he sees within the text.

Unwatched children are becoming more and more frequent in today's society. Witness the case of Charles Boyd, a six-year-old, who, while left unattended, decided to drive to his father's place of employment 20 miles away, on his own. Finding the car keys, which had carelessly been left lying around, young Charles started the car and managed to drive five miles before running off the road.

Charles showed great imagination in driving the car, but this does not change the fact that he is only six years old and could have caused an accident on the highway. It was sheer luck that no one was hurt and Charles was stopped before an accident occurred. Even so, when he stopped, he was far from home and could have fallen victim to any number of hazards, not the least of which was possible kidnapping. Luck was again with Charles, that a kind man was in the car behind him and was able to help him.

Not all children would be so lucky. There are many cases where such situations end in disaster. But what can be done about the problem? Certainly, the first thing is to try not to leave such young children unattended. Have a neighbor look in on the child once in a while. But if it is necessary to leave the child alone, make sure he knows what he can and can't do. Also, don't leave any hazardous or tempting things (like car keys) lying around. Educate the child well and try not to leave him unattended for too long a period. Remember, the safety of your child is your responsibility, whether you are there all the time or not.

# A PARTICIPANT/SPECTATOR CORRELATION

When we contrast the texts of participants and closely involved spectators with Neil's distant spectator text, we find that the "once" has been transformed. Where the participant-spectator was eager to *realize* the event, to capture the intensity of the moment, the remote spectator sees the once as a "case," as representative of what can happen to "unwatched children." Charles, who had been "Charlie" to Lisa, becomes "the child" to Neil's editorialist. The particularities of the case are selected out to fit the narrator's evaluative framework: the keys had "carelessly been left lying around"; Charles had been "left unattended"; the man in the car behind had been "kind"; it had worked out all right in this case, but "not all children would be so lucky." The event, now represented in the past tense, is subsumed in the general "truth," in the present continuous: "Unwatched children are becoming more and more frequent. . . ." The event becomes subordinate to the message, the informative to the conative, as the present and the past give way to the future, and the indicative and interrogative give way to the imperative:

> Have a neighbor look in. . . .
> Don't leave the child alone. . . .
> Educate the child well. . . .
> Remember. . . .

The correlation now becomes richer:

> Participant:   parataxis / particularization
> Spectator:   hypotaxis / generalization

But again, this is not surprising. We know that we simply cannot store, neurologically, event upon event, instance upon instance, without typifying. The event becomes a type; the once, representative; the particular gives way to the general. And while we may remember and savor the particularities of daily events, especially those that have made a difference in our lives, the "instances" give way to sorting, classifying, contrasting, generalizing, evaluating. We find that we do not need to *teach* these fundamental acts of mind; we merely make them explicit.

The movement from participant to spectator, and an understanding of what such a shift entails in terms of textual options and constraints, are the fundamentals that we aim for. We offer this theoretical framework to our students incrementally, trying to sense the moment, the occasion, when such framing will provide them with a handle—a grasp on the issues involved in their making of texts. They accept the frames as a means whereby they can reflect on the texts they have already made. In this sense, most of our "teaching" involves a retroactive pedagogy, a set of aids to reflection.

As teachers of composition, we must envisage and frame our own autonomous *terminus ad quem*. For us, this is a mind within each student that has come to appreciate more fully what is involved in the production of a text, a clearer and more confident sense of the available options, a more sophisticated sense of textuality and of utterance. By the end of a fourteen-week semester, our students will have produced about twenty-five texts—including some abandoned false starts and prototexts to be completed in their own time. And lodged somewhere inside their heads they will have a reasonably well-ordered sense of this correlative pattern:[12]

| PARTICIPANT | parataxis | particularity | private | present tense | ellipsis | uncontextu-alized and unevaluated |
|---|---|---|---|---|---|---|
| SPECTATOR | hypotaxis | generalization | public/ social | past/ future | redundancy | contextu-alized and evaluated |

# SUNDRY FILLERS, SUNDRY REACTIONS

Finally, we present three fillers that have sparked much creative merriment in our classrooms. First is a goose story:

### GOOSE IS COOKED

*PITTSBURGH (UPI)—Charles Wood Jr. found out what a pet goose is worth in court—at least $140.*

*Wood, 18, of Pittsburgh, was found guilty of criminal mischief Friday, fined $40 plus court costs and directed to pay $100 restitution to Gary and Andrea Simpson, who owned the pet goose, Pebbles, which disappeared May 27.*

*Acting on a tip, Mrs. Simpson said she and a Humane Society officer found goose feathers in the basement of Wood's home down the street shortly after Pebbles disappeared from their back yard May 27.*

The Herald Journal, Logan, Utah, June 12, 1983

Here are three reactions to the "goose" story:

So what? So it cost me a hundred and forty bucks for a goose dinner. I still maintain that it was the most satisfying meal of my life.

Whatever gave Mr. and Mrs. Simpson the idea that a goose would make a good pet anyway? What earthly good could a goose be to anyone? Watch dogs, okay; but watch geese, come on! The whole idea is revolting! I hate geese.

But, anyway, I may as well say from the start that I didn't intend to kill it. In fact, I didn't even intend to go near it. Like I said, I hate geese. It wasn't really my fault that my basketball careened off the rim, bounced over the Simpsons' fence and into their back yard. I had only been shooting baskets for five minutes, and I had planned to put in an hour or two of practice since my parents had the car and I couldn't make it to the gym. I was trying to stay in form for next season. It was really important to me, if you see what I mean.

Well, my ball was gone, my practice rudely interrupted, and the Simpsons weren't home. Their fence gate was locked, and my ball was lying on their back lawn in the middle of a pile of goose guano. It was a real predicament. Like I said, I hate geese. But something had to be done. I wasn't about to leave my ball back there with that goose. So, I boosted myself over the gate and dropped down into the Simpsons' yard.

Not wanting to alarm the goose, I tiptoed carefully and quietly through the goose droppings toward my basketball. I picked the ball up cautiously, not wanting it to touch my clothes, and held it at arm's-length from my body.

As I sadly surveyed the bird-soiled condition of my official-sized, simulated-leather basketball, I began to pick my way back to the gate. The smell of the place was unbearable. I was anxious to get safely back onto my own driveway, wipe off the ball (thoroughly, and preferably with soap and water), and resume play.

But no sooner had I started back toward the gate, when I turned my head and saw a huge white shape rushing headlong straight at me, squawking and flapping like an avenging angel. I took off toward the fence as fast as I could. No time to worry about where to put my feet now. Three more steps. I made a desperate leap for the gate, but my footing was slippery and my feet slipped out from under me. I landed flat on my back and continued sliding in the guano until my feet hit the base of the gate. I whirled around on my back to see the goose's face and long neck only inches away—coiled, hissing, ready to strike. Thoughts of cobras squirmed through my brain. In my panic, I looked around me for a weapon. Nothing. Ah, but in my hands—the basketball! In one incredibly smooth move I jumped to my feet, raised the ball high above my head, and beaned that goose with a slam dunk that would have put Dr. J. to shame. Perfect scoring play. The world suddenly had one less goose.

Then, who could blame me for what happened next? How could I waste the good meat? What better way to dispose of the "corpus delicti" than to roast and eat him? So what that they caught me? So what that they fined me one hundred and forty dollars? The only good goose is a dead goose. Anyone for basketball?

Lind Williams (U)


"That damn goose. Every time I walk down this sidewalk he comes squawking around the corner. Listen to him honk. Hey, hey, get back you crazy bird! Damn, he goosed me again! I'm going to kill myself running from that monster." . . .

O, shit, here he comes again, flapping those huge wings and hissing like a snake. Hey, get away you—ow! He nipped me again. That's it, that's enough, I can't stand it. . . .

Ok, I think it's plenty dark tonight. The biggest problem was the Simpsons, but I saw them leave. Car's still gone. Good. All right, you stupid goose—Hey, sh, shut up—my heck, what a racket, I'll catch you yet, you're a gone goose for sure, Aha! Into the gunny sack. Ha Ha. . . .

Burp! What a meal! I've never enjoyed one so much. This goose is cooked. Ha! Ha!

Adrienne Morris (U)


As a cop, I've seen a lot in my time, but the day the lady came crying bloody murder was a dilly.

"Oh, I can't believe it. Poor Pebbles, oh Pebbles my baby!" She was sobbing about a baby.

I said, "Lady, calm down please. What about your baby?"

"Oh, officer, that Charlie Wood killed him!"

I immediately stopped everything, and took her arm.

"Step over here and tell me, please, what happened?"

"Oh, I can't believe it! He came to my house last night and took Pebbles and killed him with an ax!"

I think to myself, "My god, an ax!" I buzz homicide, and try to calm the lady.

"Please stop crying, now, it's important to get the facts."

She calms down a little, and then screams, "And he ate him!"

By then my hair's standing on end, and I say to Detective Smith as he comes up, "We've got a bad one, Dave."

"What is it," he says softly over the sobbing woman.

"Lady says her baby was murdered—with an ax, and then, so help me Dave, she says he was eaten."

Dave turns green; the lady looks up at me and says, "It was my pet goose, my baby!"

Hysterical women make me ill.

Adrienne Morris (U)

Next we present a "solo" event and one student's reaction:

## CLASS BY HIMSELF

BRADFORD, Pa. (UPI)—D. Edgar Cohn took all the door prizes at his 75th high school reunion—he was the only member of the class able to attend.

There are two other survivors from Cohn's class, but one was too ill to attend and the other couldn't be located, school officials said.

Being the lone classmate at the reunion didn't bother him too much, he said.

The Herald Journal
Logan, Utah, June 12, 1983

### CLASS BY HIMSELF

Shaky hands to knot my tie
Why won't that collar stay in place
I'll wear the vest—the weather's fickle
    Is that Jenny drivin' up?

Reunion—umm—Sarah's gone
Why am I sprucing?
Walter's feeble—will he come
I'm exhausted with this fussin'
    Is that Jenny drivin' up?

234

Friday—today is Friday
Have I missed the "doo"?
Lunch and pictures . . . reminiscing
Is that Jenny drivin' up?

Joyce Oldroyd (U)

And, finally, here is a filler about a New York cabbie. We can still hear the laughter when Ernel read this text aloud to the class.

## CABBY DOESN'T WANT TO FEEL LEFT OUT

*A whimsical departure from the myriad signs telling riders what not to do in taxicabs is a hand-lettered one, in a childlike scrawl: PLEASE!*
*NO KISSING IN BACK SEAT OF TAXI*
*(unless driver included)*

*New York Times*
May 11, 1984

No kissing in back seat of taxi (unless driver included). Is this guy trying to be funny? Maybe it is a problem. Do that many people actually kiss in taxis that it's a distraction, or is he trying for a laugh? It isn't funny. If I want to kiss, that's my business. I pay my fare. It's a private matter. Who'd want to kiss him anyway? He should keep his eyes on the road and not worry about the back seat. 'Course he isn't bad looking. He is clean and he has a nice smile. I wonder what he is like. If I were to kiss him, how? Would I say, "Stop, I'm ready." Would he keep the meter running? Would he be nice, or gross? He probably would be vulgar. Still, he has nice hair. But there's a pimple on his neck.

Ernel Anderson (U)

# NOTES

1. Denise Levertov, *Light Up the Cave* (New York: New Directions, 1981), p. 149.
2. *New York Times*, July 1, 1984.
3. Edith Bone, *Seven Years Solitary* (London: Hamish Hamilton, 1957).
4. Jacobo Timerman, *Prisoner Without a Cell, Cell Without a Number* (New York: Knopf, 1981).
5. Barbara Herrnstein Smith, *On the Margins of Discourse* (Chicago: University of Chicago Press, 1983), p. 85.
6. Erving Goffman, *Frame Analysis: An Essay on the Organization of Experience* (New York: Harper & Row, 1974), p. 53.
7. Ibid., p. 57.
8. Smith, *On the Margins of Discourse*, p. 92.
9. Ibid.
10. Goffman, pp. 14–15.
11. George Kelly, *A Theory of Personality* (New York: Norton, 1963).
12. Part of this section was first written at the invitation of Donald McQuade for inclusion in *The Territory of Language: Linguistics, Stylistics, and the Teaching of Composition*, due for publication Summer, 1985 (Carbondale: Southern Illinois University Press).

# CHAPTER ELEVEN

# GENERATIVE FRAME
## Familiarization and Defamiliarization

*The two most engaging powers of an author are to make new things familiar, and familiar things new.*
Samuel Johnson

The dynamics of social interaction, which are always present – however obscurely or obliquely – in the relationship between writer and reader, assume specially direct or piquant force when the writer engages in an act of familiarization or defamiliarization.

In the first case, the aim or impulse is to share, to make available. Contrarily, the impulse behind defamiliarization is to tease, as riddles tease; to withhold, to mislead, to disconcert and surprise.

In the first, the role of the writer is that which we occupy in our daily social or professional lives when we introduce someone to something that is familiar to us and new to them. In the second, the role is an unsettling or alienating one, whereby the writer rejects familiar frames of recognition, of agreed "meaning," and offers an accurate and defensible representation that depends on a deliberate *mis*-reading – an alien reading.

# Part I
## Familiarization—
## Instructing, Sharing

# FAMILIARIZATION AS AN ACT OF INSTRUCTION

F amiliarization seems to occur in two main contexts: social and vocational – that is, sharing and instruction. In vocational contexts, it is used for the purpose of initiation. In social situations, it seems to be used for the purpose of confirming and/or strengthening a bond. It is a way of sharing bits of valued experience, "sacred objects."[1] The desire is not primarily to transmit information but to share values. *A* familiarizes *B* with *X*, because the act of familiarization is, in itself, socially satisfying – for a variety of reasons that you can uncover by exploring your own recent past and its moments of sharing.

### *Agassiz's Jellyfish*

Consider now a text by Louis Agassiz, the distinguished nineteenth-century biologist and teacher. Consider it as an act of familiarization. And as you read, use your mind's eye.

Seen floating in the water *Cyanea Arctica* exhibits a large circular disk, of a substance not unlike jelly, thick in the centre, and suddenly thinning out towards the edge, which presents several indentations. The centre of that disk is of a dark purplish-brown color, while the edge is much lighter, almost white and transparent. This disk is constantly heaving and falling, at regular intervals; the margin is especially active, so much so, that, at times, it is stretched on a level with the whole surface of the disk, which, in such a condition, is almost flat, while, at other times, it is so fully arched that it assumes the appearance of a hemisphere. These motions recall so strongly those of an umbrella, alternately opened and shut, that writers, who have described similar animals, have generally called this gelatinous disk the umbrella. From the lower surface of this disk hang, conspicuously, three kinds of appendages. Near the margin there are eight bunches of long tentacles, moving in every direction, sometimes extending to an enormous length, sometimes shortened to a mere coil of entangled threads, constantly rising and falling, stretching now in one direction and then in another, but generally spreading slantingly in a direction opposite to that of the onward movement of the animal. These streamers may be compared to floating tresses of hair, encircling organs which are farther inward upon the lower surface of the disk. Of these organs, there are also eight bunches, which alternate with the eight bunches of tentacles, but they are of two kinds; four are elegant sacks, adorned, as it were, with waving ruffles projecting in large clusters, which are alternately pressed forward and withdrawn, and might also be compared to bunches of grapes, by turns inflated and collapsed. These four bunches alternate with four masses of folds, hanging like rich curtains, loosely waving to and fro, and as they wave, extending downwards, or shortening rapidly, recalling, to those who have had an opportunity of witnessing the phenomenon, the play of the streamers of an aurora borealis. All these parts have their fixed position; they are held together by a sort of horizontal curtain, which is suspended from the lower surface of the gelatinous disk. The horizontal curtain is itself connected with the disk, fastened to it as it were by ornamental stitches, which divide the whole field into a number of areas, alternately larger and smaller, now concentric, now radiating, between which the organs already described are inserted.[2]

## Applying Jakobson's Frames to Agassiz

Roman Jakobson has postulated six frames of discourse:[3]

1. An addresser (the person talking or writing)

2. An addressee (the listener or reader)

3. A contact that joins them

4. A message that is passed from 1 to 2

5. A context, which makes sense of the message

6. A linguistic code, whereby the participants "construct" their messages and refer to "the world."

Let us now apply these frames of discourse to Agassiz's text:

1. Agassiz is the addresser—not as private person (husband, father, neighbor, or whatever) but in role as biologist/teacher of biology, explainer of biological phenomena.

2. The addressee, clearly, is someone who is absent, not present, otherwise Agassiz would not need to use text; the addressee is reader, not listener.

3. The contact is presumably a shared interest in jellyfish: on the part of the absent reader, a desire to know more, to satisfy curiosity, to enlarge knowledge; on Agassiz's part, a willingness to do the work necessary to inform the reader, to create an illusion of presence.

4. The message is clear enough; it's there on the paper. But it will get over only if both writer and reader recognize and exploit the resources of language to conjure up an image, to see, especially, not only the parts but the whole.

5. The context is a book. It has been opened by the reader. The reader has a wish, a need, an intention, that is expressed by the opening of the book. In a larger sense, the context is biological science, subsection marine biology as it existed in the late nineteenth century. The macrocontext is the Western world, its scientific tradition, the discipline of observation in the empirical sciences.

6. What, then, of the code? What are the conventions of that discourse known as English as used by biologists when addressing readers who do not know as much as the writer? (We *infer* that the reader addressed knows less than the writer. If the text had been intended for specialists, we would probably have found it mostly incomprehensible.) We can see that the

text is not text as transcript of utterance, for there are none of the "crutches" that occur in such texts—it contains no "er" or "like" or "sort of"—the kind of hesitation phenomena that characterize relaxed, informal utterance. Nor does the text seem to be a transcript of formal, expository talk— the kind of talk we might encounter in a formal, prepared lecture-demonstration.

And yet the prose sounds "natural" in the sense that Peter Medawar, a distinguished twentieth-century biologist, uses the term:

> *At some stage in his life a young scientist will inevitably have to give a paper to a learned society though not before he has tried it out on his mates at, for example, a departmental seminar. The latter is a friendly and relaxed occasion, but a paper to a learned society requires a little more address.* Under no circumstances whatsoever should a paper be read from a script. *It is hard to overestimate the dismay and resentment of an audience that has to put up with a paper read hurriedly in an even monotone: Speak from notes, young scientist; to speak without is a form of showing off and only creates the impression (perhaps well founded) that the same story has been told over and over again. Notes should be brief and never consist of long paragraphs of stately prose. If a few cues aren't sufficient to get a speaker into motion then he must go over the topic repeatedly—not necessarily aloud—until the right words come at the appropriate stimulus. I early found it to be a great help when trying to expound a difficult concept to write (EXPLAIN THIS) after it appears in the notes—a device that of course forces a speaker to find natural words.*
>
> *A torrential outpouring of words may make the speaker think that he is being brilliant, but his audience is more likely to think him glib. A measured delivery with perhaps a touch of gravity is what Polonius would surely have recommended.*[4]

But this is, *pace* Peter Medawar, not nature but *second nature.* Behind the text, we can infer many years of lab work, of teaching, of explaining, of demonstrating. Out of this funding, Agassiz has fashioned a clean prose style whose patterns follow the sequences of demonstration. And we infer that he was especially good at explaining biology to nonspecialists, because he is especially adept at finding/ offering clarifying analogies—umbrella, tresses of hair, bunches of grapes, rich curtains, and so on—analogies that depend only on commonly shared perceptions.

# FAMILIARIZATION AS AN ACT OF SHARING

## *Sharing Sacred Objects*

We invited our students to share some of their valued experiences by sharing with us—representing and presenting—an object that had taken on great meaning in their lives, something that was not just an object in their environment but was treasured by virtue of its associations, its power to evoke some of their most important values.

Rare are the times that I leave the house for any length of time that the faded, blue-gray, ratty old rucksack is not with me. It is my security blanket. My thumb to suck when I must face the world. More often than not it is my friend and companion, a confidant that is always there and rarely gets sassy. I am quite certain that if my neurotic Labrador did not accompany me on my frequent forays into the hills and fields, I should find myself talking to it. Perhaps even patting it on the head and searching for eyes to look into.

That canvas rucksack, from England, fits my needs and wants most perfectly. It came to me as a present from an understanding wife when I graduated from college: A replacement for another, which, no longer structurally sound, hangs in honor in my most private basement corner. In its barrel-shaped form less than two feet high and a foot wide, I can carry all that I need to enter a vicarious world of simplicity that seems to be more elusive each year. No flashy, high-tech indestructible nylon with whistles, bells, toggles, and pockets for toilet paper rolls, it is made of honest cotton duck that ages, that takes on character, and that, like me, will some day wear out.

The straps are simple and stout, and are beginning to wear. A simple top with one strap provides almost water-proofness to the contents and the ice axe loop on the back has carried ice axes, shovels, ski-poles, and rifles. The recent addition of a bright red strap to the crampon rings on the lid was a deliberate wish to add a bit of color to a saddening face, worn with time and distance.

No stay-at-home, this sack has been throughout the United States, including Alaska. It has been up many mountains and served in many ways. I once left it for a grizzly—hoping he would find it more appetizing than the painfully mortal flesh of a scared Utahnian far from home. A walrus once rolled on it, to my horror, and I knew it was lost forever.

Far more important than the exterior, which exists only to give shape to the memories within, is the wonderful interior. For it is here that I have carried the finest books that I have read, the finest wines that I have drunk, the finest fishing flies that I have tied, and the journals that have guided my recollections of times and places long ago and far away.

At any given moment a stranger should hesitate to put their hand into this cavern. The bottom is usually littered with the foil wrappers of ski-wax tins, stale pipe tobacco, dried-up mustard, sardines that somehow dropped in and were forgotten, and rolls of film that I meant to develop months ago. I washed it once, perhaps twice, but have put that foolishness behind me now. No, this is not for looking pretty or for carrying a truckload of hardware up some mountain. I have three other rucksacks for that. This is for carrying my memories and expectations, and the key to myself.

David Foxley (U)

## THE BRASS WATER BUCKET

Those of you who have always had hot and cold running water, will not know about washstands. Well, ever since I can remember, a large brass water bucket sat on our washstand along with a dipper, wash basin, soap dish, and soap; the hand towel hung on a corner post of the rack on the back of the stand.

Our drinking water came from a fresh water well about forty feet from the back door of our house. Attached to a strong thick rope, which ran over a big pulley bolted to a crossbar, was a three-gallon galvanized bucket. We would lower this bucket down into the water, draw it up, then pour the water into the brass water bucket, carry it back to the house and set it on the washstand in the kitchen.

The heavy brass bucket had been carefully molded to about an eighth inch thickness on the sides and a quarter inch thickness on the slightly rounded nine-inch bottom. Its almost nine-inch-long sides slope outward and are rolled over into greater thickness at the wider, thirteen-inch slightly oval top. A sturdy iron handle passes through heavy brass grommets riveted to opposite sides of the bucket. There are no seams in the bucket.

My oldest sister told me that the brass bucket must be at least sixty-five years old. She recalled a particular day when Papa hitched the horses to the wagon to go to town for groceries and other supplies. This was the day he brought the brass water bucket home.

The empty bucket was heavy all by itself. I can well remember drawing water from the well, but only filling the pail halfway, because I could not lift it when it was full. The water was always deliciously cold, even on hot summer days. White lines formed on the inside of the brass bucket because of the minerals in the water. When we polished the outside of the pail with Brasso, we also had to scour the inside in an attempt to remove the white lines.

Years passed by and the family moved to town and to modern conveniences. The old brass water bucket was relegated to the basement. Then one day Papa took it back to the farm and used it to dip oats out of the bin for his riding horses, or to carry milk to an orphan calf, and various other and sundry uses. The dents in the bottom of the pail attest to the hard knocks it had endured. However, from lack of care, the bucket's interior and exterior became discolored.

I do not know how many years the brass bucket remained at the farm, but after Papa's death in 1966, my youngest sister, Elaine, and my youngest brother, Mel, claimed ownership to the pail, and when he discovered Elaine planned to plant flowers in it, he declared the brass bucket was his and that was all there was to it. So the old bucket remained in his possession.

Several years ago, on one of my summer visits to my family in Southern Alberta, I told Mel I would clean and shine the brass bucket for him, so he could use it as a magazine rack, or whatever he wished to do with it. As I worked with Brasso to remove years of oxidation, the outside of the bucket took on a rich shiny glow again, evidence of its enduring qualities and beauty. It seemed, however, that no amount of scrubbing and scouring could restore the inside of the pail to its original beauty; the years had taken their toll.

When my task was completed, I showed the rejuvenated brass water bucket to Mel, and it was then he asked me if

I would like to take the pail home with me. I was so delighted that I could hardly contain myself. The loan, however, was made on the condition that I affix his name to the inside of the bucket. The brass antique, built to last an eternity, does not leak and could still serve as a water bucket.

This priceless treasure now occupies an honored place in my living room between a large upholstered chair and the piano. The old brass water bucket is not only filled with magazines, but is also filled with nostalgic memories of the past—both bitter and sweet.

Grace B. Peterson (U)

# Part II
## Defamiliarization— Teasing, Evoking

If familiarization is a significant part of social life, then defamiliarization also has a part to play. We know it as the unsettling experience of returning to a familiar place after an absence and seeing it as strange, odd, or new; while those who never left see it—or don't see it—through eyes that take it for granted. We also know defamiliarization in the form of teasing, of withholding—of guessing games and as riddles. All cultures, it seems, find a place for riddles. In Western cultures, childhood—ages 6 to 11—seems to be the peak years for riddling. (In adolescence our bodies, identities, and futures become in themselves riddles.) Later, many of us return to riddles in the form of mystery and detective stories: "There it was," we say, "the main clue, right under my nose, and I didn't recognize it!" We know it also in science fiction and science fiction movies—the familiar world seen through alien eyes, or seen at some far-removed time—as with Los Angeles in *Blade Runner.*

Defamiliarization is at the root of *Gulliver's Travels.* When Gulliver returns to the familiar world he fails to recognize it because he has meanwhile become habituated to the unfamiliar. In one alien place, Gulliver, the "average" man, is translated into a giant; in another, he is seen to be as small as an insect.

# ELIZABETH BISHOP SEES WITH ALIEN EYES

Here is Elizabeth Bishop writing as an alien:

## 12 O'CLOCK NEWS

*As you all know, tonight is the night of the full moon, half the world over. But here the moon seems to hang motionless in the sky. It gives very little light; it could be dead. Visibility is poor. Nevertheless, we shall try to give you some idea of the lay of the land and the present situation.*

*The escarpment that rises abruptly from the central plain is in heavy shadow, but the elaborate terracing of its southern glacis gleams faintly in the dim light, like fish scales. What endless labor those small, peculiarly shaped terraces represent! And yet, on them the welfare of this tiny principality depends.*

*A slight landslide occurred in the northwest about an hour ago. The exposed soil appears to be of poor quality: almost white, calcareous, and shaly. There are believed to have been no casualties.*

*Almost due north, our aerial reconnaissance reports the discovery of a large rectangular "field," hitherto unknown to us, obviously man-made. It is dark-speckled. An airstrip? A cemetery?*

*In this small, backward country, one of the most backward left in the world today, communications are crude and "industrialization" and its products almost nonexistent. Strange to say, however, signboards are on a truly gigantic scale.*

*We have also received reports of a mysterious, oddly shaped, black structure, at an undisclosed distance to the east. Its presence was revealed only because its highly polished surface catches such feeble moonlight as prevails. The natural resources of the country being far from completely known to us, there is the possibility that this may be, or may contain, some powerful and terrifying "secret weapon." On the other hand, given what we do know, or have learned from our anthropologists and sociologists about this people, it may well be nothing more than a numen, or a great altar recently erected to one of their gods, to which, in their present historical state of superstition and helplessness, they attribute magical powers, and may even regard as a "savior," one last hope of rescue from their grave difficulties.*

*At last! One of the elusive natives has been spotted! He appears to be—rather, to have been—a unicyclist-courier, who may have* met his end by falling from the height of the escarpment because of the deceptive illumination. Alive, he would have been small, but undoubtedly proud and erect, with the thick, bristling black hair typical of the indigenes.

From our superior vantage point, we can clearly see into a sort of dugout, possibly a shell crater, a "nest" of soldiers. They lie heaped together, wearing the camouflage "battle dress" intended for "winter warfare." They are in hideously contorted positions, all dead. We can make out at least eight bodies. These uniforms were designed to be used in guerrilla warfare on the country's one snow-covered mountain peak. The fact that these poor soldiers are wearing them here, on the plain, gives further proof, if proof were necessary, either of the childishness and hopeless impracticality of this inscrutable people, our opponents, or of the sad corruption of their leaders.[5]

In the margin of her text, Bishop provided the following glosses; see if you can identify them in her text: ink bottle, pile of manuscripts, typewriter, ashtray, typewriter eraser, typed sheet, envelopes, and gooseneck lamp.

# OUR STUDENTS SEE WITH ALIEN EYES

## *An Exercise in Defamiliarization*

With Bishop's text as a model, we ask our students to defamiliarize an object that is so familiar no one ever pays it attention—in this case a small ball of crumpled ruled paper. Defamiliarization plays with one's powers of recognition. Only when it was attended to did the object become interesting. Attention was rewarded by the observation of many interesting features: texture, form, associations. Here are their texts—written within a three-minute time limit:

1. White, sphere-shaped, craterous, rough surfaced, weathered appearance.
2. I'm near a mountain of snow. It seems like this mountain has tunnels that lead nowhere.
3. A white spherical object, evidently manipulated to minimize surface area. Probably used for liquid absorption.

4. A white circular ridged mass, containing various forms of craters . . . maybe a meteorite.
5. A huge mass of rock, possibly a mountain, with lots of caves and small indentations, which form small shelters. Some caves end suddenly. Many have little cracks that lead into other caves and tunnels. Some go all the way through; some go around in circles.
6. A unicolored spherical mass of compressed fibers stands before me. Its surface is marked by small niches and large crevices. Its purpose cannot be readily determined.
7. A highly colored round object with various sorts of craterlike indentations on the surface. It looks like one of the planets in our galaxy.
8. Very big soft, white, spherical object, with irregular edges. Probably folded from a flat form haphazardly. The surface is marked by irregular blue and red lines.
9. It is a huge three-dimensional structure, circular in shape. Although its weight is quite light, the structure seems to be a solid, not hollowed. There are crevices everywhere. Some are deep, some shallow. The surface is dry. We cannot detect any life-form.
10. White irregular shape has sharp pointed edges at indefinite intervals. Fine lines are seen on this massive object. The lines are darker than any solid ivory surface . . . plenty of folds, nooks, and crannies.
11. A huge white spherical mass with sharp indentations and protrusions in which there is no consistent pattern.

What the texts offer is varying *degrees* of defamiliarization. Some students chose to change the scale drastically, so as to conceal the actual size, and thus *deliberately* misconstrued (and therefore "misrepresented") the object, as if seen through midget alien eyes—as in Bishop's poem and the first part of *Gulliver's Travels*. Some forms of representation are offered, while others—those that would signal familiarity and facilitate recognition—are withheld. *Indentations, protrusions, edges, folds, nooks, crannies, ridges, cracks, niches,* and *crevices* are all allowed. They are indeed features of a crumpled ball of paper, but they are clearly not crucial aids to recognition. And some of those words do point in the direction of a change of scale: *niche* and *crevice*, for example.

It was only through the conferring of close attention that students transformed a perfectly banal object into a richer possibility. This, then, was an exercise that stretched, challenged, and provoked their representational resources. And they discovered the canny wit of John

Constable's remark: "I must paint what I see, not what I know is there." They all "knew what was there"—a mere crumpled ball of paper; but when they accepted the constraint of representing what they *saw,* the world—a little fragment of it—transcended the conditions of stale familiarity.

The social and interpersonal dimensions of defamiliarization are very rich: to give and simultaneously to withhold; to tease one's reader/ audience with meticulous representations that *should* afford instant recognition and yet yield up their identity slowly. The obvious analogy, as we have remarked, is the riddle. Powerful dynamics arise between riddler and "victim." When the victim solves the riddle, the riddler's pleasure is different from but as rich as when the victim fails to solve the riddle.

## More Extended Defamiliarization Texts

We offer our students a choice of three nonnormal (different) frames within which to construct such texts: the child's, the alien's, and the animal's. Here now are some more extended examples. (For "solutions," see page 255.)

1.  The vegetation is particularly dense in this part of the jungle. The long shoot-like trees are thicker at the base and taper towards the ends. Occasionally we come upon unusual metal structures. The base of the structures are cylindrical and extend far into the earth. The top of the structure is like a bowl, curving outward from the base to thinner edges. The inside is scooped out with a hexagonal object in the center. Initial search crews believed the structures to be objects related to primitive religious worship. But further evaluation seems to indicate the structures are part of an intricate communication system, the structures being found at equal distances from one another. At regular intervals these structures emit a vapory liquid substance making landing or departing next to impossible. We are attempting to determine how to control these structures, and in so doing identify the dominant life form of the planet.

    Karl Smart (U)

2.  Marvelous! The world is marvelous. Oh, hell! Here it comes again. Up. Hoisted up, again up, again up I go. What a bore. Come on now—let me go. I'm going to get angry. Go ahead and howl. I am going to go my way.

Hmm. I wonder what that sound is. Maybe it is yummy. I'll sneak up and see. I smell it—it is yummy. Gonna get it. No way out for it. I'm going to get yummy . . . going to get yummy. Here I go slowly . . . slowly. Ha, cotcha! Bop it back and forth. Ha. Looks good, smells good. Yummy.

Oh, hell, here the big it comes. Hurts my tail. I'm going up and fast. Up and up and up. It might follow. Better climb out there. It is so big that it can't follow. Hang on. Everything is shaking. I'd better leap and get out of here. Run! Damn its. Such pests. The little it ups me and the big it won't leave me alone. Damn its.

I know—I'll get a little sleep. Under the color thing. Oh damn, here comes the it again. Oh, it didn't see me. Good! Ah, marvelous.

What! What's this. It-rain! Why can't the its leave me alone. It-rain! Out I go and fast fast fast. Damn its. Mash, and up, and rain. I'm leaving.

The black earth is always so hot and hard. I'll run. Good! Now I'm in belly-highs. Ah, I love belly-highs. They tickle my undersides. Maybe that it will tickle my belly. I love belly tickles.

Hey, it! I'll rub its lifters. Ah, wow, ecstasy. Belly tickles! Wow. This is a good it.

I think I'll go home. Damn it, quit! Can't you see I'm finished. Want to leave. Come on, I'm finished! I'm getting angry. Stop, it. Out go my stickers. Smart it! Thanks and bon voyage.

Hmm. I'm still tired. I think I'll find cool. Where? Oh right over there. That big color thing. No its. Soft belly-highs. Wow! Marvelous. Life is marvelous.

That was some little yummy I had there. I'll think about yummies. Easier to rest. Almost see one in the belly highs. Marvelous. What a life. I love belly-highs. I love yummies. I love big color things. I love cool. I love its that tickle my belly. Life is marvelous. Simply marvelous . . .

Lonnie Kay (U)

3.     We have made a safe landing and our search crew has packed necessary supplies for the day's search. We have found the surface of the planet slick and shiny and of unusual design. It reminds us of our formal gardens at home, but is strangely two-dimensional. It provides very little

traction for our vehicles. Our crew agronomists wonder how it is kept so neat and manicured. It seems that this unusual strain of vegetation has mass produced itself in a strikingly similar manner, and is now arrested in growth. We have detected no change in it since our landing two days ago.

From the vantage point of our spacecraft the structures to our west are cubical and rectangular. The buildings are devoid of habitation, at least we have not yet discovered any forms of life. Some of the structures appear hinged on the front allowing complete exposure to what's inside. Crew sociologists believe a "let it all hang out" attitude accompanies this exposure of one's living quarters to the community. Above us is a strange squarish orb with two bright spots emitting light, no doubt the sun of the planet.

Due east we come upon a cubical structure quite different from the row of hinged buildings. The surface is extremely slick, much slicker than the initial landing surface. Initial attempts at scaling the structure proved futile. Our men could not cling to the surface. The structure seems important to the life form of the planet, centrally located in our search area. An amount of heat is emitted from the structure, but not so much as to penetrate our space suits. A party to the northeast has found a long tubular piping running from near the bottom of the structure on the far side to the top. The tube, somehow connected to the white stone behind the structure, may be part of an intricate communication system. The piping is within our reach and we are able to use it to scale the structure. When reaching the top we find the pipe connected to an object monitoring something. There is a dial-like configuration surrounded by a strange alien alphabet. A quiet hum comes from the mechanism.

The top of the structure's surface is similar to the slick sides, but is interrupted by four circular platforms. These platforms seem to be a source of power. Three of them are dark in color and cool to touch. The fourth is a brilliant orange-red and emits a tremendous amount of heat. On the brilliant red platform is a metallic structure the same diameter as the platform. One can hear a strange gurgling sound from within and a vapory substance rising from the top of the metallic structure. Due to the heat, we are unable to scale the structure. However, our aerial observer indicates that some life form exists inside the metallic object. The life form is extremely active and able to withstand intense heat.

The humans, if that is what they are called, are almost identical in size, shape, and color: tubular, hollow in the middle, half the size of one of our men, and a bland whitish, yellow color. They seem oblivious to our presence and engaged in a ritualistic orgy, the source of their energy and power. A dead specimen was found on the far side of the structure, but was completely lifeless and did not respond to us in any way. We conclude that the intense heat and the liquid surrounding these creatures give them some sort of life, and if they leave this environment or are exposed without protection, they die.

As evening approaches we take this specimen back to our mother ship. It is late, and the analysis of this strange life form will keep crew scientists busy for months. We shall explore further tomorrow.

Karl Smart (U)


4.                                                        June 5, 1919
                                                          Earth


. . . we flew near one of many for closer inspection. The head was supported by a long neck, brown at the bottom, and growing greener toward the top. This neck was bent and wavy with both horizontal and vertical lines visible in ordered patterns.

The very top or head of this structure was domed yet flat on top. Raised spots dotted this dome in concentric circles from a single center with lines linking dot to dot. It looked much like the eyes of our mounts only magnified tenfold.

From this pale green head streamed the hair downward, broad and in varying lengths. The color of this hair was a mixture of green, both pale and dark with red streaks. It looked scraggly and uncombed with some hair close to the neck and other projecting out away. This broad hair looked like chutes, narrower and darker at the bottom. Each chute was bumpy and veined inside and twisted and curled toward the bottom. A ride down one chute would send one through space to land on a carpet of analogous objects. We were tempted, but refrained.

Lyle Wakefield (U)

# OF MERCURY AND MARS

Finally, to end this chapter, we present two remarkably ingenious texts, the first by Edwin Morgan, the second by Craig Raine. We leave you to decide what part familiarization and defamiliarization play in these texts, in the "situations" represented by the texts, and in your relationship with the texts!

## THE FIRST MEN ON MERCURY

—We come in peace from the third planet.
Would you take us to your leader?

—Bawr stretter! Bawr. Bawr. Stretterhawl?

—This is a little plastic model
of the solar system, with working parts.
You are here and we are there and we
are now here with you, is this clear?

—Gawl horrop. Bawr. Abawrhannahanna!

—Where we come from is blue and white
with brown, you see we call the brown
here 'land', the blue is 'sea', and the white
is 'clouds' over land and sea, we live
on the surface of the brown land,
all round is sea and clouds. We are 'men'.
Men come —

—Glawp men! Gawrbenner menko. Menhawl?

—Men come in peace from the third planet
which we call 'earth'. We are earthmen.
Take us earthmen to your leader.

—Thmen? Thmen? Bawr. Bawrhossop.
Yuleeda tan hanna. Harrabost yuleeda.

—I am the yuleeda. You see my hands,
we carry no benner, we come in peace.
The spaceways are all stretterhawn.

—Glawn peacemen all horrabhanna tantko!
Tan come at'mistrossop. Glawp yuleeda!

*—Atoms are peacegawl in our harraban.*
*Menbat worrabost from tan hannahanna.*

*—You men we know bawrhossoptant. Bawr.*
*We know yuleeda. Go strawg backspetter quick.*

*—We cantantabawr, tantingko backspetter now!*

*—Banghapper now! Yes, third planet back.*
*Yuleeda will go back blue, white, brown*
*nowhanna! There is no more talk.*

*—Gawl han fasthapper?*

*—No. You must go back to your planet.*
*Go back in peace, take what you have gained*
*but quickly.*

*—Stretterworra gawl, gawl . . .*

*—Of course, but nothing is ever the same,*
*now is it? You'll remember Mercury.*[6]

## A MARTIAN SENDS A POSTCARD HOME

*Caxtons are mechanical birds with many wings*
*and some are treasured for their markings—*

*they cause the eyes to melt*
*or the body to shriek without pain.*

*I have never seen one fly, but*
*sometimes they perch on the hand.*

*Mist is when the sky is tired of flight*
*and rests its soft machine on ground:*

*then the world is dim and bookish*
*like engravings under tissue paper.*

*Rain is when the earth is television.*
*It has the property of making colours darker.*

*Model T is a room with the lock inside—*
*a key is turned to free the world*

*for movement, so quick there is a film*
*to watch for anything missed.*

*But time is tied to the wrist*
*or kept in a box, ticking with impatience.*

*In homes, a haunted apparatus sleeps,*
*that snores when you pick it up.*

*If the ghost cries, they carry it*
*to their lips and soothe it to sleep*

*with sounds. And yet, they wake it up*
*deliberately, by tickling with a finger.*

*Only the young are allowed to suffer*
*openly. Adults go to a punishment room*

*with water but nothing to eat.*
*They lock the door and suffer the noises*

*alone. No one is exempt*
*and everyone's pain has a different smell.*

*At night, when all the colours die,*
*they hide in pairs*

*and read about themselves—*
*in colour, with their eyelids shut.*[7]

## "Solutions" to Defamiliarization Texts, Pages 249–252

1. The aliens have landed on a large grassy area. The metal structures are sprinkler heads.

2. Glossary: it—children; belly-highs—grass; color thing—bush; lifters—legs; it-rain—sprinkler; yummy—smaller animal, mouse.

3. These aliens have landed in a kitchen. The linoleum has a symmetric floral pattern. There are cupboards (hinged structures) lining one wall. The stove is the prominent object standing alone against one wall. A small clock sits on the back of the stove, with a cord running down to a plug. The circular platforms are coils to the stove. On one coil is a metal pan full of boiling macaroni.

4. An old dandelion top after the yellow has turned white and blown away.

# NOTES

1. It was W. H. Auden who defined a poem as a means of paying homage to a sacred object, "Making, Knowing and Judging," in his *The Dyer's Hand* (London: Faber & Faber, 1975), p. 31.
2. Louis Agassiz, *Contributions to the Natural History of the United States* (1857–1862). (Reprinted, New York: Ayer, 1978.) "Cyanea" reprinted in George Quasha and Jerome Rothenberg, *America, A Prophecy* (New York: Random House, 1973), p. 411.
3. Roman Jakobson, "Concluding Statement: Linguistics and Poetics" in ed. T. A. Sebeok, *Style in Language* (Cambridge, Mass.: M.I.T. Press, 1960), p. 353.
4. Peter Medawar, *Advice to a Young Scientist* (New York: Harper & Row, 1981).
5. Elizabeth Bishop, *Geography III* (New York: Farrar, Straus & Giroux, 1976).
6. Edwin Morgan, *Poems of Thirty Years* (Manchester: Carcanet New Press, 1982), p. 259.
7. Craig Raine, *A Martian Sends a Postcard Home* (London: Oxford University Press, 1980), p. 1.

# CHAPTER TWELVE

# OVERVIEW
## The Shape of a Semester

*Every construction that helps anybody is also a boundary.*
*Philip Roth*

*My method is not to sunder the hard from the soft, but to see the hardness of the soft.*
*Ludwig Wittgenstein*

Our purpose in this chapter is to try to offer a sense of the "shape" of a semester's work in composition: not so much a curriculum or syllabus, but rather an exploration of aspirations, forms, and purposes; and to do so within the framework of various interacting dialectics. We see our own roles, as instructors, in dialectical terms—now supportive or protective, now demanding or applying pressure—and we see the semester as falling broadly into two parts, each characterized by its own distinctive tone or style.

# DIALECTICAL FRAMES AS GENERATIVE

In the words of T. M. Knox, the philosopher Hegel "found a place for everything—logical, natural, human, and divine—in a dialectical scheme that repeatedly swung from thesis to antithesis and back again to a higher and richer synthesis."[1] In a similar vein, F. Scott Fitzgerald argued that a necessary feature of a well-honed mind is its ability to hold two opposing ideas at the same time and go on functioning.

The pedagogical and heuristic potentialities of dialectic—arguing both within the self and with others—as a mode of thinking and as a way of shaping texts, these potentialities, we propose, will never be exhausted.

One of Hegel's first critics, Trendelenburg, observed that Hegel had failed to distinguish between two forms of dialectic: (a) a *logical* contradiction of A as opposed to non-A, the non-A being the negative transformation of A; and (b) an actual, concrete contradiction of A as opposed to B. Whereas non-A can be invented simply through applying logic and need exist only as an idea, B must be *experienced as an opposite to A*. Thus in (a) "perfection" produces its logical opposite, "imperfection," and their interaction gives rise to a synthesis that incorporates elements of both; in (b), on the other hand, B is not simply the logical negative transformation of A but an independently existing opposite: beautiful—ugly; firm—floppy; hot—cold; simple—complex.

In the pursuit of textual variety, we have discovered that our students find both of these contradictions useful. Let us now enumerate some of the dialectics that underlie, or inhere in, our work and theirs— sometimes implicitly, sometimes explicitly. Appropriately disposed, as frames for pedagogical, learning, and textual considerations, these dialectics offer us a more useful and effective alternative to the current orthodoxies offered by the term *process*, which however flexibly offered represents an "idealized" lock-step sequence for pre-writing, drafting, revising, rewriting, and end product. What we seek and desire has to do with *matter*—what is being attended to—as much as it has to do with means. Similarly, we find that dialectical frames invariably provide more intelligent and intelligible alternatives to the rather ossified and preemptive categories of conventional rhetorical forms offered by most textbooks and handbooks. Here, then, is a sampling of dialectics. You will have no difficulty in recognizing those that apply to features of a text, those that are pedagogical, and those that can be both.

| | | |
|---|---|---|
| 1. | Utterance | Text |
| 2. | Speakable | Unspeakable |
| 3. | Simple | Complex |
| 4. | Self | Other person |
| 5. | Self | World |
| 6. | Actuality | Fantasy |
| 7. | Truth | Untruth |
| 8. | Individual | Social group |
| 9. | Individual | Social class |
| 10. | Teacher | Taught |
| 11. | Writer | Nonwriter |
| 12. | Literacy | Orality |
| 13. | Female | Male |
| 14. | Actual (what is) | Potential (what might be) |
| 15. | Seed | Tree |
| 16. | Private | Public |
| 17. | Esoteric | Exoteric |
| 18. | Engagement | Disengagement |
| 19. | Common | Uncommon |
| 20. | Normal | Eccentric |
| 21. | Expert | Novice |
| 22. | Positive | Negative |
| 23. | Considered | Unconsidered |
| 24. | Participant | Spectator |
| 25. | Included | Excluded |

| 26. | Pragmatic | Mathetic |
| 27. | Mediated | Immediate |
| 28. | Hectic | Calm |
| 29. | Unity | Multiplicity |
| 30. | Direct | Indirect |
| 31. | Utterance | Silence |
| 32. | Significant | Insignificant |
| 33. | Dependence | Independence |
| 34. | Dependence | Autonomy |
| 35. | Text | Metatext |
| 36. | Natural | Cultural |
| 37. | Imposed | Elected |
| 38. | Arbitrary | Inhabited |
| 39. | Short | Long |
| 40. | Chronological | Achronological |
| 41. | Synchronous | Diachronic |
| 42. | Stable | Volatile |
| 43. | Fixed | Fluid |
| 44. | Rigid | Flexible |
| 45. | Transient | Permanent |
| 46. | Careful | Carefree |
| 47. | Considerate | Inconsiderate |

From the first day of a semester, these are some of the dialectical contradictions brought into play—not only between themselves but also in interaction with other pairs—generating a context of increasing richness and productive suggestiveness. From the very beginning, a fundamental dialectic is that of text and metatext: we insist that students write not only texts but also commentaries on their texts (labeled in this book "Reflections"). This immediately involves them in the writer's dialectic of participation-spectator: now "inside," now "outside"; now writer, now reader; first impulse and second thoughts; insouciance and consideration. The subtle fluctuations of attentiveness, shifts of focus, continuities and discontinuities, hunches, gropings, and floodings in the mind as one writes are as elusive as most inner speech. One can catch them only by a sudden glance out of the corner of one's eye. But however diverse individual idiosyncracies may be, what we wish above all to avoid is the promotion of self-consciousness in places where it doesn't belong, where it is counterproductive. Our sublime model in this matter is Goethe, who managed to incorporate in his work both the doing and also the reflecting on the doing, both acting and considering the wherewithal, the modus operandi, of his action; both synthesizing and analyzing; both producing as participant and reexamining as spectator—reexamining both what had got made (text) and also some of the movements of mind that had gone into its making (consciousness, attentiveness, relationship between self and not-self).

In the event, we are now convinced beyond any reasonable doubt that our students' reflections (metatexts) are among the most valuable texts they write—valuable both for themselves, in the discovering of meaningfulness and of ways of faring forward, and for us as those who wish to enable. When an assignment begins with the rubric: "This is what we want you to do," students are alerted to the dialectical alternatives (logical and/or concrete): "This is not what I want to do," "This is not what you should want us to do," and so on. And through engagement in the act of writing, they may discover this blessed dialectic: "This text that I have written began as imposed (37) and apparently arbitrary (38), but as I wrote I became engaged (as opposed to disengaged) to such a degree that I ended by discovering that I had written a text that I genuinely inhabited and that I would have elected to write if I myself had thought of such a possibility." In the subsections that follow, we outline some of the means—cognitive games—by which we elicit such texts.

## Cognitive Games

### Writing an Unspeakable Sentence

The following texts were written after the group had looked at Fuller's "unspeakable sentence" (see p. 76) and had then been instructed/invited: "Now write a 150-word sentence."

> Inasmuch as mothers are expected to be perfect and self-sacrificing, to live their lives for others besides themselves, to be giving and caring, loving and serving, long suffering and patient, in a way which is superhuman and perhaps even divine, may we analyze that which is being done to women all around us by their children and may we decide if this treatment is fair to those mothers who have given of

their time and talents, love and strength in the womb, given life to and nurtured their offspring in such a way that they should be revered and honored daily by said children with the honors bestowed on the saints of old, but not bestowed on those of the present who are, of course, now held in low repute, so that those children seem only to be giving derision rather than praise, pain rather than honor, hate rather than love, and demands rather than concessions to their birth mothers who deserve all that they do not now receive so that the mothers feel used and abused by the very people who could make them feel most loved and worthwhile on this earth.

Grace Marshall (U)

Given the tedium of thousands of miles of rutted blacktop through unpopulated Nevada deserts punctuated only by occasional service stations with their filthy, littered restrooms smelling of the sickly sweet deodorizers they use to cover the stench of the stale, day-old urine which lies in puddles on the floors, and given the constant dialogue of steadily increasing volume between the children in the back seat about who inflicted which kind of damage on whom at what particular point in time and whether this child or that child was the first to inflict said damage or was merely acting out of perfect justification and self-defense as he or she returned even worse damage on the accused, but professed innocent, instigator, I firmly resolve during the remainder of the week to drive no further than fifteen miles in any direction within any twenty-four hour period or to the nearest 7-Eleven store, whichever comes first, and to do it alone.

Lind Williams (U)

Because of a dismal lack of daring, bravado or venture in early life, which might be attributed to some innate shortcomings or to the overprotection of gentle, caring parents early in childhood and adolescence, only to be further perpetuated by a loving husband who unfortunately left this earth at much too early an age, I, missing those qualities in myself, have chosen Napoleon Bonaparte as the most appealing, entertaining, and enlivening historical character to write of, for he exhibited the daring, the bravado, the love of venture I secretly seek, when he fooled armies of men massively outnumbering him by taking unbelievable risks, when he returned from exile on Elba to lead his band of loyal followers while French Bourbons sought his death at every corner, and when he undertook the greatest venture of all, by gambling not only with his own life but with the fate of a nation, yes even nations, in so far as he desired and fought for a united Europe, while I, on the other hand, am unable to make the decision as to whether to risk $300 or $400 on the purchase of a new power lawnmower.

Ruth Johnson (U)

## Who Would You Like to Be?

Interestingly, Ruth Johnson's text is a synthesis of *two* assignments, her "synthesis" coming from the discovery that two texts can, paradoxically, be written as one. A prior assignment had been to characterize the historical or fictive character she would most like to be. And that assignment was derived from an apparently frivolous *New York Times* entertainment, in which famous people were asked to name the character from fiction that they would most like to be, and to explain why. The transforming dialectic involves seeing the "hardness" of the "soft," the "seriousness" of the "frivolous," the "weight" of the "trivial." Here are some of the segments of that feature that we read aloud to the students:[2]

### MARGARET ATWOOD
#### Author

To be *rather than* to have written? *Fiction? Not many women characters in fiction have a very good time. Elizabeth Bennet, in "Pride and Prejudice," manages to, but her scope is somewhat limited. How about Professor Challenger, in Arthur Conan Doyle's "The Lost World"? He gets travel, pterodactyls (which I've always lusted after) and temper tantrums (which I've never been able to have but feel I ought to). Also, he's a pig with women, and it would be interesting to know what that feels like from the inside. Nonfiction? Lady Hester Stanhope. Or Anna Jameson, who took her smelling salts and parasol into the 19th-century north woods and wrote about it.*

### WOODY ALLEN
#### Actor

*Gigi. I want more than anything to be Gigi. To meander, featherlight, down the boulevards of belle époque Paris in a little blue sailor dress, my sweet face framed by a flat, disk-shaped hat with two ribbons dangling mischievously past my bangs. And I would be squealing, "Maman! Regardez! Maman!" And my room would be paneled and perfect and cluttered with overstuffed pillows and a Victorian chaise and my bed, meltingly soft, with embroidered silk sheets, and everything would be warmly lit by sconces and table lamps whose globes were painted with buds and floral themes. And I would sit and brush my hair and put it up over my eyes, trying out new styles and giggling. And dinner would consist of a cup of thick chocolate beaten up with the yolk of an egg, some toast and grapes and for breakfast, soft-boiled eggs with cherries in them. (I would awaken refreshed each day in a nightgown and stretch like a kitten, rubbing the sleep from my saucer eyes with my tiny fists.)*

*And then, joy of joys—Gaston (who had delighted in me as a young girl but never dreamed that eventually I would blossom to stunning womanhood) would come to visit and, unable to believe his eyes, would suddenly realize that I am no longer the innocent, frail wisp of a child he has known but I have, obeying destiny, ripened into a creature of breathtaking loveliness. Now I toss my head, allowing my hair to bounce from shoulder to shoulder, offering Gaston the scent of perfume from my neck. Unable to resist, he cups my delicate face in his hands and asks me to go with him to Maxim's. From here it gets a little vague and the image of my black-rimmed glasses and shopping bag from Zabar's intrudes but by then I'm usually radiant and sobbing.*

### LAURIE ANDERSON
### Performance Artist

*I would like to have been Sei Shōnagon, who lived 1,000 years ago in Japan. She wrote "The Pillow Book," which was a series of impressions and lists ("Things That Cannot Be Compared," "Things That Quicken the Heart," "Things That Have Lost Their Power"). The only things we know about her life are the roles she gave herself: gadfly, social critic, stranger, voyeur.*

## Sei Shōnagon's *Pillow Book*

Laurie Anderson's remarks on Sei Shōnagon offered yet another dialectic:

1. This text (Laurie Anderson's) is what it is and no more.

2.  This text (Laurie Anderson's) is a seed that could be planted in well-tilled ground and grow in unpredictable directions.*

In terms of *sequence* or articulation, then, the fictions/fantasies/ metamorphoses of Atwood, Allen, and Anderson can be used as signposts to lead us in any one of a number of directions. Our own preference (based on past experiences) is to allow it to serve as an introduction to Sei Shōnagon. And, again, Shōnagon's *Pillow Book* exemplifies the dialectic (a) this is merely what it is and (b) this has several generative potentialities. It is explicitly what is and implicitly what might be.

Here, for example, are some brief extracts from Shōnagon's *Pillow Book*.[3]

### THINGS THAT GIVE AN UNCLEAN FEELING

*A rat's nest.*
*Someone who is late in washing his hands in the morning.*
*White snivel, and children who sniffle as they walk.*
*Little sparrows.*
*A person who does not bathe for a long time even though the weather is hot.*
*All faded clothes give me an unclean feeling, especially those that have glossy colours.*

### THINGS THAT HAVE LOST THEIR POWER

*A large boat which is high and dry in a creek at ebb-tide.*
*A woman who has taken off her false locks to comb the short hair that remains.*
*A large tree that has been blown down in a gale and lies on its side with its roots in the air.*
*The retreating figure of a* sumō *wrestler who has been defeated in a match.*
*A man of no importance reprimanding an attendant.*
*An old man who removes his hat, uncovering his scanty top-knot.*
*A woman, who is angry with her husband about some trifling matter, leaves home and goes somewhere to hide. She is certain that he will rush about looking for her; but he does nothing of the kind and shows the most infuriating indifference. Since she cannot stay away for ever, she swallows her pride and returns.*

---

*Cf. D. H. Lawrence: "The tree of life is a gay kind of tree that is forever dropping its leaves and budding out afresh quite different ones. If the last lot were thistle leaves, the next lot may be vine. You never can tell . . ." (*Fantasia of the Unconscious*).

## THINGS THAT GIVE A CLEAN FEELING

*An earthen cup. A new metal bowl.*
*A rush mat.*
*The play of the light on water as one pours it into a vessel.*
*A new wooden chest.*

## THINGS WITHOUT MERIT

*Rice starch that has become mixed with water. . . . I know*
*that this is a very vulgar item and everyone will dislike my men-*
*tioning it. But that should not stop me. In fact I must feel free to*
*include anything, even tongs used for the parting-fires. After all,*
*these objects do exist in our world and people all know about*
*them. I admit they do not belong to a list that others will see.*
*But I never thought that these notes would be read by anyone else,*
*and so I included everything that came into my head, however*
*strange or unpleasant.*

## SQUALID THINGS

*The back of a piece of embroidery.*
*The inside of a cat's ear.*
*A swarm of mice, who still have no fur, when they come wrig-*
*gling out of their nest.*
*The seams of a fur robe that has not yet been lined.*
*Darkness in a place that does not give the impression of being*
*very clean.*

## HATEFUL THINGS

*One is in a hurry to leave, but one's visitor keeps chattering*
*away. If it is someone of no importance, one can get rid of him by*
*saying, "You must tell me all about it next time"; but, should it be*
*the sort of visitor whose presence commands one's best behaviour,*
*the situation is hateful indeed.*
*A man who has nothing in particular to recommend him*
*discusses all sorts of subjects at random as though he knew*
*everything.*

Such revelations are in themselves of interest, if only because they
exemplify some most revealing and enlivening social dialectics: 4, 5,
9, 13, 16, 17, 19, 20, 22, 23, and 25, for example.

When our students begin to make entries in their own pillow books,
they write mere jottings. This is what is. But irresistibly they discover

that as their jottings accumulate, they come to constitute a representation of the self—oblique, ostensibly impersonal (a text about the world, not about the psyche); and interesting patterns, collocations, correlations, and contradictions emerge within and between the elements, within and between the discrete parts and the fact of their coexistence within one life, one consciousness. With a simple dialectical switch from self to other (dialectic 4), they can then compose a representation of grandmother, mother, friend, or whoever. And again, the text that they compose is both what it is and also potentially something more —something more complex, more ambitious, more demanding, more coherent, more integrated, played for higher stakes.

Conversely, a relatively difficult text can be deconstructed into elements of a pillow book, so that students have a clean and usable handle on a text that might otherwise daunt them. "This," says William Stafford, in effect, "is what we know about the people of the Northern Ice." We know what things frighten them, what questions they can answer/not answer, what they believe in, what gives them strength, and so on.

### SAYINGS FROM THE NORTHERN ICE

*It is people at the edge who say*
*things at the edge: winter is toward knowing.*

> *Sled runners before they meet have long talk apart.*
> *There is a pup in every litter the wolves will have.*
> *A knife that falls points at an enemy.*
> *Rocks in the wind know their place: down low.*
> *Over your shoulder is God; the dying deer sees Him.*

*At the mouth of the long sack we fall in forever*
*storms brighten the spikes of the stars.*

> *Wind that buried bear skulls north of here*
> *and beats moth wings for help outside the door*
> *is bringing bear skull wisdom, but do not ask the skull*
> *too large a question till summer.*
> *Something too dark was held in that strong bone.*

*Better to end with a lucky saying:*

> *Sled runners cannot decide to join or to part.*
> *When they decide, it is a bad day.*[4]

## Auden's *Eden*

Similar possibilities are exemplified by another, closely related form of cognitive play exemplified in W. H. Auden's representation of his vision of an ideal world:

### EDEN

Landscape
*Limestone uplands like the Pennines plus a small region of igneous rocks with at least one extinct volcano. A precipitous and indented sea-coast.*

Climate
*British.*

Ethnic origin of inhabitants
*Highly varied as in the United States, but with a slight nordic predominance.*

Language
*Of mixed origins like English, but highly inflected.*

Weights & Measures
*Irregular and complicated. No decimal system.*

Religion
*Roman Catholic in an easygoing Mediterranean sort of way. Lots of local saints.*

Size of Capital
*Plato's ideal figure, 5040 about right.*

Form of Government
*Absolute monarchy, elected for life by lot.*

Sources of Natural Power
*Wind, water, peat, coal. No oil.*

Economic activities
*Lead mining, coal mining, chemical factories, paper mills, sheep farming, truck farming, greenhouse horticulture.*

Means of transport
*Horses and horse-drawn vehicles, canal barges, balloons. No automobiles or airplanes.*

Architecture
*State: Baroque. Ecclesiastical: Romanesque or Byzantine. Domestic: Eighteenth Century British or American Colonial.*

Domestic Furniture and Equipment
*Victorian except for kitchens and bathrooms which are as full of modern gadgets as possible.*

Formal Dress
*The fashions of Paris in the 1830's and '40's.*

Sources of Public Information
*Gossip. Technical and learned periodicals but no newspapers.*

Public Statues
*Confined to famous defunct chefs.*

Public Entertainments
*Religious Processions, Brass Bands, Opera, Classical Ballet. No movies, radio or television.*[5]

Consider, even at this precise moment, the town or city that you find yourself in; imagine that it is the *intended* realization of a blueprint such as Auden's, using Auden's categories and any others you may find necessary. Compose that blueprint or vision, so that what *is* now is an exact and complete fulfillment of it. Who would have conceived such a plan? Were they mad? Perverse? Idealistic? Wicked? Now consider your own ideals. Using Auden's categories, produce a blueprint of your ideal world. Then consider your mother, your grandmother, your closest friend: construct a plan for their utopia. Such are some of the writings that we invite students to try, after meeting Auden's wry plan.

## Writing Action Portraits

An equally evocative format is offered by the following representation of a wicked man in the Chinese *Book of Rewards and Punishment* of the fourth century A.D.

> *He leaps over wells and hearths; over food and men. Destroys young children and unborn infants. Does many secret and perverse things. Sings and dances on the last day of the month or year; shouts in anger on the first of the month or in the morning; weeps, spits or behaves indecently towards the north; hums and mutters before the hearth; uses the hearth fire for burning incense. Prepares food with dirty firewood; goes abroad at night exposed and naked. Inflicts punishment during the "eight periods"; spits at shooting stars; points at the rainbow, at the sun, moon and stars in an irreverent manner; stares at the sun and moon. Fires brushwood and hunts in the spring; curses toward the north; and kills tortoises and snakes needlessly.*[6]

How, we ask, using the same format, would you characterize your-self—what *actions* of yours would illustrate that characterization, bring it to life? Now, in the same way, characterize someone you love or someone you disapprove of.

## *The Elementary Ideas Underlying Such Games*

Underlying most of these relatively modest "games"—games that all have the potential to assume deeper resonances, stronger significances —is something akin to Adolf Bastian's "elementary ideas": ideas of birth, death, initiation, sacrifice, the transcendental, and the immanent, such as he found to occur in various forms in all religions. Our "ele-mentary ideas," however, have a different center. They are primarily *social* in a fairly intimate and informal sense—that is, they offer various ways in which students can explore aspects of their social lives as experience, memory, aspirations, representations, anticipations, cele-brations, regrets, and so on. In a word, they offer various modest loca-tions in which they can record or represent their meanings. And they are asked to do this in ways that involve a variety of syntax, voice, role, intention, and audience. At this point, Joseph Campbell's observation is à propos:

> *In this sensitive and trickish field (Goethe's wondrous realm of "The Mothers") the poet, the artist, and a certain type of roman-tic philosopher (Emerson, Nietzsche, Bergson, for example) are more successful; for, since in poetry and art, beyond the learning of rhetorical and manual techniques, the whole craft is that of seiz-ing the idea and facilitating its epiphany, the creative mind, ade-quately trained, is less apt than the analytic to mistake a mere trope or concept for a living, life-awakening image. Poetry and art, whether "academic" or "modern," are simply dead unless informed by Elementary Ideas: ideas, not as clear abstractions held in the mind, but as cognized, or rather re-cognized, vital factors of the subject's own being. Though it is true that such living ideas be-come manifest only in the terms and style of some specific histori-cal moment, their force nevertheless lies not in what meets the eye but in what dilates the heart, and this force, precisely, is their essential trait.[7]*

For emphasis, let us repeat Campbell's words: "Though it is true that such living ideas become manifest only in the terms and style of some specific historical moment, their force nevertheless lies not in what meets the eye but in what dilates the heart, and this force, precisely, is their essential trait." For Campbell's own purposes, his use of the concessive "though . . . nevertheless" was quite necessary; we, conversely, could legitimately substitute "because." And to reinforce our sense of where we must aim to go with our students, we recall De Quincey's remark in his review of the works of Pope:

> There is, first, the literature of knowledge; and, secondly, the literature of power. The function of the first is—to teach; the function of the second is—to move: the first is a rudder; the second, an oar or a sail. The first speaks to the mere discursive understanding; the second speaks ultimately, it may happen, to the higher understanding or reason, but always through affections of pleasure and sympathy.[8]

It should be clear by now that we believe that our students' texts may constitute essays in the literature of power, while their metatexts are contributions to the class's literature of knowledge.

# PART ONE OF THE SEMESTER: A SAFE PLACE FOR RISK TAKING

A fifteen-week semester is an absurdly short period in which to try to make a positive difference both to students' attitudes to writing and to their performance. But such constraint has the negative virtue of concentrating the mind—as Dr. Johnson said of knowing that you're going to be hanged. How, then, can we make the most of it? How can we shape, articulate, establish sequence, in such ways as will give students an adequate sense of purpose and direction; how can we open up for them a good realm of being?

One convenient answer is to see the semester as falling into two main segments, each with its own distinctive ethos and range, its own tone and reach. Risking a stereotype, let us think of the first of these two segments as primarily maternal—while conceding that the archetype treads on potentially dangerous ground. The idea tempts us, in part because Ted Solatoroff uses it so persuasively in his essay "A Few Good Voices in Your Head," one of the most winning and ingratiating essays on writing that we know.

He is writing of a review of E. E. Cummings's poetry that he wrote when he was a student for his professor, Herbert Barrows. Solatoroff remembers having written the review "with a kind of 'Look, Mom' élan" and goes on: "According to the English psychoanalyst A. W. Winnecott [actually, D. W. Winnicott], who has a great deal to teach about these matters, that's how creativity begins: exploring, self-expressive play under the auspices of a mother who frees the child of anxiety; who is, in effect, one's first and determining audience. . . . As the sort of 'holding' figure [Winnicott] speaks of, Barrows enabled me to relax, to open up, to trust my imagination, and to stop pretending, which is really a form of compliance bred by anxiety."[9]

In the first segment of a semester, our aim as "holding figures" is to elicit a great deal of writing, in the form of short texts—many and varied texts of a relatively modest scope such as we displayed in Chapter 1 and on pages 261–270. These are texts that are not to be agonized over; texts in the writing of which the stakes are not dauntingly high; texts in which an element of play is undeniably present; texts in which a relative failure is *quickly* followed by a relative success; texts in which the stance of the writer is often openly experimental. These number twenty-five to thirty texts, each just a page or two; each comprising a particular form of discourse; each realizing a particular social intention or purpose. Many are begun in class and completed at home; many involve a degree of risk taking, a dash of insouciance, a willingness to take a leap, to innovate, to move beyond the safety of the familiar, the well trodden.

Such texts we open up to readers. It is important that they not sit in files or folders for weeks on end, that they meet with a more or less immediate response—a response (let us typify it as quasi-maternal) that is offered primarily in terms not of grading but of acceptance and relative recognition—a recognition of the nature both of what was attempted and of what was achieved. This response is not only from us but also from the "sibling" members of the class.

Thus in eight weeks or so—about twenty hours of class time and twenty hours of homework—students build a modest repertoire of texts, which provide a grounding, a series of forays, a sequence of experiments, some of which they can elect to take further, build on, and some of which incorporate tentative approaches toward the distinctive features of academic discourse. We offer, as examples, two types of exercises. The first is based on a recognition of the distinction between esoteric and exoteric; the second is a sequence based on shifts of frame: from participant to participant become spectator to impersonal spectator.

## Going for Esoteric Arcana

One of the primary effects of academic discourse is to divide its readers into two societies: those who "know" and therefore recognize its meanings, its intentions, its effects; and those who do not. It includes, and by the same token, it excludes. This is partly a matter of an esoteric or arcane lexicon and partly a matter of the kind of activity or operation any piece of academic writing constitutes—a deeper question, involving not merely surface verbal features but familiarity with representative or typical activities, procedures, purposes, and functions—what academics "do."

"Machado says somewhere that in order to write a poem you have to invent a poet to write it."[10] Analogously, in order to write specialist or academic prose, you have to invent a specialist or academic to write it. Another way of putting this is to recognize that one needs to reinvent oneself as a specialist, to discover the specialist within oneself. However unacademic the culture of a student may be, somewhere in the recent past he or she can uncover or reconstruct some form of relatively specialized activity, involving an appropriate language variety.

One of our assignments, then, is to ask students to write as a specialist to/for another specialist, in such a way that the nonspecialist (the nonparticipant, the innocent observer) will find such a text impenetrable. Both in actions and in words, the specialist participant functions in a world that is effectively closed to the nonspecialist spectator. In a very modest sense, this exercise is, in effect, a venture into reflexive ethnography—presenting a segment of a way of life through representing actions typical of a specific subculture, and presenting a segment of language as constituting one significant element of that subculture—its system of signs.

The texts, and their esoteric varieties of language, come from all manner of places—CB radio, automobile repair shops, drug dealing, the sciences, the social sciences, music, and so on. Here, first, is a student in role as a drug dealer:

> Cat got clipped again, and they set him up with two grand uncles, so that's why I went to Phoenix, you know, we heard that Phoenix was real hot 'cause the Box got packed every night, but all I brought back from Phoenix was Uncle Franky's smile, and he only smiled three times, so I became a mailman and sold lots of stamps, but I sold too much and the stamp collector heard about the deal, but before he got to make his bid, I skipped with my two grand uncles, yeah,

I was smiling with them until my Aunt Lala killed them both. Nah, she died too, so I sold some oranges around my arm and unclipped cat, but cat put his collar right back on, and this time, here I am buddy, waiting for cat to run around, yeah, I gotta get rid of cat, I only get scratched.

Sakura Khan (Q)

And here is a text written in a very different role:

March 5, 1985

Dear Sir,

I am very disappointed with the quality of the spectrophotometer which I have received from your company. I have used many spectrophotometers in the past and have determined that the defect is this: The incident beam seems to be of an irregular size, making the curvette of all objects seem abnormal. This, needless to say, distorts the path of the transmitter beam, and since no radiant energy is being absorbed, the galvonometer's performance is adversely affected by the inadequate intensity of the transmitter. In addition, the optical density scale is missing from the base.

I am returning the spectrophotometer to your company. Please send me another at your earliest convenience. Your cooperation in this matter is greatly appreciated; I look forward to doing business with your company in the future.

Yours sincerely,

Marianne Holden (Q)

A complementary exercise is to write of the same matter for a nonspecialist reader. In both cases, the student must also invent plausible contexts in which such communications are likely to be found, and found to be serving a recognizable purpose. Without a recognition of the contexts in which such communications make sense, have purpose, satisfy need, do a job, the exercise is inevitably deprived of some of its crucial elements.

## A Sequence of Frames

In our second example, we ask students to choose a memorable experience from their own past and to write first as a participant (themselves, then, there, in it), then as a spectator (themselves, now, here, outside it). Characteristic features arise in these two complementary texts. The participant text tends to be (we quote a student's notebook) "apparently simultaneous (concurrent), discrete, dramatic, paratactic, discontinuous, fragmentary . . ."; long on sensation, and short on reflectiveness. The spectator text, conversely, reaping the benefits of time for reflection, reconsideration, appraisal or reappraisal, is relatively complex, connected, coherent, hypotactic, and is able to offer an evaluation.

The third part of this task is to switch from a personal spectator role to an impersonal spectator role—to become, for example, a historian or a sociologist and to reconstruct, contextualize, and reconstrue the same event so as to reveal some of its public meanings. The move is from a stance that may well be naive, "merely personal," even private, to one that involves an appeal to some notion of significance at a social, political, ideological, or philosophical level.

Here is one student's sequence, on the Bicentennial celebrations of 1976. First, his text that represents the voice of the 10-year-old participant, synchronously:*

> What a beautiful day! I am glad my parents have brought me to Manhattan. The streets are so crowded, but there are no cars. All the streets are closed to cars. The big ships should sail down the river soon. Here they come! There are ships from all over the world. The fireboats even have colored fountains of water. I wish these big people would move. I can't see a thing anymore. We might as well take a walk around the park. There are many jugglers and comics. Some of them are good enough for television. It is so hot and crowded though. I wish we could take a rest.
>
> That sandwich shop was just as crowded as everything else. At least I cooled off a little. Here comes the parade down Broadway. There are many politicians in the parade. I think I see Mayor Beame. There are also many bands and houses. The fireworks should start soon, but we have to leave. It is not safe to take the trains too late. Crime is around even on the Bicentennial. I am still satisfied to have seen this great event. I wish it was more than one day.
>
> Jeffrey Mollin (Q)

---

*If we wanted to offer a "model" for such a text we would probably use T. S. Eliot's "Coriolan."

### *Reflections*

It is very difficult to write as when you were ten years old. Not only is it hard to use a smaller vocabulary, but I found it a struggle to adopt some of my old attitudes. Unfortunately, I am much more cynical and sullen than I was back then.

Jeffrey Mollin (Q)

Next, his spectator text, written *in propria persona:*

Looking back on the Bicentennial, I realize how fortunate I was to have taken part in this great event. At the time, I could not grasp that this was a once-in-a-lifetime opportunity. As I recall, I was more concerned with the heat and crowds. However, as the years went by, I realized that this was a special Fourth of July, which none of the later ones have seemed to match. Although the Bicentennial was highly commercialized, it still retained a special meaning. Despite the many troubles in the country at that time, there seemed to swell up a quiet but strong pride among the people. This pride and patriotism were more based on the survival of our Constitution and democratic system, in contrast to the packaged and vague patriotism of the last year.

On a more personal level, the Bicentennial helped encourage my great interest in history. I wanted to learn more about the United States and what had happened in those two hundred years. This interest is one that has not subsided, unlike many of my previous interests. Furthermore, the Bicentennial took place during an election year, and this made the whole period seem even more momentous. On the whole, the summer of 1976 was a very enriching one, from both an emotional and an intellectual standpoint.

Jeffrey Mollin (Q)

### *Reflections*

I found it much easier to write the "spectator" text. It was quite surprising to me how much I had organized and integrated this event into my memory. As a matter of fact, I found it very pleasing to think back on past events and forget about what exam is next on my schedule.

Jeffrey Mollin (Q)

Finally, Jeffrey's text written in role as a historian:

## THE BICENTENNIAL IN RETROSPECT

The Bicentennial marked the two hundredth anniversary of the signing of the Declaration of Independence. That famous document declared the separation of the United States from the colonial empire of England, although it would take seven years of hard fighting to bring its goal to fruition. With the ratification of the Constitution in 1789, the young nation had a strong framework on which to build. This unique document was drafted by wealthy merchants and landowners to protect the existing social order, but it was to prove quite able to adapt to a growing nation and a changing population.

During its first century, the new republic strove to maintain its independence and to harness its vast resources. Constantly threatened by the old nations of Europe, the United States sought to stay out of foreign affairs, a policy it would not totally abandon until the 1940s. The Napoleonic Wars forced the United States into the so-called War of 1812 with England. Although far from conclusive, this war helped confirm the independence of the nation and allowed it to concentrate on its own affairs. Foremost among these was the settlement of the West. By the purchase of the Louisiana Territory and the acquisition of territory during the Mexican War, America had spread itself from coast to coast along the North American continent. With the development of industry in the Northeast, the nation seemed on its way to world greatness.

The issue of slavery, however, slowed down that march to greatness. The feudal institution of slavery conflicted with the growing industrial base in the North and seemed hypocritical in light of the noble-sounding Constitution. Only by an extremely brutal struggle between North and South was slavery abolished and the unity of the republic assured. It was in the context of these events that the Centennial was celebrated in 1876. After a bloody Civil War, the nation appeared on the road to recovery. Railroads were being built all through the land and big business was coming into its own. There was little trouble from abroad and all seemed to be going well. Thus the expositions of that year seemed to stress the unity of the nation and its growing industrial power. However, there was also a touch of solemnity due to the many losses of the recent conflict.

The mood of the nation during the Bicentennial must also be seen in the context of preceding events. The century from 1876 to 1976 marked the emergence of the United States as a world power. During the 1890s and early 1900s, the industrial growth of the nation was spurred by the influx of cheap immigrant labor from Eastern and Southern Europe. This growth in industry coincided with the growing United States role in world affairs, as evidenced by the war with Spain and Theodore Roosevelt's efforts at international diplomacy. America's flurry of activity climaxed with her entry into World War I in order to save democracy. After the war, she resorted to isolationism again in order to savor the prosperity of the 1920s and solve the economic crisis of the 1930s.

With the emergence of fascism, America joined forces with Britain and Russia to defeat the Axis Powers. At the end of World War II, America seemed to be invincible. Not only did the United States have the atomic bomb, but she had emerged from the war with her factories and land undamaged. Russia, however, was not about to let a Pax Americana be imposed on the world. The Communist power challenged the United States for influence in Europe and Asia, but this time the United States did not back down or hide. NATO was established, and America constantly frustrated Russia during the 1950s.

It was, however, the 1960s and early 1970s that most profoundly affected the nation that celebrated the Bicentennial. The Vietnam War and the Civil Rights movement helped spark a reappraisal of America's social, political, and moral values. Established institutions such as the church, the schools, and the government were brought under scrutiny. The "old neighborhoods" began to die. . . . There seemed to be no order left. Even the President was caught in the Watergate scandal and forced to resign in 1974. At the same time, the United States was forced out of Vietnam while Russian power and influence grew.

The nation seemed to have sunk to new lows in 1976. The populace, however, realized how much the country still could survive, that their Constitution had survived all the turmoil of recent years. Thus the Bicentennial was not marked by a gloomy reflection on past glories but by a quiet determination to solve the nation's problems and to persevere. The recent upsurge in American power has confirmed these hopes. With hope, we will be able to proudly celebrate the Tricentennial.

Jeffrey Mollin (Q)

# THE LARGER DIALECTIC

B efore going on to a characterization of the second part of our semester, let us consider the following question: What are our students participants in? A "real" soap opera, a "merely personal" story, a private fiction? The larger dialectic that guides/shapes the last segment of our work with students (normally weeks 10 to 15 of a semester) is one that is designed to re-frame their *personal* lives in ways that will force them ineluctably to re-construe them (cf. Campbell's *though*, our *because*; p. 271); to read them as history, social, economic, political; to read them as ethics, morality; to read them as manifests/signs of ideology, witting or unwitting.

An image will help us here. It appears in a poem by William Stafford, a poem that is difficult in two ways: in that it enacts its meaning, riddlingly, and in that it characterizes love as "of the surface" and insists that there is something deeper, more enduring, fixed, and inexorable: difficult, then, in that it consigns love—one of the primary values of a life conceived in merely personal terms—to the "map of roads":

### BI-FOCAL

*Sometimes up out of this land*
*a legend begins to move.*
*Is it a coming near*
*of something under love?*

*Love is of the earth only,*
*the surface, a map of roads*
*leading wherever go miles*
*or little bushes nod.*

*Not so the legend under,*
*fixed, inexorable,*
*deep as the darkest mine*
*the thick rocks won't tell.*

*As fire burns the leaf*
*and out of the green appears*
*the vein in the center line*
*and the legend veins under there,*

*So, the world happens twice —*
*once what we see it as;*
*second it legends itself*
*deep, the way it is.*[11]

It is the last two stanzas of the poem that especially concern us. We observe, in passing, the ingenious cunning of Stafford's syntax — "the legend veins under there," where "legend" can be both adjective and noun, and "veins" both noun and verb — and we are left to consider the enforced distinction between two accounts, two representations, of the world: one "what we see it as" and the other "the way it is" — which for Stafford can be represented adequately only by a "deep legend," a reflexive act of "legending."

Such teasing thoughts remind us of Joseph Campbell's insistence that "myths are a function of nature as well as of culture, and as necessary to the balanced maturation of the human psyche as is nourishment of the body."[12] And Stafford's image of "the vein in the center line," both central and deep, calls to mind Philip Roth's use of a remarkably similar metaphor — not only the vein of a leaf but the very vein that sustains the life of the body: "No, one's story isn't a skin to be shed — it's inescapable, one's body and blood. You go on pumping it out till you die, the story veined with the themes of your life, the ever-recurring story that's at once your invention and the invention of you."[13]

The very title of Stafford's poem is sufficient to alert us to the presence of a teasing, provocative, and unsettling dialectic; and the beautiful paradox of Roth's "at once" (who is inventing? who is invented?) reinforces the interplay, of complementarity, of subject as object, the paradox of the self inventing and reinventing itself. It is such texts as Stafford's and Roth's that reinforce our belief that what our students do with us matters; and that it matters because it is an attempt, at its most ambitious, to work for a synthesis of the thesis of self and the antithesis of the other (both others and "the world"); so we are guided by Wittgenstein's proposition that "The sense of the world must lie outside the world. In the world everything is as it is, and everything happens as it does happen: *in* it no value exists — and if it did exist, it would have no value."[14]

What value, then, is it that "letters," as the nineteenth century called humanistic studies, can have for our students? What are "letters" good for? Matthew Arnold's answer is one that we can still endorse: "The animation of mind, the multiplying of ideas, the promptness to connect, in the thoughts, one thing with another, and to illuminate one thing by another, are what are wanted; just what *letters*, as they are called, are supposed to communicate."[15] As for what the "one thing" and the "another" may *usefully* be, we have no hesitation in proposing that for the purposes of any composition course, "one thing" will be some such thing as our students will be predisposed to construe in merely, exclusively, personal terms, and "another" will be some such phenomenon as they tend to think of as impersonal, remote, theoretical. Our aim, then, is to nudge them into a dialectic whereby the inseparability of the "personal" and the impersonal (the ideological, the political, the public, the civic) will be revealed. Seeing again, this time through a bifocal lens, they will discover that the meanings of that which they had embraced as merely personal are inescapably social, historical, economic. The legends—and here we divert Stafford's metaphor for our own purposes—the legends will be not so much the "natural" legends of "elementary ideas" but, rather, the "legends" made available to us by the instruments of our culture—anthropology, sociology, political science, ethnography—the legends of the intellect. And in pursuing such purposes, we find that we depend not only on the mythopoeic gifts of such as Stafford and Roth but also on the far-reaching synthesis of action and reflection, offered by those whose work exemplifies the ideals of Wilhelm Dilthey: "Opposed to the trend in the historical sciences to approximate the methodological ideal of the natural sciences, Dilthey tried to establish the humanities as interpretative sciences in their own right. He considered as fundamental to this notion the interaction among personal experience *(Erleben)*, its realization in creative expression, and the reflective understanding of this experience."[16]

# PART TWO OF THE SEMESTER: THE LONGER REACH

A sublime example of a relatively young writer achieving a "longer reach" is Wordsworth's *Prelude.* It is not our purpose to propose that students of composition attempt a personal epic in blank verse. Wordsworth's text, nevertheless, offers us two suggestive paradigms, or forms, which lend themselves to the shaping of a more philosophical, more considerable, reach for meanings. It offers a synthesizing coordination of the personal and the public, of autobiography and history, of personal action and ideology. Above all, it offers a moral quest, a considered evaluation of experiences that may, indeed must, be construed as more than merely personal if we are to see the stories of our lives as more than naive anecdote floating outside time, outside social and political fact, outside those elements that we must either accommodate to or assimilate.

In the second part of our semester, then, having so to speak allowed them to play in a little world that we have held steady for them, we edge our students out of the nest and toward a longer reach, a more inclusive, a more complex counterpoint. And we borrow from Wordsworth the paradigms of "spots of time" and of thread, strand, or river —some motif or theme that runs as a line, a sustained preoccupation or a continuing tendency, through their lives.

## Oscillating Frames

In some cases, students elect to alternate the "voices" of participant and spectator within the same text. This alternation allows for an interpenetration of the individual experience and social values, respecting the intensity and density of the particular moment—a moment of being—and ventilating it, informing it, with the benefits of reflection. For example, Claire Windsor-Shapiro established a fairly intimate relationship between spectator voice and participant voice, gaining from their interaction an almost synchronous effect of both "in" and "out"— of both the pressured and hectic immediacy of the almost overwhelmed participant's vulnerable view and the more inclusive, detached, considering, reflecting, and conclusion-drawing distance of the spectator's view. To her text, we have appended a few of our own observations, which we wrote so that other students could appreciate more fully the cooperation within Claire's text of the two roles, the two stances, the two "voices." It is partly through an appreciation of others' texts that students can envisage the possibilities of and for their own writing.

(1)     There was nothing even remotely sinister about being on the same beach where Dr. No had attempted to discount 007 permanently. Perhaps it was the lack of ominous background music.
(2)     Love Beach, Nassau, the Bahamas, the site of scenes from the first James Bond movie, is lushly tropical, with high palm trees, cotton-soft bone-white sand, and Caribbean

blue water running into greens as bright as an Irish meadow. The day was sunny, sleepy, and not quite real to a temporarily transplanted New Yorker who'd worn boots and a ski jacket thirty hours before.

(3)     Fifteen people were scattered at intervals along the beach worshipping the sun, serving as sacrificial offerings to be burnt or tanned, depending on heredity and cosmetic chemistry. Waves no bigger than a foot flopped lethargically on the shore and even the breeze was lazy, barely stirring scents of coconut and hibiscus.

(4)     If I hadn't already rented the face mask and snorkel, nothing could have induced me to move—not that the water wasn't inviting, but bodies at rest tend to remain at rest when they're perfectly content to do so.

(5)     I contemplated moving for quite a while, but orders from my brain to my body filtered through my muscles and seeped out my toes. "I'm going . . . I'm going to move . . . I'm going to move! One . . . two . . . THREE! . . . four, five, six." I sat up, yawned widely, and nearly fell back down. The heat, the sun, or inertia held my eyelids to pencil-slim slits, which was just as well since my mind was not prepared to deal with big scenes. Nearby, in the shade of a scenically arched palm tree, my husband slept peacefully, blissfully, intelligently. (He hadn't rented snorkeling gear.)

(6)     The sea temperature was so delightfully warm that nothing dispelled the illusion that I was sleepwalking through a dream day, not even the normally daunting, eye-opening step—the crotch-wetter. This time it tickled and I smiled, enjoying several instant replays before moving on.

(7)     Snorkeling in the tropics is akin to visiting an underwater fairy land. Coral castles seemed to be inhabited by brightly colored knights in fins courting unseen mermaids or blonde fish princesses. I followed a bulging-eyed porkfish past several rock beauties before joining a school of sea anemones. Like Cinderella at a ball with no clock, I was timelessly enchanted.

(8)     Many images and unknown minutes later I lifted my head out of the water to stare at the unbroken line of the Caribbean Sea. There was nothing on the horizon except water and sky. I turned toward shore and blinked. It wasn't there. I turned right again, looking at the sea and then left where the island should have been. Disoriented, I tore off

my face mask and snorkel, swiveling in circles to get my bearings. If I hadn't had a sharply lucid thought in hours, I more than made up for it in a dozen split seconds. Where was the island? Who's playing games with me? Slamming hard heartbeats punctuated each thought. I was a half-mile or more from the beach. Was my husband still sleeping? Did he know I was swimming? Could he see me? Would anyone hear if I screamed? If I waved my arms would they see me? Was there anyone on the shore who could swim this far fast enough to help me? With a rapidity that rivaled that of a computer, bad news registered. There was no lifeguard on the beach and no row boats for emergencies. There were no boats behind me. The one person in sight with the skill and training to rescue anybody was about to drown.

(9)     Like a dybbuk taking possession, panic imploded. Machine gun palpitations hammered my ribs, making breathing impossible. Muscles twitched in spastic frenzy. I was strangling and suffocating and drowning. I was going to die . . . here . . . on Love Beach. Me and James Bond.

(10)     In a childish terror tantrum I started to cry, furiously pumping my legs to keep my head above water, gasping for air. I sobbed and choked, shivering with fear. Lack of oxygen was a cloud covering the sun, and day became night. It was dark, literally dark. I couldn't breathe. I was gulping air but not breathing. On the verge of hyperventilating I pushed my head back and tried to float. Even then I couldn't draw a deep breath. I was hiccuping and whimpering. I couldn't breathe. I sank and swallowed water, or the water swallowed me. Nothing was clear except terror and a need to breathe. I fought my way back to the surface and forced myself to float.

(11)     Look at the clouds. The clouds look soft. Breathe. Breathe. Meditate on the clouds. Concentrate on the clouds. Breathebreathe . . . breathe. I'm floating further away from the shore! Oh God! Help! Somebody! Help me! Breathe . . . breathe . . . breabreathe . . . breathe. Look at the clouds and breathe. I needed the litany, the rhythm for breathing.

(12)     Fighting panic for possession of myself, for the life of me, I struggled to breathe. Each breath was a new battle. Panic rules reason. Let me breathe. Panic is the killer. On land, on sea, in the sea, in the air, panic is the enemy. Let me breathe. The mind views panic, and the brain releases chemicals into the bloodstream that cause people to self-

destruct. The chemicals were killing me! Breathe! Don't panic. How dumb! As a swimming instructor I'd drummed the words into my students as they'd been drummed into me. Don't panic. The first, foremost, primary rule of life-saving . . . the one they printed in capital letters, "DON'T PANIC!" So dumb! The rule should have read "FIGHT THE PANIC!" Breathebreathebreathe. Breabreathe. Breathe! Fight the panic. Float on your back and breathe. Breathe. Other rules flipped through my mind. Never swim alone. Never swim without a lifeguard present. Extraneous! Extraneous to breathing. Objection! Sustained! Breathe! Float on your back and breathe. Look at the clouds and breathe.

(13)     Gently, very gently, I pointed myself toward shore, trying to gauge the direction without seeing the distance. Now easy . . . easy . . . kick your legs just a bit. It was a game—a war game. Don't let the panic know what you're doing. It was alive in my chest, between my collar bones. I could feel it just below my throat. I could hear it. I didn't know you could hear panic.

(14)     Float on your back and breathe. Look at the clouds and breathe.

(15)     I was clutching my face mask and snorkel unconsciously, like a security blanket. If I threw them away it would be an admission that maybe I wasn't going to make it. I needed them. I had to return them. I'd only rented them. They had to be returned.

(16)     Float on your back and breathe. Look at the clouds and breathe.

(17)     Never have I disciplined my thoughts and movements with such rigid, concentrated, single-minded determination. I could have written books, built cities, and cured diseases with that telescoped intensity. And I needed it, all of it. I had the adrenaline for ten times the energy I required, but my body was dead without my mind. If the panic got my mind the adrenaline would be used against me. Why did the panic feel bigger and stronger than me? I had created a monster and it wouldn't let go.

(18)     Float on your back and breathe. Look at the clouds and breathe.

(19)     Again and again I repeated the sequence, over and over until I felt calm enough to swim. Swim slowly, easily, with effortless strokes. Two yards forward, one yard back. The current giveth and taketh away. It played leader as if

I'd forgotten to say "May I?" Three kicks to each arm stroke, roll your head, breathe when the right arm is raised. Don't look at the shore. Don't look! It was back! It hadn't left! The panic was growing again! Breathe breathe. Float on your back and breathebreathe breathe. Look at the clouds and breathe. Float on your back and breathe. Think of your training. Remember your training. Remember your training. . . .

(20) I was the youngest in the lifesaving class, not yet thirteen, and the teacher was slightly sadistic. At least I'd thought so at the time. On the final lifesaving test she had played victim, yelling and thrashing about in the lake. Float . . . breathe . . . Look at the clouds and breathe. It was my turn to save the teacher. I jumped in—lifesavers don't dive. You can't lose sight of the victim. I swam until I was about 5 feet in front of her and then I did a surface dive. You have to. You can't give the victim a chance to grab you around the neck because victims have a tendency to panic. That's funny. Panic. Breathe . . . breathe . . . float on your back and . . . breathe. I approached her underwater, turning her legs, keeping my hands in contact with her body. I surfaced behind her, avoiding her clutches, and grabbed her securely in a lifesaving carry. Breathe . . . breathe. . . .

(21) Using her far greater height and strength my teacher had flipped over and gotten me in a stranglehold, pulling us both underwater. She'd trained us so well that I had felt only minimal panic . . . breathe breathe . . . float on your back . . . look at the clouds. After all, she wouldn't really let me drown. Automatically I'd followed the lifesaving manual, forcibly subduing her—if need be knock her out or shove her head underwater until she is unconscious or stunned. Any lifesaver is a potential victim, so do what you must to save the victim, and if it's impossible then just save yourself. Breathe . . . breathe . . . I'd dragged my teacher to the shore eventually. She must have been black and blue and aching like crazy after testing 15 kids that day. I can't remember her name. That's sad. Breathe . . . She saved my life and I don't remember her name. Float . . . breathe. . . .

(22) Totally hypnotized by the words, the rhythm, and the memories, I didn't know I had reached the shore until the snorkel scraped bottom. My legs buckled twice before I could stand and I staggered, whimpering, wounded.

(23) "You idiot! What kind of moron swims out that far? You friggin' lunatic! You should have your head examined.

You have less brains than a peapod. You scared me half to death. Do you know how easily you could have drowned?" My husband screamed at me nonstop until he ran out of words. I stared at him blankly, ankle deep in water with my teeth chattering. It made no sense. If he knew I was in trouble why hadn't he come to help me, or why hadn't he sent someone to help me? Or had he realized that with the distance between me and the shore no one could have helped me but myself? It didn't make sense, but I was too drained and much too tired to think sensibly. I even stopped shivering. I didn't have the strength for it. I walked, talked, dressed, ate, and functioned in a zombie-like state for at least twelve hours. When the shock hit and registered I cried uncontrollably, hysterically until I was cried out. Then I slept for a long, long time.

(24)     Having had more training than most people in water safety, how the hell do I forgive myself for breaking a dozen basic rules? How many times can I call myself stupid? Eventually, for the sake of my own self-respect, I've had to put it out of my mind. But stupidity aside, there's got to be a way to teach people about panic so that they can save themselves. Somewhere in our school systems, in the early grades, someone should be teaching "Panic Survival." Parroting the words "Don't panic" is senseless because given a terrifying situation you can't prevent panic any more than you can prevent a knee-jerk reaction. How you *fight* that panic is a matter of life and death. To my knowledge no one has ever suggested a course or class in panic training. Is it possible that there are so few of us who have experienced panic and lived to tell about it?

Claire Windsor-Shapiro (Q)

## Commentary

Claire begins by contextualizing—"placing" the events of her text both in time and in place. She can do this because she is now—writing—a spectator of her own past experience.

Line 3 of paragraph 1, and line 2 of paragraph 3 foreshadow the calamity of the climax. As readers, we appreciate these only on a second reading.

Paragraph 5 sustains the spectator frame but also marks a shift toward a participant text, by quoting and referring to very specific small details.

Paragraph 7: Meanings are to be found in the differences; the fantasy or fairytale, enchanted tone of this paragraph works effectively to lull the reader—as the writer herself had been lulled—into a state of euphoric relaxation.

Paragraphs 8–10 nudge closer and closer toward a participant text; and paragraph 11 plunges us into participation, establishing a rhythm that becomes the recurring *motif* of her struggle to overcome panic. The last sentence of paragraph 11 and the first two sentences of paragraph 12 shift quickly into spectator text (note the verb tenses) and represent her own explanatory commentary: they serve to distance us momentarily and allow us to catch our breath.

Paragraphs 13–20 fluctuate between participant and spectator, parataxis and hypotaxis, shifting out of an exclusively participant text as she escapes from her panic. But we as readers have, as it were, "felt" her panic precisely because of the effectiveness of her participant text.

The last sentence of paragraph 19 alerts us to the shift in paragraph 20, the reminiscence of her lifesaving experience, punctuated by her present litany "Float . . . breathe." The memory mostly reassures her, but it also occasionally scares / disconcerts her.

Paragraph 22: narrative economy as a means of avoiding a crudely chronological, moment by moment, narrative. Paragraph 23 gives us a spectator within the text, her husband expostulating; and then her confused and tense questions "If . . . why?" But she's still too exhausted to "think sensibly"—that is, achieve a satisfactory evaluation. It is only with paragraph 24 that she represents a point in time from which she, as distanced spectator, can now express a coherent, definitive, evaluation of those awful events.

Like Claire's, Donald Liebell's text oscillates between participant and spectator. And it, too, offers an evaluation. In Donald's text, an amalgam of elegy and celebration, the personal and the public interpenetrate; one person's quest for what is almost lost opens a larger ecological perspective.

> A thriving deciduous forest full of flora and fauna once existed in some areas of Queens. One could walk out the back door of the house and become part of nature, coexist with it . . . be it. Thirty years ago, Little Neck could hardly be considered to be New York City, so I am told. The term *city* seemed inappropriate for an area rich with creatures, greenery, and earth. Neighbors who were around then tell me how they could go toad hunting in their own yard or chase a raccoon out of the garbage cans and maybe even

spy on a huge orange pheasant while looking through the bedroom window. It must have been a paradise for the nature enthusiast. I would have loved to be a part of it. I think of the menagerie of creatures I could have had in my own back yard. A veritable potpourri of objects of my intrigue existed there. Today there are only memories . . . or are there?

A remnant of the past does exist. There is a place where I can go to be a part of the past. I can see how things used to be. This other world is only half a mile away. A small section of forest still remains alive in between the condominiums, garden apartments, and private houses. Once every so often I set aside a couple of hours to forget the urban world and take a long walk through the natural world. The following is an account of such a venture. This particular one is done in a series of trips back to the forest in search of a goal: to find the spring peeper, a tiny frog which I had read so much about but had never actually seen.

The call comes from low marshy ground in the open or from pools and marshy land in the woods; from sun-exposed ponds or from swamps deep into the forest. It can be distinctly heard almost a quarter of a mile from its origins. I can approach the forest by car on a fully paved urban roadway and still hear this loud chorus resembling a jangle of sleigh bells. To isolate a single voice would be a difficult task.

I visit the forest solitarily, carrying a small container just in case I find an interesting creature. There are many to be seen and heard. The spring peeper, a tree frog, no more than an inch in length, is only heard. After hearing the musical chorus year after year in the forest, I have to admit that the peeper is still only a voice. I must somehow unravel the mystery.

It is the second week of March. The temperature is a cool 55 degrees. I leave for class an hour early to visit the forest. I pull my car alongside the forest fringe and step out into the street. The peepers are singing! I follow the song until I reach a shallow pond surrounded by sweetgum and oak trees. This is the source. A simple peeper can be heard along the water's edge in a patch of moss and rotted leaves. There is nothing to be seen. Searching among the leaves reveals nothing. The tiny animal is still only a voice. I must leave now.

Two weeks have passed, and I try again to find a peeper. The sun is shining. The temperature is 64 degrees. The chorus can be heard before I leave the car. Stepping from stone to stone beside the pond, I notice a painted turtle sunning itself along the rock, undisturbed by the ear-splitting sound of the tiny frogs. Still I wonder. Where are the frogs? The sound surrounds me, but they are nowhere to be found. Searching through the muck and leaves is futile still. I once again retreat. The mystery continues.

I try again in May. Spring flowers are in bloom and the leaves are out on the trees. The shoreline of the pond has receded slightly. I slowly tiptoe towards the edge of the water and then remain motionless. The calls start and stop randomly with fluctuating intensity. Even though I get wet, I walk into the water a few steps. The calls surround me again. The search has finally ended. A tiny froglet, no more than half an inch long, appears on a lichen-covered twig. He leaps onto a clump of leaves and begins to sing. It is hard to believe that something so small could create so much sound.

The little fellow finally notices me and scampers away to safety. It is a joyous moment; I have finally seen a peeper after all these years. It is in a way a personal victory. A goal has been attained. I have spent some time in a different world. I have seen what few people ever see, and in a way I have tasted the past.

Donald Liebell (Q)

### Reflections

I enjoyed writing this because it was something personal.* I wasn't assigned to do it. I didn't have to do it. I wanted to. There was true motivation involved.

Donald Liebell (Q)

# TO WHAT END?

Depending on what the students' chosen starting point may be, their particular spot of time or their chosen river, we then nudge or elbow them in one or more appropriate directions in a search

---

*By "personal," Donald seems to signify "meaningful" or "charged with value." He writes of a valued experience, but it is not a "merely personal" one.

for, and an invention of, larger resonances, meanings, or significances that both contain and transcend the merely personal. We aim to bring them to see any "personal" experience as inescapably saturated, informed, packed, by public meanings. The nudgings involve group discussions, one-on-one conferences, the recommendation of books, articles, films, television programs—whatever seems appropriate to their contextualizing of the personal within the public. The problem of alienation—a failure to connect the energies of the self to the potential charge of something "out there," a failure that characterizes much academic activity for too many students—is fended off by respecting *their* experience, *their* life, *their* microcosm. But to allow them to rest there, naively, cozily, uncritically, is to allow their myths to remain intact. And insofar as these myths derive from the media, with their chronic evacuation of all ideology, all politics, all social criticism, from the personal realm, to do so would be simply to leave them prey to a privatized illusion. It is our purpose not to corrode or undermine our students' values, beliefs, or pieties; rather to ventilate those values with the cool and refreshing air of a spirit of inquiry: to ask why, to examine and challenge their own tacit assumptions.

For some of our students, those starting points or preoccupations are obsessions that, if turned inward, become disabling. A number of our students are children of Holocaust survivors, who upon looking at their own lives may conclude—as one student recently did—that their own lives, in the context of their parents', are uneventful, meaningless. History, for them, has already happened, and they are left—in some cases with a heavy silence (their parents do not tell stories), in others with words and stories they need to do something with.

Annie Landa, in the following text, "speaks" as her own mother, a Holocaust survivor, who recounts a scene that is "burned somewhere into [her] memory" and, "in moments of reflection and pain," pulled out. One of those "moments" was President Reagan's visit to the Bitburg Cemetery, where German SS troops are buried. The event exploded into protest and entreaty. American veteran groups, Jewish groups, foreign representatives, all pleaded with the President not to attend this memorial service. Annie's text is convergent: the voice of the mother is that of a spectator, looking back on that in which she had participated forty years earlier. Now, when the events to many are history, she shows that they are not, that events collocate, one being sparked by the other through the shaping power of the memory, the continuing need to evaluate—to make sense of that which is, in the final analysis, inexplicable—and the urge to speak out, to protest against actions that violate memory and her version of history. The personal here is not merely personal. A daughter in looking at her mother's past looks square into the eyes of the present and says, "No, this is not the way to read the past."

*For My Mother:*
*A Survivor and a Heroine*

## VICTIMS

For years I tried to forget that scene. But no more could I forget it than I could forget how to breathe. It is burned somewhere into my memory to be taken out and dusted in moments of reflection and pain. As the years wore on, the memories of what had happened in that dreadful time slowly dulled. There are, however, certain moments, fragments of time, like snapshots that refuse to lose their sharpness or strength. That scene, whether recalled every day or once in five years, will always be as clear to me as if it were happening before my eyes. Now brought back again by the President's unsettling words, I see that it taught me what innocent victim, guilty murderer, and true evil and injustice really mean.

I will never forget . . .

It was a foggy spring day with the sun sneaking in through the clouds only to tease its victims. There was no spring or summer in the camps, only death and winter. The air had a certain dampness probably caused by the forgotten sweat and tears of our forgotten souls. The stone-cold barracks stood against the once innocent countryside. We were encircled in a barbed wire of fear and submission. By that time most of us had lost all hope and human emotion. The one thing that made me persevere was the thought that I had to survive as a testimony to this inconceivable horror.

One has to understand that their aim was to physically and psychologically make us believe we were less than human and that they were superhuman. They did this through a calculated method of force. They forced us to realize that because they had the physical strength we had to obey their commands, no matter how insane, inhuman, or futile. One example of this was that when there was no work we were kept outside to be counted, just to be shown that our lives were no longer our own. Hundreds of skeletal shadows and images, which were once people, lined the courtyard. For hours we would be kept outside, in line, like ignorant sheep led by a small pack of killer wolves. The one rule that had to be obeyed was that we could, under no circumstances, step even an inch out of line. If we would it usually meant instant death. It was as if we were locked into a psychological strait jacket of a square-foot prison.

On that day I had been put into a line with some of the newer prisoners who still had that mixed look of confusion and empty hope. A few rows in front of me stood a woman, who I later found out was part of a group from one of the smaller towns in Western Hungary which had just arrived with the last transport. It was only the day before that they had been separated from their families and selected for life or death. She had been separated from her twelve-year-old daughter, assigned to a different barrack, and had not seen her since. I had noticed her searching the blank faces of the prisoners in each of the endless lines. I didn't think anything of it until she met eyes with her daughter. Before we could warn her, she left the line to share a moment of embrace and comfort with her lost daughter. This the officers, the so-called "victims of Nazism and fascism," could not tolerate. Ordinarily, from a warped sense of compassion, the officer would make sure the transgressor was instantly killed with a bullet or a blow to the head. But in this instance, a *female* officer felt personally offended by the woman's act of bravery in the face of hopelessness. The officer felt it her duty to remove her leather belt and whip the woman in violent lashes. This sound echoed throughout the courtyard. Once the woman was on the ground, the officer wrapped a riding crop around the prisoner's neck and dragged her through those impenetrable lines, like a calf being captured for slaughter. Once the deed was done, the officer had a sadistic smile of accomplishment at having caused such a perfect, painful, slow, and violent death. As the mother lay dead on the ground looking almost holy and untouchable, I realized that in the master plan of turning us into animals, they were the ones who were transformed into beasts . . .

Now, years later, this scene jumps out into my consciousness as a remembrance of the martyred souls and those inhuman murderers. I cannot accept the words of our respected leader in creating an analogy between the true victims and those who perpetrated the victimization. Would he still believe that they, those brutal officers, were victims just as we were if he understood what had really happened? It frightens me to think that the hellish evil of that time is still being perpetuated in the ignorance of this, our children's time.

Annie Landa (Q)

If we speak of our bias as tending toward ethnography, it is because we wish to suggest that the exploration of any personal meaning is to be challenged, complicated, and moved toward a greater fullness by involving the personal in an intimate dialectic with the public. If, then, a student chooses to write a text in memory of a revered grandparent, our task is to help the writer "place" that life in the context of an appropriate segment of social, economic, and political history. We recall, for instance, a student whose paper was conceived as an affectionate portrait of her grandmother and mother, exploring their characteristic idiosyncrasies, quirks, virtues. In the end her text emerged as "Grandmother, No; Mother, Maybe; Myself, Yes"—an exploration of changes in sexual mores as exemplified by the lives of three women; a scrutiny, moreover, of the social, religious, and political agencies that bear down on women and attempt to make their decisions for them.

Similarly, when a student chose to write an account of the early immigrant trials, troubles, and achievements of his grandfather's boyhood, we argued that the individual experience had to be construed as typical/atypical (to some degree) of a larger demographic convulsion, cultural dislocation, social crisis. It is history as encapsulated in one life; one life having historical significance—two sides of the same coin. The biographer, handling familiar and familial material as a participant observer, deriving anecdotes, stories, memories, from the central participant, also must take on the responsibility of working as a cultural historian/spectator/ethnographer, establishing appropriate contexts, offering relevant statistics, distinguishing between discomfort and pain, crisis and calamity. Most important, his or her task is to balance the respective claims of proximity and distance, the inner and the outer, and to validate the benefits of bifocal vision.

Many of our students in Queens are Jewish; a large proportion of them have spent time in Israel. When they come to choose a topic for their longer paper, they find that it is they who are chosen, by the irresistible power of memories of their experience of Israel. The sheer eventfulness of their months there is one thing—a matter in which they are, indeed, expert. But to bring consideration to bear, to construe and reconstrue, involves them in a great variety of reflections—political, religious, ethnic, ethical, historical, and ideological. Theirs is the opportunity, extending over a period of six or seven weeks, to raise valued experience above the level of the casual anecdote, the stock response, the glib shorthand ("It was a great trip"). Theirs is the opportunity, simultaneously, to respect and honor the quiddity of *their* particular experience, thus enforcing an interplay of personal and public—a dialectic that discovers the public nature of the personal, the personal significance of the public; an interplay, too, of participant and spectator roles. It is this opportunity that invites, provokes, students to enter, to take on, "academic" roles without falling into the lassitude and apathy of alienation. And they discover, in the process, that political, social, ideological consciousness enriches, not denies, the phenomenal richness of what has happened to them, personally, what they have personally known.

Dell Hymes, the distinguished ethnographer, has observed that "there is an inescapable tension between the rhetorical and literary forms considered necessary for the persuasion of colleagues, and the narrative form 'natural to the experience of the work, and natural to the meaningful report of it in other than monographic contexts' "; also, that "the scientific styles often imposed on ethnographic writing may produce, not objectivity, but distortion. This is an old problem—I was told of a Berkeley ethnographer in the 1930's who said, data in hand, 'Now all I have to do is take the life out of it.' "[17]

The task involved in the longer reach can be seen as one of conjunction and integration: on the one hand are the moments of being, spots of time that were apprehended directly, preanalytically, compelling and enlivening participation in a mode of being.[18] Now they are recalled, reconstructed, sometimes so vividly as to seem reexperienced, reentered, but imbued with the benefits of time: retrospective reflection, consideration, a move toward conceptualization and evaluation, aided by relative detachment. On the other hand are the "legends": ways of thinking, modes of analysis and appraisal into which we can initiate our students. And between the two, at best, exists a symbiotic and synergistic interplay, a dialogue, which may happily result in a conversation, a flowing together, of the experiential and the philosophical. Such conjunctions can be almost disconcerting, as when one student recently brought the techniques and methods of political science—a recent discovery for him—to bear on one of his abiding passions, a noteworthy and controversial high school baseball coach, and so produced an exploration of the nature of charisma, power, and influence. "Only connect. . . ." The fruits of such connection are that the valued experience, the sacred object, is not diminished, drained of value, deconsecrated; even when demystified, placed, and typified, it can be construed in a more complex, a richer way, revaluated, reinterpreted, seen again in the light of insights that the "innocent" mind cannot ever know.

At the end of a semester's work, we hope to leave our students both exhausted and satisfied; with a sense of recent accomplishment and of future possibility; with a clear recognition of a discovered commitment—in Donald Liebell's words: "I enjoyed writing this . . . I wasn't assigned to do it. I didn't have to do it. I wanted to . . . I now know that I can enjoy writing. In February I thought I had nothing to write about. Now, writing is no longer just a tool for obtaining a grade." Through negotiation and collaboration, and through a balancing of support and demand, we strive to come reasonably close to a synthesis of the students' needs and our desires, their best wishes and our proper hopes; in Makarenko's words: "The maximum possible demands with the maximum possible respect."

# NOTES

1. *Encyclopaedia Britannica,* 15th ed., s.v. Hegel.
2. *New York Times,* December 2, 1984.
3. Sei Shōnagon, *The Pillow Book,* trans. Ivan Morris (Harmondsworth: Penguin, 1971).
4. William Stafford, *Stories That Could Be True* (New York: Harper & Row, 1977), p. 54.
5. W. H. Auden, "Reading," in his *The Dyer's Hand* (London: Faber & Faber, 1975), pp. 6–7.
6. *The Book of Rewards and Punishments,* quoted in Alasdair Clayre, *The Heart of the Dragon* (Boston: Houghton Mifflin, 1985), p. 51.
7. Joseph Campbell, *The Flight of the Wild Gander* (Chicago: Regnery Gateway, n.d.), p. 48.
8. Thomas De Quincey, "Review of the Works of Pope," *North British Review,* August 1848.
9. Ted Solatoroff, "A Few Good Voices in Your Head," in *In Praise of What Persists,* ed. Stephen Berg (New York: Harper & Row, 1983), p. 246.
10. C. K. Williams, "Beginnings," in *In Praise of What Persists,* p. 272.
11. Stafford, *Stories That Could Be True,* p. 48.
12. Campbell, *The Flight of the Wild Gander,* Chapter 1: "Bios and Mythos."
13. Philip Roth, *Zuckerman Bound* (New York: Farrar, Straus & Giroux, 1985), p. 782.
14. Ludwig Wittgenstein, *Tractatus Logico-Philosophicus,* trans. D. F. Pears and B. F. McGuinness (London: Routledge Kegan Paul, 1969), p. 3.
15. Geoffrey Summerfield and Peter Smith, *Matthew Arnold and the Education of the New Order* (London: Cambridge University Press, 1969), p. 221.
16. *Encyclopaedia Britannica,* 15th ed., s.v. Wilhelm Dilthey.
17. Dell Hymes, "An Ethnographic Perspective," *New Literary History* 4 (Autumn 1973); cited in Elizabeth Fine, *The Folklore Text* (Bloomington: Indiana University Press, 1985), p. 100. Cf. Hugh Brody, *Maps and Dreams* (New York: Pantheon, 1982).
18. It seems to us crucial that students in composition at any level continue to write *from within.* As Henry Glassie observes of a story-telling community, "All seem reasonable from within, strange from without, silent at a distance. The way to study people is not from the top down or the bottom up, but from the inside out, from the place where people are articulate to the place where they are not, from the place where they are in control of their destinies to the place where they are not." Henry Glassie, *Passing the Time in Ballymenone* (Philadelphia: University of Pennsylvania Press, 1982), p. 86.

# Bibliography

## Literature

Agassiz, Louis. *Contributions to the Natural History of the United States (1857–1862)*. Salem, N.H.: 1978.

Agee, James, and Walker Evans. *Let Us Now Praise Famous Men*. New York: Ballantine Books, 1970.

Anderson, Sherwood. *Selected Letters*. Edited by C. E. Modlin. Knoxville: University of Tennessee Press, 1984.

Barth, John. *Lost in the Funhouse*. New York: Bantam, 1969.

Beckett, Samuel. *Watt*. New York: Grove Press, 1981.

Bishop, Elizabeth. *Geography III*. New York: Farrar Straus & Giroux, 1976.

Bogarde, Dirk. *A Postillion Struck by Lightning*. New York: Holt, Rinehart & Winston, 1977.

Bone, Edith. *Seven Years Solitary*. London: Hamish Hamilton, 1957.

Didion, Joan. *The White Album*. New York: Simon & Schuster, 1979.

Eliot, T. S. *The Family Reunion*. London: Faber & Faber, 1960.

Fuller, Buckminster. Entry for *Who's Who*. *Saturday Review*, March 2, 1968.

Gosse, Edmund. *Father and Son, A Study of Two Temperaments*. Harmondsworth: Penguin, 1979.

Hoban, Russell. *Riddley Walker*. London: Picador, 1982.

Hudson, Virginia Carey. *O Ye Jigs and Juleps!* New York: Macmillan, 1962.

Hughes, Ted. *Wodwo*. London: Faber & Faber, 1971.

Joyce, James. *Ulysses*. New York: Vintage Books, 1961.

L'Anselme, Jean. *The Ring Around the World*. Translated by Michael Benedict. London: Rapp & Whiting, n.d.

Levertov, Denise. *Candles in Babylon*. New York: New Directions, 1982.

Lewis, Cecil. *Sagittarius Rising*. Harmondsworth: Penguin, 1977.

Mailer, Norman. *Marilyn*. New York: Grosset & Dunlap, 1973.

———. *Of Women and Their Elegance*. New York: Tor Books, 1981.

Malouf, David. *An Imaginary Life*. London: Picador, 1980.

Morgan, Edwin. *Poems of Thirty Years*. Manchester: Carcanet New Press, 1982.

Queneau, Raymond. *Exercises in Style*. Translated by Barbara Wright. London: John Calder, 1981.

Raine, Craig. *A Martian Sends a Postcard Home*. London: Oxford University Press, 1980.

Renard, Jules. *Journals*. Edited and translated by Louise Bogan and Elizabeth Roget. New York: Braziller, 1964.

Roth, Philip. *Zuckerman Bound*. New York: Farrar Straus & Giroux, 1985.

———. *The Professor of Desire*. New York: Farrar Straus & Giroux, 1977.

Rushdie, Salman. *Midnight's Children*. New York: Bard/Avon Books, 1980.

Shōnagon, Sei. *The Pillow Book*. Translated by Ivan Morris. Harmondsworth: Penguin, 1971.

Stafford, William. *Stories That Could Be True*. New York: Harper & Row, 1977.

Steinbeck, John. *The Grapes of Wrath*. New York: Penguin, 1976.

Sterne, Laurence. *The Life and Opinions of Tristram Shandy, Gentleman*. Boston: Houghton Mifflin, 1965.

Woolf, Virginia. *Moments of Being: Unpublished Autobiographical Writings*. Edited by Jeanne Schulkind. Orlando, Fla.: Harcourt Brace Jovanovich, 1978.

Wordsworth, William. *The Prelude, 1799, 1805, 1850*. Edited by Jonathan Wordsworth, M. H. Abrams, and Stephen Gill. New York: Norton, 1979.

Yourcenar, Marguerite. *Memoirs of Hadrian*. Translated by Grace Frick and the author. New York: Farrar Straus & Giroux, 1981.

## Theoretical and Critical

Auden, W. H. *The Dyer's Hand*. London: Faber & Faber, 1975.

Auerbach, Eric. *Mimesis: The Representation of Reality in Western Literature*. Translated by Willard R. Trask. Princeton, N.J.: Princeton University Press, 1974.

Barthes, Roland. *Roland Barthes*. Translated by Richard Howard. New York: Hill & Wang, 1977.

————. *Mythologies*. Translated by Annette Lavers. New York: Hill & Wang, 1981.

Bartholomae, David. "Writing Assignments: Where Writing Begins." In *Fforum*, edited by Patricia Stock. Montclair, N.J.: Boynton/Cook, 1983.

Bell, Quentin. *Virginia Woolf: A Biography*. 2 vols. Orlando, Fla.: Harcourt Brace Jovanovich, 1972.

Berg, Stephen, ed. *In Praise of What Persists*. New York: Harper & Row, 1983.

Berger, Peter L., and Thomas Luckmann. *The Social Construction of Reality*. New York: Doubleday, 1967.

Blakemore, Colin. *Mechanics of the Mind*. London: Cambridge University Press, 1977.

Bollnow, O. F. "Wilhelm Dilthey." Encyclopaedia Britannica. 15th ed. Vol. 5. p. 804.

Britton, James N. *Prospect and Retrospect*. Edited by Gordon Pradl. Montclair, N.J.: Boynton/Cook, 1982.

Brody, Hugh. *Maps and Dreams*. New York: Pantheon Books, 1982.

Bruner, Jerome. "Teaching a Native Language." In *Toward a Theory of Instruction*. New York: Norton, 1968.

Campbell, Joseph. *The Flight of the Wild Gander*. Chicago: Regnery Gateway, n.d.

Cavell, Stanley. "The Availability of Wittgenstein's Later Philosophy." In *The Philosophical Investigations*, edited by G. Pitcher. New York: Doubleday, 1965.

Crystal, David, and Derek Davy. *Investigating English Style*. London: Longman, 1969.

DeQuincey, Thomas. "Review of Alexander Pope." *North British Review,* August 1848.

Donaldson, Margaret. *Children's Minds.* London: Fontana/Collins, 1979.

Fader, Dan. "Narrowing the Space Between Writer and Text." In *Fforum,* edited by Patricia Stock. Montclair, N.J.: Boynton/Cook, 1983.

Farrell, Thomas. "I.Q. and Standard English." *CCC,* XXXIV, N.C.T.E., December 1983.

Fine, Elizabeth. *The Folklore Text.* Bloomington: Indiana University Press, 1985.

Glassie, Henry. *Passing the Time in Ballymenone.* Philadelphia: University of Pennsylvania Press, 1982.

Goffman, Erving. *Frame Analysis: An Essay on the Organization of Experience.* New York: Harper & Row, 1974.

Halliday, M. A. K. *Learning How to Mean—Explorations in the Development of Language.* London: Arnold, 1975.

——. *Language as Social Semiotic.* London: Arnold, 1979.

Harding, D. W. "The Role of the Onlooker." *Scrutiny* 6 (1937):247.

——. "Psychological Processes in the Reading of Fiction." *British Journal of Aesthetics,* 2, no. 2 (1962).

——. *Experience into Words.* London: Cambridge University Press, 1982.

Hardy, Barbara. *Tellers and Listeners: The Narrative Imagination.* London: Athlone Press, 1984.

Harré, Rom. *Personal Being.* Cambridge, Mass.: Harvard University Press, 1984.

Heaney, Seamus. "The Makings of a Music: Reflections on the Poetry of Wordsworth and Yeats." The Kenneth Allott Lecture. Liverpool: Liverpool University Press, 1978. Reprinted in *Preoccupations, Selected Prose 1968-1978.* London: Faber & Faber, 1980.

Heathcote, Dorothy. *Collected Writings on Education and Drama.* Edited by L. Johnson and C. O'Neill. London: Hutchinson, 1984.

Hughes, Ted. *Poetry in the Making.* London: Faber & Faber, 1967.

——. "Myth and Education." In *Writers, Critics and Children,* edited by G. Fox et al. London: Heinemann, 1976.

Hymes, Dell. "An Ethnographic Perspective." *New Literary History* 4, Autumn 1973.

Jakobson, Roman. "Concluding Statement." In *Style in Language,* edited by T. A. Sebeok. Cambridge, Mass.: M.I.T. Press, 1960.

James, William. "On a Certain Blindness in Human Beings." In his *Talks to Teachers.* New York: Norton, 1958.

——. *Principles of Psychology.* 2 vols. New York: Dover Publications, 1950.

Kelly, George. *A Theory of Personality: The Psychology of Personal Constructs.* New York: Norton, 1963.

Keniston, Kenneth. *Youth and Dissent.* Orlando, Fla.: Harcourt Brace Jovanovich, 1971.

Kermode, Frank. *The Sense of an Ending: Studies in the Theory of Fiction.* London: Oxford University Press, 1967.

Knox, T. M. "Hegel." *Encyclopaedia Britannica,* 15th ed., vol. 8, p. 728.

Labov, William. "The Transformation of Experience into Narrative Syntax." In *Language in the Inner City*. Philadelphia: University of Pennsylvania Press, 1972.

———. *Sociolinguistic Patterns*. Philadelphia: University of Pennsylvania Press, 1972.

Langer, Susanne. *Feeling and Form*. New York: Scribners, 1977.

———. *Philosophy in a New Key*. Cambridge, Mass.: Harvard University Press, 1976.

Lawrence, D. H. *Fantasia of the Unconscious*. Harmondsworth: Penguin, 1978.

LeGuin, Ursula K. "It Was a Dark and Stormy Night; or Why Are We Huddling About the Fire?" *Critical Inquiry* 7, no. 1 (Autumn 1980).

Levertov, Denise. *The Poet in the World*. New York: New Directions, 1973.

———. *Light Up the Cave*. New York: New Directions, 1981.

Maimon, Elaine P., et al. *Writing in the Arts and Sciences*. Cambridge, Mass.: Winthrop, 1981.

Martin, Nancy, et al. *Writing and Learning Across the Curriculum*. London: Ward Lock, 1981.

Medawar, Peter. *Advice to a Young Scientist*. New York: Harper & Row, 1981.

Meisel, Perry (ed.). *Freud: A Collection of Critical Essays*. Englewood Cliffs, N.J.: Prentice-Hall, 1981.

Mitchell, W. J. T. (ed.). "On Narrative." *Critical Inquiry* 7, no. 1 (Autumn 1980).

Morgan, Edwin. "There Is a Poetry Before Poetry." In *Worlds*, edited by Geoffrey Summerfield. Harmondsworth: Penguin, 1974.

Neel, Jasper P. (ed.). *Options for the Teaching of English: Freshman Composition*. N.C.T.E., 1978.

Ong, Walter J. *Interfaces of the Word*. Ithaca, N.Y.: Cornell University Press, 1982.

Oakeshott, Michael. *The Voice of Poetry in the Conversation of Mankind*. London: Bowes, 1959.

Pachter, Marc (ed.). *Telling Lives: The Biographer's Art*. Ithaca, N.Y.: Cornell University Press, 1979.

Percy, Walker. "Symbol, Consciousness and Intersubjectivity." *Journal of Philosophy* 55 (1958), 632–41.

Rosen, Harold. "The Nurture of Narrative." IRA Convention, Chicago, April 1982.

Rosengarten, Theodore. "Stepping over Cockleburs: Conversations with Ned Cobb." In Pachter, op. cit.

Sapir, Edward. "The Status of Linguistics as a Science." In *Culture, Language, and Personality*, edited by David G. Mandelbaum. Berkeley: University of California Press, n.d.

Shattuck, Roger. *The Forbidden Experiment*. New York: Washington Square Press, 1981.

Smith, Barbara Herrnstein. *Poetic Closure*. Chicago: University of Chicago Press, 1974.

———. *On the Margin of Discourse*. Chicago: University of Chicago Press, 1983.

Solotaroff, Ted. "A Few Good Voices in Your Head." In Berg, op. cit.

Stock, Patricia L. (ed.). *Forum: Essays on Theory and Practice in the Teaching of Writing.* Montclair, N.J.: Boynton/Cook, 1983.

Summerfield, Geoffrey. *Fantasy and Reason.* Athens: University of Georgia Press, 1985.

———. (ed.). *Worlds: Seven Modern Poets.* Harmondsworth: Penguin, 1974.

Summerfield, Geoffrey, and Peter Smith. *Matthew Arnold and the Education of the New Order.* London: Cambridge University Press, 1969.

Tufte, Virginia. *Grammar as Style.* New York: Holt, Rinehart & Winston, 1971.

Turner, G. W. *Stylistics.* Harmondsworth: Penguin, 1973.

Vendler, Helen. *The Odes of John Keats.* Cambridge, Mass.: Harvard University Press, 1984.

Vygotsky, Lev S. *Thought and Language.* Cambridge, Mass.: M.I.T. Press, 1962.

White, James Boyd. "The Invisible Discourse of the Law: Reflections on Legal Literacy and General Education." In Stock, op. cit.

Williams, C. K. "Beginnings." In Berg, op. cit.

Winnicott, D. W. *Playing and Reality.* London: Tavistock, 1971.

Wittgenstein, Ludwig. *Tractatus Logico-Philosophicus.* Translated by D. F. Pears and B. F. McGuinness. London: Routledge, 1969.

# About the Authors

**Judith Summerfield** (formerly **Fishman**) has taught composition and literature since 1963; at Queens College since 1972, she has served as director of the Writing Skills Workshop, co-director of the Queens English Project, a federally funded articulation project, and associate director of the composition program. A former member of the CCC Executive Committee, she has conducted workshops for teachers throughout the country. She is co-author, with Sandra Schor, of the *Random House Guide to Writing* and editor of *Responding to Prose: A Reader for Writers* (Macmillan). She is now at work on an interdisciplinary study of narrative as it informs autobiography, fiction, and nonfiction prose. Recent articles appear in *WPA, Linguistics and Stylistics, The Journal Book* (ed. Toby Fulwiler), and proceedings from the 1984 New Hampshire Conference on Reading and Writing, where she delivered a keynote address, "Framing Narratives."

**Geoffrey Summerfield** is best known in his native England as co-editor of the poems and prose of John Clare (Oxford University Press), for his poetry anthologies, *Voices* and *Worlds* (Penguin), and for his work on Matthew Arnold (Cambridge University Press) and on composition (Batsford). In the United States, he was a member of the Dartmouth Seminar (1966), and has taught at the University of California at Berkeley, Northwestern University, New York University, and the University of Nebraska; he is currently an adjunct professor, teaching composition, at Queens College, New York. His most recent publications are *Welcome* (Deutsch/Dutton), poems for young readers, and *Fantasy and Reason*, a "prelude" to Wordsworth's *Prelude* (Methuen/University of Georgia Press). In 1980, he lectured in Australia and New Zealand; in 1982, he settled in the States. He married Judith Fishman in 1983. In addition to this text he has co-authored with her a freshman composition text, *Frames of Mind* (Random House).